Renewing the Covenant

A Theology for the Postmodern Jew

BOOKS BY EUGENE B. BOROWITZ

A Layman's Introduction to Religious Existentialism
A New Jewish Theology in the Making
How Can a Jew Speak of Faith Today?
Choosing a Sex Ethic
The Mask Jews Wear
Reform Judaism Today
Understanding Judaism
Contemporary Christologies, a Jewish Response
Choices in Modern Jewish Thought
Liberal Judaism
Explaining Reform Judaism (with Naomi Patz)
Exploring Jewish Ethics

Renewing the Covenant

A Theology for the Postmodern Jew

EUGENE B. BOROWITZ

The Jewish Publication Society

Philadelphia   New York   Jerusalem   5752/1991

This book, the first publication sponsored by
the Ilona Samek Institute
of Hebrew Union College–Jewish Institute of Religion,
is gratefully dedicated to the memory of
    ILONA SAMEK
in appreciation of her beneficence.

Copyright © 1991 by Eugene B. Borowitz
First edition   All rights reserved
Manufactured in the United States of America

Library of Congress Cataloging-in-Publication Data
Borowitz, Eugene B.
    Renewing the covenant : a theology for the postmodern Jew / Eugene B.
Borowitz.
        p.   cm.
    Includes bibliographical references and index.
    ISBN 0–8276–0400–9
    1. Judaism—20th century.   2. Commandments (Judaism)—History of doc-
trines—20th century. 3. Covenants (Jewish theology)—History of doctrines—
20th century.   I. Title.
BM601.B62   1991
296.3—dc20   91–23536
                                                                  CIP

for
Zachary Aaron

Contents

III   The Torah Born of Covenant

Preface

In my 1961 article "Crisis Theology and the Jewish Community" (in the July *Commentary*), I introduced the term "Covenant Theology" to characterize an emerging paradigm shift in non-Orthodox Jewish thought. I thought then, as I do now, that the critical intellectual questions of belief have little to do with our conventional community labels, Conservative, Reform, Reconstructionist. Rather, a very large part of modernized Jewry—including many nominally Orthodox—is made up of Jews who know that their Judaism must allow greater personal freedom than the one they inherited, though no consensus has emerged as to how. I was one of a number of thinkers seeking to speak out of and to the Jewish faith of this transdenominational group. To try to keep my meaning clear, I shall speak of this reference group as "non-Orthodox," though in prior writings I have also used the term "liberal" for it and in certain contexts will do so here as well.

In the ensuing three decades I have tried to clarify what it meant to speak intellectually of Judaism as "Covenant," not as law, ethics, ethnicity, or nationality. This book presents a comprehensive theology pivoting on my understanding of "Covenant," a task I now begin by calling attention to a stylistic matter. I distinguish between the historic relationship between God and the Jewish people and that between God and humankind by using "Covenant" for the former and "covenant" for the latter.

For all its reach, this book deals with but one aspect of my theology. To my surprise and consternation, the theological task I early set for myself refused to remain unified, but ramified into three independent, if correlated, foci of interest: (1) the response to our culture, (2) the dialogue with Jewish tradition, and (3) the testing of these ideas in Jewish action.

By 1963 my growing sense of what we have since come to call the "postmodern" mood had clarified sufficiently that I could specify the critical methodological change we required. In a paper to the Central Conference of American Rabbis meeting that year (published in the 1963 *Yearbook* as "Faith and Method in Jewish Theology") I argued against supinely accommodating Judaism to the general culture's models of truth, which in that era were essentially rationalistic ones. Instead, out of self-respect as well as belief in Judaism's continuing truth. I called for carrying on a Jewish critique of the reigning intellectual systems while also learning from what remained spiritually compelling in them. So to speak, I wanted to reverse the liberalistic procedure of having the culture tell us what remained true in Judaism and instead do Jewish theology from the inside out.

I soon discovered how elusive a goal I had set for myself. Basing my initial effort on my doctoral work in rabbinic theology and further graduate study in contemporary philosophy of religion. I attempted to accomplish both the apologetic and traditional goals by explicating the theological entailments of what I divined to be the implicit key concept of classic (i.e., biblical-rabbinic) Judaism, namely, the Covenant. I abandoned this approach when I realized that my assertion of a conceptual core to Jewish religiosity repeated the methodological error I decried in the liberals.

The problem of the Jewish authenticity of a new non-Orthodox Jewish theology now became very much more challenging: it could not simply be done "from the inside out." Even in the loose, wary sense in which I employ the term "theology"— meaning orderly reflection about Jewish belief—the enterprise has no biblical or talmudic warrant. Jewish theology and philosophy arise out of Jewish marginality in cultures that esteem Hellenic ratiocination. This situation is common to Philo and Maimonides but not to Babylonians like Rava and Abbaye or East Europeans like the Besht and the Vilna Gaon, none of whom worked at theology. Systematic thinking about Jewish belief inevitably involves some initial accommodation to the surrounding culture. Thus, authenticity can only mean a resolute confrontation between the culture's truth and as faithful an understanding of classic Jewish faith as learning, belief, and practice can provide. As long as one remains on this speculative/historical level, the undertaking remains much the same for Orthodox and non-Orthodox thinkers. The distinctions emerge only as non-Orthodoxy manifests itself in the modification of a classic Jewish affirmation because of a recognized truth in the general culture. In my case, it was a root belief that personal dignity means having substantial self-determination.

I next attacked this issue on the basis of the later thought of Ludwig Wittgenstein. Wittgenstein had given contemporary philosophy—and much of our culture—a decisive linguistic turn by demonstrating the extent to which our efforts to make sense of reality involved creating specialized language patterns, "language-games," as they came to be called. This philosophic turn opened up the possibility of a nonreductive yet intellectually respectable understanding of religious faith. In classic Judaism, explicit theologizing is done as *aggadah*. These rabbinic comments seem by Hellenic standards to have no structure but, if Wittgenstein was correct, their "odd" form only showed that they had an uncommonly impenetrable set of syntactic game rules. If I could manage to determine the "logic" of the *aggadah* I could then theologize in the authentic Jewish manner.

I therefore spent many years studying the nature—that is the rhetorical-logical patterns—of aggadic theological utterance, concentrating eventually on a substantial talmudic sample. As that work began to draw to a conclusion I discovered its futility for my purpose. For I learned what perhaps I should have known in advance: that the rules of the aggadic language-game did not finally control its glorious freedom. Rather, its limits were set externally, mostly through its sister rabbinic language-game, *halakhah*. If so, my quest for Jewish theological authenticity could be achieved only by eliciting the Jewish aspect of my thought from the *halakhah* itself.

In recent years I have therefore worked on the problem of deriving from the *halakhah* the Jewish ground of my theology. My experience with several forbearing seminars has emboldened me to specify the process of research and reflection that, God granting me the vigor and insight, will finally allow me to bring to publication this aspect of my theology, the second motif in my prior list: the dialogue with tradition. In the present volume I can only point to these years of study as the basis for my generalizations about the classic Jewish faith that confronts us with its claims.

This growing concern with the *halakhah* confirmed an old Jewish understanding of mine. Over the millennia Judaism has been far more concerned with action than with thought, a consequentialism still manifest among Jews today and central to contemporary Jewish religious thought. I therefore had long believed I could test something of the Jewishness of my thinking by employing it as a meta-*halakhah* and seeing what obligations it directed me to. I have mostly carried on this inductive program by working on specific issues in applied Jewish ethics, such as our societal, sexual, business, and interreligious responsibilities. In my recently published collection of these papers, *Exploring Jewish Ethics* (Wayne State University Press, 1990), I have carried out the third item on my agenda: the testing of these ideas in Jewish action. As such, it constitutes the functional companion volume to this work, which concentrates on the first theme, mediation between Judaism and contemporary culture.

Despite the length of this book, I still have had to omit many matters that concern me greatly, three of them so important that I must offer some explanation.

The first is feminist Jewish theology. Though I engage the ideas of many theologians in this book, feminist Jewish thinkers are not among them. I read feminist theologians with great interest and benefit but do not know how to join in discussion with them without importing a male and hence, from their perspective, problematic grounding experience. Since men have long determined how women ought to think, I think it best to listen and learn in respectful silence until women clarify how men can join them in common deliberation. I hope, however, that feminists will find that much of what concerns them has a significant place in these pages. That manifests itself in gender-free language with but one exception, the word "God." Of all the substitutes, some of which inclusivist syntax has required of me, I find none as satisfactory as this troubled old word that still trails sanctity despite its penumbra of masculinity.

Another, more longstanding influence on my thought finds no explicit mention here, namely, Steven S. Schwarzchild, *zikhrono livrakhah*, whose untimely death occurred when I was well into this book. For forty-some years he and I debated rationalism versus nonrationalism, philosophy versus theology, radical versus meliorative ethics. After a while we didn't even need to butt heads; we merely sent each other our papers, knowing full well how the other would react. The preeminent Jewish neo-Kantian of our time, he devoted himself to demonstrating the incomparable philosophic adequacy and truth of Hermann Cohen. He stands, muttering I would guess, behind my ongoing dissent from Cohen's and other philosophic rationalisms.

I also make no mention of my lifelong intellectual and human companion, Arnold Jacob Wolf. He has been the most consistently cogent and loving critic of my insistence on setting personal freedom at the center of Jewish existence. Although I have, as always, tried to keep his strictures in mind, I know I shall again trouble him, for I do not write so much about my doubts as about my beliefs—and I seem to be serenely certain about them. I have no lack of perplexities, though mine do not seem to me to be as continually tormenting or anguishing as the spiritual agony others report. I do not know why, but to some extent it comes from my regular experience that my certainties-of-disbelief make less sense than the inconclusiveness-of-my-faith. In any case, I find many writers speak more authoritatively and illuminatingly about doubting than I can—though I not infrequently feel that some indulge themselves in the romanticism of unbelief. Few Jews write about what they personally believe, and far fewer give their reasons for believing it. I feel I can be more useful to the Jewish community by sharing what I affirm. Sensitive readers will recognize that the ceaseless casuistry of this book testifies to my *a posteriori* doubt about whether I am being true and responsible. I have, as it were, borrowed the German social philosopher Jürgen Habermas's hermeneutic of suspicion and shifted it from his social to my personal context in order to be as honest and faithful as I can about what my Jewish faith does and does not contain and entail.

This book serves as a testimony to the life and good works of Ilona Samek and is the first project of the institute established in her name at the Hebrew Union College–Jewish Institute of Religion for special activities in the fields of theology and liturgy. Ilona Samek was a refugee from Central Europe who rebuilt her life in the United States and, after her death, left a substantial portion of her estate to carry on these Jewish religious activities. I am deeply grateful to my old friend, George Lotker, who, as a fellow lover of philosophy, was the intermediary for the establishment of the Ilona Samek Institute. May its works be a proper tribute to her memory and bring George much satisfaction.

I have been the happy beneficiary of Sheila Segal's sensitive reading of my manuscript and her judicious editorial suggestions for its improvement. Her warm reception of my suggestion that this book be written and her kindly insistence that I use it to take my thought as far forward as I could spurred me to do more in this effort than I originally thought possible. I am greatly in her debt. It is also a pleasure to acknowledge here my happy experience in working with the staff of the Jewish Publication Society charged with various responsibilites related to this volume. They have given me a cordial reception and thoughtful guidance and I am grateful indeed to them.

Over the years I have been intimately conscious that what I have been able to accomplish in my life or work has involved the goodness of God as much as anything I might have brought to them. The period in which I worked on this book had its special trials and so it is with even fuller than usual gratitude that my ultimate acknowledgment is to God, and I say with the Psalmists

אַשְׁרֵי הָעָם שֶׁיְיָ אֱלֹהָיו . . . וַאֲנִי בְּחַסְדְּךָ בָטַחְתִּי; יָגֵל לִבִּי בִּישׁוּעָתָךְ;
אָשִׁירָה לַיְיָ, כִּי גָמַל עָלָי:

"Happy is the people whose God is *Adonai* . . . and I, I have
trusted in your lovingkindness. My heart exults in Your saving
power, I sing to *Adonai* for God has been generous to me."

Eugene B. Borowitz
Port Washington, N.Y.

Renewing the Covenant

A Theology for the Postmodern Jew

Introduction: The History That Shapes Us

ELIEF HAS BEEN so intimately associated with historical experience and memory in Judaism that some thinkers have felt they could present the contemporary meaning of Jewish religious ideas by tracing their evolution. I shall not be giving much attention to our premodern history in this book—more precisely, I simply take our general academic understanding of it for granted—so that I can concentrate on the problems and possibilities of Jewish belief today. Modernity challenges us to mediate between the Jewish truth we have inherited and cherish, and that which our surrounding culture deems worth embracing. However, before proceeding, I want to indicate my sense of the historical context in which our generation's special religious quest has arisen.

It seems to me that Jewish spirituality has been decisively molded by six momentous folk experiences: Covenant, Settlement, Rabbinism, Diaspora, Emancipation, and post-Holocaust disillusionment. Note, please, that I am speaking in terms of our people's experience, not that of one or another individual or that of humankind universally. Were I concerned with religion in general, either of those considerations would be worthy starting points. I am interested, rather, in emphasizing what I believe to be the specific quality of *Jewish* belief so that Judaism can function as an independent partner in its ongoing dialogue with culture. As I explicate later, I believe it critical to Jewish authenticity to try to think out of our corporate experience. Here this implies identification with the belief of a significant segment of our community in response to its recognized spiritual leaders. Though I can only speak as an individual, I seek to do so as one of this people, elucidating what I understand to have been our formative communal spirituality. I present my views to my fellow Jews in the hope that they may recognize in them their own religious self-understanding.

Promise, Fulfillment, Destruction, Rebuilding

The first and most formative experience in the development of Jewish spirituality was entering into the Covenant. As traditionally

1

put, the one God of the universe made a pact with Abraham, renewed it with his descendants, confirmed it in the Exodus, and made it specific in giving the Torah to the people of Israel at Mount Sinai. True, God also had a prior covenant with all humanity, as specified in the story of Noah, but humankind remained obdurate and disobedient. In response, God called Abraham to live in special loyalty to God so that through him and his descendants all human beings might one day come to know—that is, to obey—God. In return, God promised to make Abraham's family a mighty nation, to give them a land, and to protect them throughout history. Thus individuals, society, and responsibility are that fundamental and interrelated in Jewish faith.

Judaism revolves about the Covenant experience of choice, promise, demand, redemption, and mission. Our liturgy reviews it every day, our calendar follows it each year. Believing Jews live in the reality of the Covenant.

The second phase in the growth of the Hebrew spirit occurred in the land of Israel. Between 1250 and 500 B.C.E. a family become a nation experienced settlement, kingdom, the establishment of the Temple, social division and decline, prophecy, the loss of ten tribes, the conquest of Judah and destruction of the Temple, exile, and, most startlingly, a return to the land and rebuilding of the Temple. Hebrew saga and legend, law and history, prophecy and wisdom, apocalyptic and story, all found fixed verbal form, giving birth to a bookish piety. These events and writings greatly amplified the Covenant, reaching a climax in the visions of a Messianic Day when all humankind, led by the people of Israel, would finally serve God fully and freely.

The third decisive stage in Jewish religiosity began when, some centuries after most of the biblical books were composed, our people created the religious life described and advanced by the writings of "the rabbis." This modest term refers to the sages who are cited in the Mishnah (compiled about the year 200 C.E.) and the talmudic commentaries on their dicta (one compiled in the land of Israel in the last half of the 4th century and another in Babylon about 500 C.E.) These rabbis framed our people's religion as we know it today. We read the Bible through their eyes; we celebrate, mourn, pray, and study in the patterns they created. Thus, when the Second Temple was destroyed, the rabbis created the synagogue style that remembers the Temple but has no sacrifices and whose service any learned Jew may lead. In the classic rabbinic texts, law, halakhah, intertwines with spiritual teaching, *aggadah*, together creating a religious way that seeks sanctity through educated participation and characterizes all succeeding Judaism.

Segregation Becomes Equality

Our Diaspora existence of the next thirteen centuries engendered the fourth step in our growth, most of whose distinctive spiritual tone arose in response to the debased social situation that Islam and Christianity imposed upon us. After the First Crusade, European Christians increasingly attacked, robbed, forcibly converted, expelled, and murdered Jews. The ghetto and *shtetl* of Europe and the *mellah* of North Africa arose relatively late in this period and symbolize the segregation that was its dominant social characteristic. We came to see ourselves as God's Suffering Servant in history and knew that our defamers, by their very persecution of us, could not be God's chosen. In the face of external hostility we created rich patterns of family and community life to sanctify our inner existence. We also did not hesitate to learn from the cultures that permitted us to participate in them. We began to systematize Judaism in legal codes and philosophic structures while also developing the speculative mysticism called *kabbalah*.

After more than a millennium of ostracism and persecution, European Jews were astounded when the French Revolution signaled a turn to political equality in Europe, including even Jews. With modernity—that is, with the radical social and intellectual changes we call the Emancipation—the fifth phase began. Slowly, often bregrudgingly, states granted Jews civil and social equality—a process not fully realized today even in the United States, the freest of modern nations. Regardless, Emancipation revolutionized Jewish spirituality, for whenever Jews were permitted to modernize, they did so avidly, and uncomplainingly accepted its accompanying secularization.

The startling effects of this fundamental shift of cultural context cannot be overemphasized. Freedom from segregated existence brought on a transition from a life oriented by revelation, tradition, and a sense of the holy to one in which religion became privatized if not irrelevant or obsolete. This had the advantage of making a Jew's religion no longer a public handicap. It also meant that as the realm of religiously neutral activity expanded, the twin questions of Jewish identity and continuity became increasingly troublesome.

Jews began to ask, "What does it mean to be a Jew today? Why should one undertake its special responsibilities?" Modern Jewish thought arose as Jews sought to respond to these questions in ways that would be culturally credible and Jewishly persuasive. To this day, the major differences between our modern Jewish ideologies and movements stem from their divergent approaches to the same essential problem of balancing tradition and modernity.

For American Jews the confrontation with Emancipation has been relatively recent. Most of us are descended from families who immigrated to this country between 1880 and 1924, mainly from countries where Jews had not been integrated into the general culture. As a result, the overwhelming majority of us have been the social equals of our neighbors for only a few generations, a short time indeed for such radical transformation.

Though our modernization has been swift, its accompanying secularization has been thorough. Wherever America has been truly free, we, the descendants of social outcasts, have happily embraced the dignity it has granted us. Though this new social acceptance seemed to require our giving up most of our distinguishing religious practices, we complied with little hesitation, believing that our new equality would enable us to have an extraordinarily rich human existence. We stopped relying on our traditional God to save us and instead put our faith in humanity's power to create justice. We now expected that education, cultural creativity, economic expansion, and political action—not observance of the Torah—would bring us to a Messianic age. Ethics became our surrogate for *mitzvot*; the concert hall, bookstore, and university replaced the *bet midrash*. Those who still talked of God largely meant an idea that unified their ever-expanding humanistic worldview. In sum, non-Orthodox American Jewish spirituality, in ways typical of every modernized Jewry, now sought human fulfillment through Western culture rather than through the Written and Oral Law.

The Survival of the Modern in the Postmodern Spirit

Our late 19th- and early 20th-century love affair with modernity and its equality still animates most of our discussions of contemporary Judaism despite the loss of our old unquestioned passion. With so much continuity from the modern to the postmodern spiritual situation I probably should not call our present development a new, sixth period in the Jewish religious journey. I have done so for

heuristic reasons, to heighten the contrast between the two sensibilities: utter confidence in human capabilities on the one hand and a
new realism about human limits on the other. This should highlight
the question that heads our theological agenda: How shall we balance
what remains true in our Emanicipation idealism with what our
post-Holocaust realism demands we never forget?

The sixth period in Jewish spirituality resulted, as many have
suggested, from Hitler's murder of six million Jews and the existence
of the State of Israel. Once Jews could confront the Holocaust in its
own satanic fullness and see it as the terrifying symbol of humankind's demonic energies, they identified Western culture as an
ethical fraud. With modernist messianism discredited, we modern
Jews, like many others in our civilization, have had to rethink our
most fundamental beliefs, particularly with regard to the age-old
Jewish concern: How, really, must we live? If we insist, against most
of what we see and hear around us, that there are things that *must
not* ever be done by anyone, that there are standards of quality that
every life must manifest to be truly human—to be a *mentsh*—then
we must seek their ground elsewhere than in our secular culture.
The slow but steady growth of this consciousness has been the basis
of the surprising emergence of an explicitly religious concern in
postmodern Jewishness; against the predictions of the pundits God
again claims our attention.

As we have recognized that our intense commitment to Jewish
survival has a parallel transcendent grounding, spirituality has become the twin of our postmodern ethnicity. We have lived this
in our response to the Holocaust, in our pride in the Jewish
accomplishments of the State of Israel, and in our revulsion at the
world's complacency at the threats to its existence. Religiously, too,
we feel ourselves commanded to fight the loss of our people's folk
vitality and the evaporation of its morale lest the millennia of its
Covenantal testimony to humankind be frustrated on our account.
Where Jewish modernity gloried in a heady universalism, postmodern
Judaism manifests a resurgent particularism.

What Truth Demands Our Mediating Stance?

Despite disillusionment with Western civilization, Jews overwhelmingly do not wish to return to the ghetto. We remain devoted
to modernity's central benefit, equality, and to the democratic
pluralism that has enabled us to live in human decency as rarely

before in our history. Most American Jews also stand by democracy's corollary principle, that individuals should decide or help decide the rules by which they are expected to live. We postmodern, non-Orthodox Jews may want to be more religious and "more Jewish" than the previous generation, but we still insist on determining for ourselves just what aspects of Judaism we will accept and observe.

The bulk of our community now finds itself spiritually situated halfway between uncritical modernity and undemocratized traditionalism. We are searching for a new understanding of the transcendent ground of our ethical and ethnic commitment; we have made a postmodern turn to our people's millennial Covenant. We surely do not yet see with any clarity what manner of faith or way of life our present religiosity might yield. But we can now seek to strengthen these fresh Jewish intuitions and make them the basis of our existence.

One way of doing so is to think carefully about what we can affirm as well as what we must deny. This work is devoted to that analytic task, and strives to clarify the nature of our contemporary Jewish religious experience, to grope for the God with whom we still stand in partnership, to articulate what we mean by reasserting that we are the people of the Covenant, and to delineate the nature of the Jewish responsibility that arises from this new/old affirmation.

Jewish Religious Experience
in Our Time

1 Modernization: The Secular Messiah

O ANALYZE the Jewish communal experience to which my theology responds, I must first, even sketchily, provide its immediate historical basis and its general social context. I therefore devote this chapter to the spiritual ethos of modernity and the following one to some religiously significant themes in Western civilization's disenchantment with it.

One can hardly overestimate the extent to which, from the late 18th century on, the Emancipation caused our people to reshape the inherited faith of Judaism. It did so essentially by liberating us from our fifteen-hundred-year ordeal of physical, social, and economic segregation. In the first half of that period—roughly from 313 C.E., when Christianity became the established religion of the Roman Empire, until the First Crusade (1096)—European Jews might be scorned but they lived in comparative personal safety. In the wake of the Crusades, pogroms, forced conversions, institutionalized degradation, expulsions, and other forms of terror became common. By the end of the 16th century, Jewish neighborhoods were becoming ghettos, walled in and locked each day at sundown. This Italian innovation came to symbolize the entire pattern of segregation imposed on Jews until the French Revolution. (The North African *mellah* and the East European *shtetl* lacked the physical separation but nonetheless debased their inhabitants in distinctive ways.) When the French proponents of liberty, equality, and fraternity seized power, they extended freedom to the Jews, though it took a three-year debate to legislate so radical a social innovation. From then on, by fits and starts, and with great regional variation, Jews began entering European society as equals. Jews in Moslem lands had to wait longer, receiving freedom only as their countries accepted European notions of modernization.

Jews who abandoned the ghetto style of Jewishness suffered enormous cultural shock. Equality required them to dress like everyone else, speak their language, live by their etiquette, accept their aesthetic, read their literature, listen to their music, attend their universities, participate in their business life, and be good citizens of their nations. In theory, a history of fifteen centuries of disdain and persecution, suffused by a virulent, irrational, and often deeply unconscious hatred, had now been overcome. Those who had granted Jews these rights expected them to take grateful advantage of them and show how they could adapt thoroughly to their new social context.

Wherever the Emancipation became effective, masses of Jews rushed from the ghetto into the modern world without anyone having to tell them to do so. The leading Jewish religious authorities of the day opposed such radical change; there had been few signs of the Emancipation in their Eastern European world, but they had heard that modernization led to the abandonment of the community's traditional ways. Few dared to innovate as daringly as the shapers of talmudic Judaism had occasionally done. Instead, they regularly opposed the rapid social and intellectual changes Jews made in response to the Emancipation.

These generalizations require much qualification. European Jewry did not have a hierarchical or institutionalized pattern of authority but an essentially atomized, localized, and informal one. Nonetheless, modernizing Jews mostly found themselves alienated from a religious leadership that defended the old ghetto-oriented pattern of Jewish living. As a result, in an astonishing break with the discipline that had ordered our people's life for well over a millennium, the bulk of our community rejected the authority of traditional Jewish law, *halakhah*, and that of its interpreters as well. This revolutionary diminution of Jewish practice—and of much of traditional Jewish belief associated with it—continues to be seen by many as the great virtue of modern Judaism.

Modernization's impact on Jews seeking equality may be gauged from the willingness of many to take the only step they felt would make them truly acceptable in general society: conversion to Christianity. In retrospect, that thousands apostatized or thoroughly assimilated to Western culture should have come as no surprise. Perhaps more surprising, considering how long Jews had been deprived of simple human dignity, is that most of the modernizers insisted on remaining Jews even though no one could tell them how to be both modern *and* Jewish. Without the modern commitment to freedom, Jews would still be in the ghetto; but as long as they insisted on practicing their Judaism as their leaders then demanded, they would continue to be stigmatized as social outsiders. The majority's stubborn Jewish insistence on an improbable "both/and" created the continuing hope and problem of modern Jewish thought: how to reconcile the liberty central to the contemporary ethos with a religion whose venerable traditionalism and institutional patterns made it relatively inflexible?

Intuitively, without knowing what lay ahead but certain that Judaism needed to modernize in order to endure, deghettoized Jews began creating the distinctive blends of freedom and tradition that crystallized into what we call Reform and Conservative Judaism. In reaction, a self-conscious Orthodoxy emerged, and the dominant institutional claims of modern Jewish religiosity were staked out.

This quick survey of religious developments should not leave out modernization's concomitant secularization of Jewry, a further transformation that continues to affect our spiritual situation. Religious institutions and rites no longer gave moderns their plausibility structure. God retreated from the center of their worldview to an uncertain place at its periphery. The universality of this secularization can easily be overstated but its transforming power cannot be denied without missing something critical to the character of modern life.

Separating the Secular from the Sacred

Sociologists have identified the city and the university as the two main instruments of secularization, and free Jews have been overrepresented in both. As the towns of Western and Central Europe grew in size and commerce in the 17th and 18th centuries, they slowly permitted the readmission of Jews they had expelled some centuries earlier. When they became cities, their Jewish populations expanded, particularly because the new economic order cared more about productivity than about religion or cultural style. Urban life thus fostered pluralism and gave Jews more effective freedom than their people had ever known in the Diaspora.

The modern university also derogated faith; it concerned itself with knowledge, often polemicizing against religion as the enemy of free inquiry. It considered the worth of every human being a self-evident truth of nature, not a religiously grounded tenet, and then provided the socialization and knowledge that enabled Jews to make their way successfully into the modern world. Jews reveled in its meritocracy of intellect and quickly made it their surrogate for the *yeshivah*. The result was a profusion of scholars and professionals whose contribution to our civilization has been inestimable.

Overwhelmingly urban and increasingly university trained, emancipated Jewry became thoroughly secularized.

The political desirability for Jews of secularization in society at large also requires mention; for had nationality remained intertwined with religion Jews could hardly have attained social equality. When states were Christian, as in the Middle Ages, non-Christians had an anomalous political status because they could not swear the Christian oaths that bound citizens to one another. Only when citizenship and faith became disentangled could Jews be fully enfranchised and become political equals. Since the secular state has opened the door to belonging and opportunity for all, modern Jews have been enthusiastic supporters of the secularization of society.

Many Christians find this Jewish attitude surprising insofar as they retain traditional Christianity's rather sharp distinction between the religious and worldly aspects of life. Most Jews have found secularization less threatening, and not merely because of the political benefits its implementation has brought us. For all our involvement with God, we have described ourselves from biblical times on as an ethnic group, a people, and not as a church. Thus, our "religion" in modern times has continually involved Jews in social and political matters that, from a classic Christian perspective, would appear to be secular rather than religious, most recently our intense identification with the national well-being of the State of Israel. But, as the Bible makes plain, for the nation called to Covenant these matters are equally religious, composing the uncommon spiritual-social mixture that Martin Buber perceptively termed theopolitical.

The same anomaly appears again in Judaism's inclusion of self-consciously irreligious Jews within the religious community. At their best, such Jews transform religious commandments into ethics, Torah into culture, and salvation into good politics rather than give themselves to hedonism, self-seeking, or cynicism. In distinctive statistical disproportion, these more fully secularized Jews devote themselves to human betterment, liberal politics, and high culture. Every decade since the Emancipation would not have produced so many Jewish unbelievers devoted to improving humankind had they not at some level believed these causes to be a fulfillment of the Jewish heritage.

Zionism epitomizes this demythologized, secularized Jewishness. Some modernizing Jews seized upon the idea of nationalism—a major 19th-century European political phenomenon—and sought to liberate our people from demeaning cultural and social dependency on its host nations. The State of Israel today, in its undoubted Jewishness yet thoroughgoing secularity, testifies to the power of their dream. While classic Judaism envisioned something more messianic in its prayers for a return to Zion, one cannot understand the Jewishness of the State of Israel or world Jewry's intense identification with it unless one recognizes it as another modern transformation of Jewish faith.

Secular philosophy also played a significant role in the process of modernizing Judaism, validating and guiding its development. It could serve this revisionist function because of our people's long ambivalence toward it. Jewish culture esteemed a number of the figures who had written philosophic works in the Middle Ages, but in traditional Judaism ratiocination had not been considered a major asset to Jewish faith. Hence, when Western and Central European Jews, seeking to harmonize Judaism with general culture, discovered secular philosophies that would enable them to give intellectual form to their new/old Jewishness, they began thinking in those terms. Hence modern Jewish thought, philosophical and theological, came into being.

Judaism for the University-Trained Mind

For most of the 19th century and much of the 20th, the thought of Immanuel Kant provided the major underpinnings of philosophical reinterpretations of Judaism. It was Hermann Cohen, the internationally acclaimed reviver of Kant's philosophy, who first gave this project academic legitimacy and became its lasting model. Cohen, who taught philosophy at the University of Marburg, reconceptualized Judaism in terms of his philosophical idealism. Like Kant, he took universal ethics to be intrinsic to rationality. This led him, for systematic coherence, to the need for an idea of God to guarantee the ethical activity that defines humanhood and to connect rational ethics with the scientific worldview by which reason construes nature. This philosophical view of reality, ethical monotheism, he regarded as the enduring rational insight of Judaism, one that made it the intellectual banner-bearer for all humanity. His philosophy thus demonstrated that only the concept of ethical monotheism could be considered permanent in Judaism, while the customs and practices that expressed, taught, and transmitted it continually changed—in Judaism as in all religions. While Cohen's technical

philosophy influenced only a narrow academic circle, his general
ideas about Judaism gained wide acceptance. These ideas gave modern
Judaism the universal ethical cast that distinguishes it to this day.

Since I will frequently refer to this theme of universal ethics, I
want to add some explanatory words about it here. After Kant's path-
breaking analysis of the rationality of ethics, any theory of what
constitutes the human good had to apply to all rational beings. It
could not be limited to one's own nation or religion or, to move to
our own time, to one's own race or gender. This radical, rational
inclusiveness directly confirmed Jewish experience. As the European
nations, often in advance of their citizenry, increasingly agreed that
political rights had to be universal, they could not ignore the case
for the emancipation of their Jews. Any theory that validated a less
embracing ethic could mean—as it did under Hitler—that Jews would
again be ostracized and persecuted. Jews have therefore had a
personal stake in universal ethics, one which, though not morally
disinterested, has been founded on the continuing personal experience
that the idea is true. While many postmodern Jews feel that Jewish
liberals overstated the Jewish significance of universal ethics, they
continue to affirm it because they too know its truth. One sees
this clearly in Hermann Cohen's critics. Despite the felt need to
reconstruct much of his interpretation of Judaism, every succeeding
non-Orthodox Jewish system-builder also has emphasized the importance of universal ethics, or its equivalent, in Judaism.

From German Philosophical Idealism
to American Naturalism

After World War I, when some American thinkers rejected
Kantian and Hegelian philosophy for pragmatism and naturalism,
Mordecai Kaplan led the Jewish effort to speculate about Judaism in
this fashion. Building his theory of Judaism on the basis of the newly
emerging science of sociology, Kaplan celebrated ethnic creativity—
in our case, that of the Jewish folk. This shift of the paradigm from
the individual mind to group behavior enabled him to explain what
the universalists could not, namely, why enfranchised moderns still
should devote themselves to staying Jewish, particularly when Jewish
identity necessarily carried with it certain minority handicaps.
Kaplan responded that sociology had demonstrated how extensively
the group shapes our values and worldview, and, therefore, our

individuality. Jews, having been born into our people and formed by its culture, should, in the natural human way of things, live by it. Not to want to do so, particularly when the Jewish people has so much to offer, indicated an unhealthy psyche, most likely caused by a faulty Jewish self-understanding. We are not another church in the Christian model but a people in the full ethnic sense of the term and we need to rebuild ourselves into a full-scale culture, or civilization, as Kaplan preferred to call it. This would include all the normal elements of folk existence: land, language, calendar, lore, art, music, custom, and religion, the capstone of every group culture.

Kaplan, therefore, considered peoplehood the only eternal aspect of Judaism. Modern historical research had made it undeniable that Jewish law could no longer be seen as Sinaitically revealed; it must rather be understood as the folk's creative effort to institutionalize its ethos and give it historical staying power. It ought to serve the needs of the Jewish people and not vice versa. Hence, it must accommodate itself to the modernity into which Jews had so happily integrated themselves. Yet on one point Kaplan remained true to his liberal forebears: While he otherwise recognized no limits to what the Jewish people might do in their ethnic creativity, he insisted that they must, like all human beings, conform to the universal ethics that he too believed reason showed to be true.

Kaplan's civilizational view of Judaism made it possible for modern Jews to find their Jewish identity through culture, a most appealing alternative to a generation who often equated modernity with agnosticism. Kaplan himself demanded—as sociology had taught him—that religion have a key place in a reconstructed Judaism. However, it had to be socially relevant. Hence, in place of supernaturalistic Jewish faith, Kaplan projected a humanistic concept of God as nature's support of human growth and flourishing. In making human needs the criterion for what Jews should now think about God, Kaplan's philosophy may be said to be the extreme case of secularizing Judaism while yet preserving a place in it for religion.

A Judaism of the Whole Person: Existentialism

A decade or so before Kaplan began to write in the United States, a radically different reaction to idealist theories of Judaism arose in Germany and gave rise to the Jewish existentialism of Martin Buber and Franz Rosenzweig.

The starting-point for the existentialists was their sense that modern thought had overestimated the competence of rationalism. Hellenic reason seeks universal patterns—but persons are quite individual. They are not merely particular instances of the general rules of biology, psychology, and sociology but unique human beings. The more rationalism had constricted itself in the 20th century, relegating ethics and aesthetics to the realm of mere emotion, the more it seemed to value cognitive precision above human reality.

The existentialists suggested a new theological paradigm. Instead of reinterpreting Judaism via an idealistic or naturalistic system of ideas, they wanted to think about it in terms suggested by reflecting on what it meant to be a whole person. In one's most immediate consciousness, for example, one felt oneself to be a unique self even before one thought much about it. Philosophically, that became the recognition that existence is simply given us and we ought to think in terms of this givenness, not try to make it conform to our reason. This applied particularly to how we should understand what we ought to do to fulfill ourselves as persons.

Buber and Rosenzweig helped pioneer the religious development of this kind of thinking. They believed that if we would stop rationalistically censoring out what might be, we could simply find God. In this mode of theorizing, religiosity did not consist of having "ideas" of God or merely being ethical, but in establishing a relationship with God upon which one then modeled one's relationships with people. Revelation, commandment, judgment, sin, forgiveness, atonement, salvation—all terms eschewed by modern rationists—now acquired new meaning as aspects of one's intimacy with God. Ironically, this personalistic reinterpretation of Judaism sounded very much more traditional, or at least more pious, than had prior modern philosophies.

Buber and Rosenzweig both considered the relationship with God to be the unchanging core of Judaism, although, as in all relationships, the specific manner of living it varied with significant changes in circumstance. Like any love, it commanded one only when the self willingly responded to it. The two thinkers differed radically, however, on what this made of Jewish duty—an issue that still troubles us. Buber espoused a radical individualism, arguing that Jewish law and tradition could no longer determine one's Jewish duty, that no prior rule could stand in the way of the present, commanding sense of God's presence. Rosenzweig intuitively knew that the *halakhah* still bound all Jews and contended that we would find its objective rules turned into personally validated behests as we observed them. However, he never explained why most Jews did not find this to be the case or how he could know the validity of classic Jewish law in advance of its personal authorization.

The critics of Jewish existentialism have charged it with being too personalistic—Buber for as good as nullifying law, Rosenzweig because of theoretical incoherence. But for all that is problematic, the existentialists nonetheless shared an important precept of modernity: that all authority, whether exercised in terms of one's rationality, ethnicity, or relationships, finally resides in the individual self.

The Jewish Ambivalence of Personal Autonomy

This issue has critical bearing on the substance of postmodern Judaism. Consider, for example, the case of Mordecai Kaplan, who would seem to have the least individualistic sense of authority since he stresses the importance of the group. Faithful to his sociological criteria, Kaplan specifies democracy as the only acceptable process by which we should determine Jewish community standards. Accepting it so fully in our everyday life, we cannot hope to remain a living culture if we do not apply it in our ethnic existence. He also suggests a pragmatic reason for utilizing the democratic process: if people share in making the rules they will be more inclined to abide by them. Yet Kaplan takes a firm stand against community sanctions for Jews who then flaunt the new rules. Though he wants the community to be a decisive factor in our lives, he also knows that community needs must bow to the modernistic notion of authority as being empowered by the individual's free decision to accept it. Today's Jews are essentially volunteers, people who choose to do something about their ethnic identity and not merely drift into the American mass. Any effort to try to make our community votes binding on individual Jews will be futile. As moderns, Jews will reserve the right to make up their own mind about what they will and will not do—and though they may be animated by deep Jewish ethnic loyalties, they will feel fully justified in this ultimate individualism.

All modernist theories of Judaism uphold the principle of autonomy, that authority ultimately is vested in the individual mind and will. In this unity they reflect the beneficent social reality of democracy and the persuasiveness of the modern idea that the true dignity of the self rests in its power of self-determination. As to the former, we Jews received our rights in the modern world as individuals, not as a religious or an ethnic community. Our precious equality and opportunity derives from this recognition of us as single selves. Moreover, we have learned the compelling virtue of self-determination by our participation in the political process. By voting and other political activity, we have a real say in who will rule, how they are to do so, and what the rules for our lives will be. Practically, our influence may be quite limited. Symbolically, occasionally realistically, seeing ourselves as effective agents of our own existence endows us with incomparably great personal stature. After our long exclusion from general society, our community has gloried in this humanizing individualism and made it a central premise of contemporary Jewish existence.

Almost all modern philosophers of the human condition, Marx excepted, maintained that legitimate authority derives from personal autonomy. From Descartes's time on, the individual mind has been the rightful judge of claims made upon the individual, accepting responsibility for only those injunctions that survived the self's critical scrunity. We deem this notion so important that we teach our children early that good reasons stand behind good rules. We soon expect them to ask us "Why?," a powerful moral question, which implies that they have a right to explanations and a responsibility to distinguish good from bad ones. Building this understanding of worthy personhood into their personal development, we teach them to equate self-regard with being able to decide for oneself. All modernized Jews have, in one fashion or another, founded their versions of Judaism on this premise.

This individualism led its adherents to exalt human creativity. Among Jewish rationalists God receded to the far background as humankind became the chief agent in creating religion and shaping history. Elated by the many wonders accomplished by a secularized humankind, Jews, like other moderns, exhibited boundless optimism about human potentiality. They epitomized this in two popular religious slogans: "the perfectibility of man [sic]" and "the Messianic Age." By the former, modern rabbis meant that once we could give people the proper education, culture, and social circumstances, they would stop doing evil and do the good. When enough good people made themselves felt in social and political affairs to control them, God's rule on earth would finally come into being. With progressive human action replacing the Messiah's miraculous transformation of reality, the dignity of the individual, writ large, had taken on redemptive dimensions. Some modern thinkers may have been somewhat more circumspect in their expectations—Hermann Cohen, for example, considering the Messianic Age an ever-nearing yet ever-distant goal—but they all gloried in human action and saw it, rather than God's holy power, as the source of our salvation.

In sum, modernization became our Messiah and we looked to it to effectuate the ideals we had for so long vainly looked to God and piety to fulfill. This was a heady, energizing faith, one which, like other aspirants to the Messiah's role, failed to live up to its promise. The way to postmodern Jewish faith was thereby opened.

2 Modernity: The Betrayer

ODERNITY, which once had a sense of historical inevitability about it, lost its cultural preeminence during the last third of the 20th century. Often, as in the resurgence of fundamentalism in Iran, one could not distinguish antimodernism from anti-Americanism, the United States having long epitomized the triumph of secularization. Suddenly our society's accepted, unbounded faith in human accomplishment began to seem ludicrous. Each day's telecasts brought into our homes numbing evidence that, along with its many benefits, modernity has also created new and intense forms of human misery. The disillusionment touches us in ways as local as the threat of drugs, violence, or the loss of meaning, and as global as pollution, terrorism, or nuclear destruction. We did not naively believe modernity would create no new problems, but we did assume that its spread meant the continual improvement of life, for no human problem appeared to be beyond its eventual competence. Yet people, institutions, and ideologies have so regularly disappointed us that hope, the driving force of a prior generation, has become rather a luxury, and cynicism and depression far more common. The term "postmodern" arose to describe the diverse movements that stemmed from our disillusionment with the modernists' messianic humanism.

We Americans share a special pain because we believed our country better than others. Our disillusionment with democracy became clearly visible in the late 1960s. Despite a strong civil rights law, blacks and other minority groups found that prejudice remained brutally strong, an impression relentlessly reinforced by experience. Since then, regardless of economic fluctuation, the gap between the white majority and non-white minorities remains shockingly large. Similar disparities continue in the opportunities and compensation available to men and to women. The struggle over the continuation of the Vietnam War made suspicion rather than respect the common attitude toward government; and the unending scandals of official corruption, from Watergate through the Iran-Contra revelations and beyond, desacralized the practice of democracy. Even pluralism, which we embraced as giving our society an appreciation of human diversity, now pains us by its even-handed legitimation of vice along with what we had long thought virtue. Every institution we had

20

expected to nurture character, not excepting that most sacred symbol of Americanism, the family, has shown itself equally capable of corrupting it.

The same corrosion ate away at the life of individuals. What began as the dignification of self-determination now widely took the form of self-interest. With authority ultimately vested in the self, social responsibility became ever more difficult to validate, and libertarianism, privatism, narcissism, and hedonism widely sapped our sense of civic virtue. With the self increasingly free to be anything, why one should be satisfied with any one thing became a gnawing problem. Psychotherapists report that instead of seeing patients morbidly burdened with guilt they more often find themselves working with people depressed that their life has no meaning.

We can generalize this dissatisfaction. Despite its prodigious accomplishments, the democratic capitalism in which we had placed so much trust has betrayed our modernistic dream that it would foster humane existence to the point of near messianism. Uniting mind, will, and energy into a self of striking efficiency, modernity also drove people relentlessly toward the unattainable goal of fulfillment, and thus to continual frustration. Every amazing benefit stimulated new demand and desire, making insatiability the power behind our social development and thereby disfiguring our lives.

So, too, our faith in high humanism failed us. For the sake of greater precision, philosophers denuded reason of the moral substance we assumed it necessarily contained, while our artists, ever more adept at stripping us of illusion and shocking us with harsh images of reality, offered no culturally compelling vision of the good person or society. A critical pillar of modernism collapsed: the belief that secular enlightenment would make people ethically self-correcting.

Losing Morality's Religious and Philosophical Basis

Liberal religion, which preached accommodation to the culture as its new messianism, must share in this indictment of our culture. It once seemed so obvious that autonomous moderns would make a place for religion in their lives if we modernized our old rites and made self-commending what God's will once imposed upon us. As long as liberalism emancipated us from the tyranny of old orthodoxies, its innovativeness elicited enthusiasm. But as a once repressive culture advanced to permissivism, freedom became more our problem than our redemption. "Why not?" became a terrifying opening to self-destruction and social rot. The apostles of change and adaptation found themselves with nothing independent to say about the limits that would keep us from joining society's onward rush into amorality. Rationalism and science, the two great mentors that we thought would be the basis of our ennoblement, lost their mythic authority. We discovered that they reinforced relativism more than they specified enduring values. And by substituting personal growth or self-fulfillment for God's revelation, liberal religion now looked to be only another social agency eating away at our faith in high standards for human responsibility.

The failure of philosophy to meet the emerging crisis of value completed the erosion of the intellectual footings of modernity. Had thinkers in this century been able to follow Kant confidently, the power of their ideas might have slowed the tidal drift to moral insecurity. But his conception of humankind as rational, and therefore intrinsically committed to universal ethical obligation, barely survived the incredible carnage of World War I and its revelations about the realities of human behavior. What remained of the identification of humanness with ethical rationality disappeared as psychoanalysis, anthropology, and Marxism persuasively contended that "conscience" mostly represented the introjected parent or group interest.

Philosophers abetted this debasing of morality by their increasing identification of certainty with scientific method and the rational with the verifiable. Movements like logical positivism and linguistic analysis demeaned ethics as only personal preference or cultural style. Ethics and reason moved so far apart that technically competent though value-neutral reasoning about human affairs could qualify as rationally exemplary. More recently, deconstructionism has advanced this work of delegitimization by construing all reasoning as word-play, not as authorized by logic, and hence perhaps engaging but never commanding. Some contemporary thinkers, like Alasdair MacIntyre, attempt to revalidate ethics by espousing communitarianism, limiting claims for ethical meaning to those speaking within a group to others sharing its values. Others, like Hans-Georg Gadamer and Richard Rorty, nobly seek to preserve humanistic rationalism but end up making such modest claims for its competence that they confirm the gnomic judgments of Nietzsche and Heidegger that Western philosophy has reached a dead end. Our secularized civilization thus no longer has a philosophic consensus as to why people *must* be ethical or how reason *commands* duty rather than offers counsel. Simply put, secular intellect no longer supplies a secure ground of value.

Postmodernity: An Intuition Seeking Self-understanding

If, then, one still knew and knew undeniably that humaneness was enjoined upon us by our humanity, our civilization's regnant ethos, modernity, had to be denied. This crisis of value, whether perceived in the terms of high or low culture, came to permeate much of Western civilization and provided the spiritual womb for the birth of postmodernity.

With the demise of the generative Kantian premise of liberal religion—that ethics was more certain than belief—the converse of the liberal axiom now asserted itself: If ethics rightly deserves a substance and power that rationalism can no longer provide, then faith must now once again provide its foundation and standard.

The zeitgeist now moved in another direction, and in many Western societies a broad-scale reaction against modernity made itself felt by championing old truths as the remedy for a restless, corrosive freedom. Cultures became newly conservative and so did much of their religious life. People who had lost the only god whom they had truly worshiped, the god of human competence, now began an intense, widespread search for a more worthy faith. Nothing in our secularized culture directly prepared us for the passion, depth, diversity, and endurance of the religious quest of the late 20th century. An examination of some of its diverse spiritual directions will provide the context in which my own postmodern Jewish theology is situated.

Reacting to the loss of the old social guides, this quest often manifests itself in a turn into the self. In its simplest, perhaps most timid form, it becomes a dedication to pleasure, a kind of latter-day epicureanism empowered by affluence and authorized by world-weariness. This devotion to knowledgeable consumption may not be much of a philosophy, but at least no one can accuse it of being other-worldly. Its most troubling extreme appears in the use of drugs, which technologize bliss, and supply meaning without the impediments of discipline, institution, doctrine, or form. But addiction also radically reduces the life of the spirit to a self-concern soon oblivious to responsibility to others, a contraction of the self that generally disturbs religionists even more than does the new openness of sexual relationships.

The inward turn takes a more positive form in the numerous psychological movements, of which EST and Esalen were the early prototypes, dedicated to helping us "get in greater touch with ourselves" and thus discover more truly who we are. Their tutelage as to how much our bodies or our unconscious minds influence our lives comes as a revelation. This meliorative wisdom suggests that further psychic exploration will provide us with a certainty from within that our old institutional forms no longer reliably provide from without. As a result, psychological sects that supply quasi-religious guidance proliferate endlessly. But the more intimately one knows one's psyche, the more one realizes its capacity for anything, thus conferring psychic validity on all feelings and simultaneously rendering them all equally insubstantial. Observing the folly that results when people decide to act out some hitherto repressed impulse of their psyche forces the issue of responsibility upon us: Which of our many impulses shall we follow, and which shall we deny? If we are to channel its animal urgings into nobility, we must move from the psyche's randomness to standards that transcend it and thus can lend it a stability and quality it cannot know on its own.

Liberal religion, which had as good as deified the self, ascribing to human consciousness or ethics a certainty it denied to God and revelation, lost much of its credibility as the self became discredited as its own savior. After all we have seen of human failure, individual and social, its optimistic humanism seemed shallow compared with the old religious paradigms of reality. They, at least, had unambiguous, worthy standards by which persons, families, communities, and nations could direct their randy freedom, whereas the liberals had such openness and tolerance that they could hardly ever tell us when we must say no to a new possibility. For all their talk of human fulfillment, they provided little specific guidance as to how to attain it, for they had nothing beyond the human to serve as a lasting, qualitative standard. Conscious that we deserved and needed far more positive guidance than we had received from liberal humanism, many people became part of that broad movement of postmodern spirituality that has sought to reclaim a source of human meaning beyond the self.

Beyond the Self, Even to Fundamentalism

To some extent the humanocentrism of modern thought has persisted in a new particularism, the effort to let our sexual, ethnic, racial or other social group fill out the self's limitations in the realm of values. Nationalism and ethnicity, advancing under the banner of pluralism, replaced both the "melting pot" theory of American society and the hope of world citizenship. Now it seemed like the height of arrogance for any one faction of society to demand that everyone else be like them. Rather, with race, religion, gender, sexual preference, folk, region, or nationality dominating individual style, a resurgent particularism appears to supply a practical transpersonal guide for much of life. But this only returns us to the issue of the right use of our freedom. Every group has its countercurrents of value and life-style, at some point turning our erstwhile guide into our immediate perplexity.

Contemplation, meditation, yoga, and mysticism are options with a humanistic appeal that move one beyond humanism as one becomes more deeply involved in them. For example, the Transcendental Meditation movement once sought a place in the public school curriculum as a secular means of helping children gain inner serenity. Yet pursued beyond the initial stages, TM, like any authentic study of yoga, leads its adepts far beyond the self to contact with Ultimate Reality. In movements such as this, modernist self-projection transforms itself through direct, personal experience of "primal Oneness" or "qualitative Nothingness," as they put it. In these spiritualities, communion with the Absolute or identification with it enables one simultaneously to utterly lose/absolutely fulfill one's self. We then complete our search not merely knowing the truth but blessedly discovering that, at our deepest level, we can be the truth.

Most people today, as in the past, do not seem open to or capable of so internal a pilgrimage, and the mystical path remains a minority option. A much greater number prefer an external, fixed route to truth, one derived from an authoritative source and exhibited in a community whose dedicated accomplishment reinforces its validity. This also has the advantage of resolving the problem of transmitting the cherished values to others, particularly one's children, a difficult task in something as subjective as inner religious experience. Not only the grounding of traditional religion but also the warmth and habituation of its long-hallowed religious practices are necessary to nullify the pernicious effects of modern culture. Something like this line of reasoning has motivated the recent revitalization of religious orthodoxies, whose unexpected range, depth, intensity, and staying-power has been the major religious phenomenon of the last part of this century.

Now, fundamentalists say, if we will only have complete trust,

God's word will fill the void created by our inner liberty. With God and our community authority setting our group's discipline of heart and deed, we will give it willing obedience, scorning the majority's amusement at our quaintness and enduring serenely such severe trials as life brings us. To end the gnawing spiritual hunger arising from our overextended modernist individualism, many formerly self-reliant moderns have gladly accepted leaders and teachings that promise to give them ultimate truth. A significant number of Americans have found spiritual security in Asian faiths and quasi-Asian cults as well as, more commonly, in the rich fare of Christian and Moslem fundamentalism or Jewish Orthodoxy.

Sophisticates of some decades ago would have thought it laughable that religious orthodoxies would ever again be the self-consciously chosen faith of large numbers of educated, cultured moderns. They assumed that the onward march of history made their view of humankind and the universe progressively inescapable. Those whose liberal certainty remains unshaken cannot believe that a shift in the zeitgeist has rendered their optimism questionable, even dangerous. But it turns out that character is not as educable, society not as malleable, and culture not as humanizing as messianic modernism, secular and religious, once taught. Now it seems plain to many that religion best serves human beings in creatively disengaging them from the society as well as adapting them to its latest passions. More of the newly orthodox than anyone anticipated have opted for disciplines that unambiguously proclaim their disdain of modernity by demanding a premodern life-style. The efflorescence of such sects provides important testimony about the spiritual motives prompting our postmodern religiosity.

Overwhelmingly, however, the move to religious orthodoxies has not taken an obscurantist form. Rather it has been accompanied by a judicious, religiously selective acceptance of some of modernity's benefits. For example, civility in disagreement and some tolerance of dissent; openness to uncommon cultural styles; recognition of the role of the body, sexuality, and emotion in our lives; science and scholarship as allies rather than enemies; and the importance of works of social ethical activism are all characteristic of American evangelicals and fundamentalists. But knowing that traditional religion has much to teach our morally feeble culture, they propose to stand up to it and correct its excesses instead of genuflecting to it. Only a religion that possesses a truth independent of the culture, secure because of its long history and depth of tradition, confident that it will long survive the present social malaise and ultimately be vindicated—hence only an orthodoxy—can hope to carry out this prophetic role.

Heschel, Precursor of Jewish Postmodernity

Among Jewish thinkers, it was Abraham Joshua Heschel who first gave this change of sentiment significant expression. To some extent his special insight had a biographical base. Heir to a Hasidic dynasty, he broke with the separatistic Polish Jewish milieu of his upbringing and embraced modernity through the Yiddish culture of Warsaw and doctoral studies at the University of Berlin. That he nonetheless retained his deep faith is attested by his dissertation topic, a phenomenological examination and validation of prophetic revelation. Fleeing Hitler, Heschel made the further transition from Europe to the United States, emerging two decades later as a gifted apologist for a modernized but quite traditional Judaism.

Heschel, like many a great religious teacher, used evocative language to open his readers to the reality that transcends the reach of reason. He knew the contemporary spirit and could speak in its terms, but used it only to initiate dialogue. He then moved on to challenge the credibility it gave to methodological skepticism. He sought to show how it had blinded us to the wonder of the simply given—including our very ability to doubt—and then contrasted its shallowness with the depth of traditional belief. He proceeded not by direct refutation, for any "logical" argument would already concede modernity's standards, but by playing off our existential perplexities against the believer's formative certainties. He employed his verbal genius in support of this tactic and thereby momentarily exposed to the reader his realm of faith. In Heschel's refusal to begin with human experience and in his determination to revalidate contentful revelation, the postmodern Jewish consciousness found early expression.

I introduce Heschel's thought here, in the context of the universal rather than the particular Jewish disillusionment with modernity, for two reasons. First, because of the agony of the Holocaust, we regularly underestimate the extent to which modern Jewry shared the general trauma that gave rise to the postmodern ethos; our secularization had been so thoroughgoing we could not avoid being badly shaken by the general collapse of our surrogate faith. Second, Heschel spoke to his readers in universal terms though he illustrates his meaning with Jewish learning and soul. Thus, in his major books he barely refers to the Holocaust, the hinge of the particular Jewish turn from enthusiastic modernity. Although he did not explain this enigmatic silence, I believe we can infer the reasons for it from the rest of his thought. He apparently believed that whatever could be given utterance had already been said in his discussion of the universal problem of theodicy—and the vastly greater suffering we had so recently experienced, to which words must ever remain inadequate, required silence.

By pressing an unwavering theocentricity on the Jewish community, Heschel attempted to move it to what we now can see was a characteristic postmodern stance: an openness to God as a present, living reality. Heschel thought he might accomplish this by awakening moderns to awe and wonder. While many a sensitive soul has found him speaking to them, I think the more common path to postmodern belief has come by way of that central modern theme, universal ethics.

In its secularizing zeal, the modern ethos had glorified our ethical power to shape our ultimate destiny, but humankind's virtuosity at evildoing brought on a general revulsion that engendered a spiritual reversal. It arose from the unexpected question forced on us by our changed intellectual and human situation. If reason only required logical competence but not ethical discipline, if, illusionless, we could finally acknowledge nature's barren neutrality, if raw history and wasted lives indicated the truth about existence, why our moral outrage? Instead of being indignant, we should become realists, admitting that this was just the way things were, giving up our ethical fantasies, and learning the survival strategies of an amoral civilization.

This ugly philosophy, now accepted by many as their secret credo, made us face up to what we most truly believed. If human nature is not essentially good but bipolar and morality results from childhood introjections or conditioning to the verities of class or culture, why should we rage at inhumanity or make sacrifices for greater humaneness? If creation is truly value-free, our ethics deserve no more credence than any other personal preferences. But the converse might also be true. If there is something primal and enduring about our ethical intuition that we cannot deny, and if we know that our moral anguish reflects something ultimate in the universe itself, then we need a new, postsecular ground of value. And it must ultimately derive from a source that the secular mind has refused to acknowledge.

I am convinced that the postmodern consciousness arose out of this rejection of the meaninglessness of a secularized reality and the affirmation of an immutable ground of universal value. Abandoning modernity's prideful method, it begins not with some certainty about human nature but with a glimpse of that which transcends us and upholds our self-affirmation. And that, quite remarkably, has brought many secularized moderns back to what the Judeo-Christian tradition called God.

Heschel would not have been satisfied with bringing Jewry only to a new religiosity, one not completed in an acceptance of the truth of God's revelation. He understood this rather traditionally and, in his own way, stands with those many postmoderns whose religiosity manifests a form of fundamentalism. Heschel firmly opposed the notion that the prophets had an independent, creative role in revelation beyond shaping the verbal style of their message. Instead, the prophet's rare empathy for God—with Moses the preeminent example—enabled him to give us an accurate, reliable understanding of God's will. Furthermore, Heschel explicitly grants to the Oral Torah of the rabbis the same authority as the prophets' Written Torah. Though his passion for ethics and concern for persons offset this traditionalistic theory of revelation, they remain subject to its strictures. Thus this theology must be characterized as quasi-Orthodox.

The Postmodern Resistance to Orthodoxies

Heschel had few followers in this aspect of his postmodernity. Most Jews rejected Orthodoxy for all the democratic, pluralistic reasons that other Americans resisted fundamentalisms. Perhaps nowhere has this recalcitrance become more dramatically evident than in Roman Catholicism, and not only in the United States. Despite the church's strongly reiterated teaching of the sinfulness of contraception, the overwhelming majority of American Catholics practice it. More important, they think they are right to do so as a matter of conscience. This amounts to asserting that self-determination is so integral to personal dignity that they must exercise it in a manner their beloved church does not empower.

Numerous other examples of issues prompting the postmodern rejection of orthodoxies could be adduced, but I think none is as telling as feminism, a matter of direct, personal appeal. Orthodoxies seem intrinsically sexist and thus inhuman and unethical. Against the argument from the universality of ethics—are women not moral agents?—the orthodoxies can only say that God's authority or the leaders God sanctions must receive greater credence than the immediate promptings of conscience. While many postmoderns accept God as the ground of their personhood, the nonorthodox stream believes they are partners with God in the determination of their religious duty. Consequently, as in the case of feminism, they often will insist on the priority of the clear mandates of morality when they believe they contradict the rules of the religious institutions they otherwise revere.

I can summarize the general spiritual development as follows: The modern replacement of traditional religion's dependence on God's revelation with self-reliance proved unrealistic in view of the human ability to be as demonic as saintly. With culture no longer empowering modernity and philosophy no longer mandating substantive ethics, the nature of humanhood itself became radically problematic. If, then, the old imperative to humaneness remains valid, it must be because of each individual's link to the God who enjoins responsibility and endows persons with inalienable worth. Many postmoderns believe, with classic religion, that God's behests of people were verbally communicated and institutionalized, resulting in secure communities that lived in God's discipline. Many others agree only in part, persisting in the Enlightenment belief that the self finds its fulfillment through God-oriented, community-guided personal choice. These believers stand between two older, more familiar ways of thinking about religion. They cannot call themselves religious liberals because they deny our human adequacy to resolve our ultimate problems and because of their willingness to acknowledge their grounding relationship with a real, independent God. They cannot identify with traditional religion because they also insist on greater personal self-determination in their intimacy with God than the Western religions have customarily allowed. The term "postmodern" indicates their mediating position well for it indicates that they carry something of modernity with them—dedication to autonomy—even as they seek to transcend it.

A Preliminary Indication of My Religious Stance

I am one of this postliberal/post-orthodox community because I live from a Jewish faith that my personhood derives from God who commands me yet also dignifies me with independent personal responsibility. I stand alongside other postmodern Westerners in typical self-conscious particularity, in my case as a Jewish believer seeking to articulate the Jewish meaning of this paradoxical linkage to God's authority with personal autonomy.

In this universal context, God and the individual self are the two axes around which my faith pivots, but I do not consider them to be of equal significance. For all my insistence on a somewhat curious "independence" of the self, I know that it derives its value from and is subordinate to God. Primacy can never be in serious doubt here since the One creates and the other is created. Yet the creatures have such stature with God that, on occasion, they may argue God's justice, as it were, face to face. When the biblical motif of covenant is restated as relationship rather than as contract—giving expanded scope to the human partner—this hallowed notion can effectively symbolize our postmodern spirituality.

Summoned by God to personal responsibility, my piety expresses itself as a personal activism that finds its motive and standard in my being privileged to serve God as a covenantal partner. Who this God of all humankind might be must yet be explored but one thing may already be said: I am one of those who no longer has such confidence in the human self as to say "God" and merely mean humanity extended.

But I must not take this sketch of my belief any further, for it is quite artificial, a hypothetical extrapolation of the universal aspect of what I know to be far more fundamentally my quite particular, ethnic Jewish faith. I do not have a relationship with God as a person-in-general but as a result of my specific human particularity as a Jew. Directly put, I share in the people of Israel's corporate Covenant with God and my fervent universalism grows directly out of that particularity. I will, in due course, want to analyze in detail each aspect of this relationship. However, I must first turn to the specific development of our postmodern Jewish spirituality, for it is the social reality to which my theology speaks.

3   Through the Shadowed Valley

UR JEWISH TURN from messianic modernism has pivoted on the Holocaust and our response to it. I seek to probe its spiritual footings afresh by analyzing the many anomalies of our religious discussion of the Holocaust.

To begin with, why did it take us until the mid-1960s to initiate a widespread discussion of its "meaning"? Why did almost all our thinkers then reject what Richard Rubenstein claimed was its critical theological challenge? Why did our years of theological discussion yield no ideas not well known before Hitler? Why did our largely agnostic community keep talking about the nature of a God it did not affirm? Why didn't liberated humanism, associated with the "death of God," conquer the Jewish community, which instead became more interested in Jewish spirituality and mysticism? Why did Orthodoxy, allegedly invalidated by the Holocaust, become newly attractive to modernized Jews yet remain a minority? Why did the State of Israel, our great answer to the Holocaust, lose its salvific significance? Why have the non-Orthodox Judaisms, all tarred by modernity's failures, retained the spiritual allegiance of most modernized Jews? And how does the religious experience underlying these developments set our Jewish theological agenda?

Breaking the Barriers to Debating the Holocaust

I begin with the historical background: Emancipation, modernization, secularization. Already in the late 19th century, believing Jewish thinkers created non-Orthodox—that is, liberal—theologies of Judaism while more skeptical types broke with religion and created secular theories of Judaism. This demythologized religion was the accepted ethos of modernized Jews everywhere well before Hitler. This meant that those modern Jews who still spoke about God did so in the terms created by the Jewish rationalists, utilizing Cohenian terms like "God-idea" or "concept of God," which reduced God to the founding premise of rational ethics, or, in the Kaplanian version, to those natural forces that further the development of our human potential.

After World War II, the new democratization of American society intensified our community's uncomfortable inner tension. Our growing acceptance depended on our being one of America's "three great religions," and our suburbanization largely limited our self-identification as Jews to the synagogue. Only this conflicted with the reality that most modern Jews were agnostics—the prewar atheistic certainties having faded—who tolerated worship with difficulty and contented themselves with supporting the synagogue for its familial and communal uses.

Socially and theologically, Jews could not easily discuss the theological implications of the Holocaust, even had they been so inclined. To raise a cry against the God who tolerated such an enormity would expose the full extent of Jewish unbelief to Christian America, thereby undermining Judaism's status as one of America's equivalent faiths. This changed only in the mid-1960s when the Protestant death-of-God movement captured the popular imagination and created a new cultural circumstance. The spiritual convulsion that rolled through much of American Christianity can most easily be explained as a consequence of its long overdue secularization. Consider two of its pivotal books: Paul Van Buren's *The Secular Meaning of the Gospels*, which argued that the Christ needed to be understood in fully human terms, and Harvey Cox's *The Secular City*, which argued for the church's becoming more worldly and political. With Jesus de-trinitized and social responsibility via politics the major focus of Christian living, God had become superfluous, a philosophical and cultural embarrassment. But if America could tolerate such a humanistic Christianity, it might equally do so for a long-secularized Judaism.

When Jews began to join this discussion they did so in a distinctively Jewish way. It had not occurred to any of the seminal Christian death-of-God thinkers—Paul Van Buren, William Hamilton, Gabriel Vahanian, or Thomas J. J. Altizer—to discuss the Holocaust. Their arguments grew from developments in philosophy, culture, or personal religious experience, not from what recent history might imply about the absence of God. Their abstractness clashed sharply with the traditional Jewish concern about God's involvement with people in history, which now suddenly became an argument against God. That critical difference noted, American Jewry quickly joined in the death-of-God discussions as an acceptable American context in which they might finally express their old/new religious doubts.

Rubenstein's Death-of-God Challenge

The form that our ensuing theological debates took shows them to be a continuation of our ongoing arguments about how best to modernize Judaism. Richard Rubenstein's collection of articles entitled *After Auschwitz* defined much of the discussion. He contended that the Holocaust had made it impossible for a responsible person any longer to believe in the God of the Covenant, the One he said Judaism considered "the ultimate, omnipotent actor in history." The sages of biblical-rabbinic Judaism had intimately identified the Covenant with God's justice. When Jews do the good, God blesses them abundantly; when they sin, God punishes them, a theme so significant that the second paragraph of the full *shema* consists of a passage expounding it (Deut. 11:13–21). This led to the further biblical teaching that God employs the enemies of the Jews to punish them, hoping through their suffering to return them to faithfulness. From the prophets until recent times, at least that of the Chmielnicki pogroms (1648), Jewish calamity evoked from Jewish thinkers the Covenantal judgment: Because of our sins God has properly brought this evil upon us.

If so, Rubenstein pointed out, we should in all piety say that God used Hitler to punish and reform us, a view that would give him some vindication, a doctrine Rubenstein considered utterly obscene. It seemed far more blasphemous than inferring from the terrifying reality of the Holocaust that an empty neutrality pervaded the universe and that, at least in our time, God, the God of the Covenant, was dead.

The critique stung and aroused much response. But to whom was it directed? Rubenstein's demand that Jews give up their retributive God, the One who tightly scrutinized actions and responded to them with immediately palpable justice, was addressed to modernized, non-Orthodox Jews. Yet such a God had long had no place in the worldview of those who fled the ghetto. For them, science, not theology, explained what happened in nature, and political commentators, not the prophets, did the same for history. As the 19th century moved on, Jewish thinkers like Hermann Cohen and their rabbinic popularizers had reworked the Jewish view of God to emphasize human agency—ethics—and so saw secular causation adequately explaining specific events.

Rejecting God's Management of History

We can gauge what had already happened to the Jewish view of history from our people's response to the 1903 pogrom in Kishinev. To the world's outrage, the Russian police stood by idly and perhaps encouragingly as forty-seven Jews were killed and ninety-two others were severely wounded by mobs. The reaction of Jews to this tragedy—most particularly of those who lived in Russia—reveals how fully God's retribution had given way to a secularistic commitment to human responsibility. Perhaps some few pietists could still suggest that Russian mobs and their governmental protectors had been God's agents; had any modern Jews suggested the notion they would have been thought ridiculous. And one would have to search hard to find a lament that Jewish sin had brought this evil upon the community. Instead, Russian Zionists called for Jewish self-defense units and Hebrew writers derided the passivity of Jews in simply accepting the slaughter. World Jewry also responded by organizing itself for political action, emergency aid, and rescue, not for fasting and prayer. No modern Jewish writer distressfully inquired where God was during the pogrom; moderns knew that human freedom, not God's retributive pedagogy, lay behind these events.

Every major Jewish philosopher of the 20th century reinforced this more reticent view of God's role in history; surely rationalism permitted little else. In its finest European variety, the neo-Kantianism of Hermann Cohen, God grounds and spurs ethics but a free humanity determines what will happen in history for good or ill. In its favorite American form, Mordecai Kaplan's naturalism, God was carefully redefined to have only limited power. Kaplan considered the notion of God intervening in human affairs to be the kind of carry-over supernaturalism that made moderns reject Jewish belief. Even in Leo Baeck's reach beyond reason to religious consciousness, God remains the mystery we sense behind our ethics, not an independent agent dominating history.

The existentialism of Franz Rosenzweig and Martin Buber did not yield a stronger view of retribution. The former denied that the Jewish people truly lives in history while the latter relegated academic, that is, secularistic, history to the realm of I—it relationships, where God, the Eternal Thou, cannot be encountered. In some ways Abraham Heschel's thought most tellingly instances this distancing of God from events because he alone of our master philosophers wrote his major works after the Holocaust. Though an exalted God dominates his theology, all but a few sentences of his rare comments about the Holocaust refer to human failure, not God's ineffable wisdom and inscrutable justice.

For many years before the Holocaust most rabbis, when they actually referred to God, used the humanized concepts of these master teachers, not a tight reading of Isaiah that might yield the idea that our God is Rubenstein's "ultimate, omnipotent actor in history." The God that Richard Rubenstein discovered as a result of the Holocaust had died, had long since been reinterpreted in other fashion by modern Jews. Consequently, when Jewish thinkers began addressing the religious issues posed by the Holocaust, they did not consider themselves obligated to defend a strong, Deuteronomic view of God's justice. Instead, they explored the implications of this awesome evildoing in the context of their modern understanding of God and human nature.

Denying the Qualitative Uniqueness of the Holocaust

Another assertion by a thinker central to the debate over the Holocaust has also been widely rejected, in this case after acknowledging its pertinence. Emil Fackenheim deems the Holocaust a qualitatively unique instance of evil and stipulates that its uniqueness not be trivialized by reducing it to the singleness of every other event in history. Rather, the Nazi effort to kill all Jews merely because of their Jewishness exposed humankind to an utterly new dimension of evil. As a result, no previous philosophic or Jewish religious response to the problem of evil can be remotely adequate to a discussion of the Holocaust. Elie Wiesel goes further still: the stupefying uniqueness of the Holocaust negates any possibility of our even formulating apt questions about it and, therefore, certainly precludes the possibility of our finding answers. Fackenheim and others, conscious that philosophizing might be a blasphemous mitigation of the horror, nonetheless believe that we must attempt to elucidate its implications for contemporary Jewish belief.

Fackenheim argues that the Nazis' unparalleled depravity arose more from their intention than from their acts. They carried out this evil fully conscious of its perversity; worse, they did it for the sheer willfulness of doing so monstrous an evil. He supports this view by citing numerous examples of the Nazis self-destructively pursuing their demonic goal, as in diverting railroad equipment desperately needed to repel the Allied invasion so they could continue transporting Jews to the death camps. Fackenheim's interpretation of Nazi intentions is ultimately unconvincing because it finds so little direct support in the vast historic evidence about the Holocaust. To the contrary, the more we study the records of the Third Reich the more we see how concretely goal-directed and therefore routinized was the progression from discrimination to degradation and then to murder. Far from consciously seeking to do evil for evil's sake they applied their fabled ethnic discipline to achieving what their demented logic had identified as a supreme "ethical" good: ridding Europe and the world of a racial strain that would otherwise destroy true human value. Most Jewish thinkers consider the Holocaust a most egregious human evil—if one may use comparative terminology when referring to events of awesome inhumanity—but one that needs to be considered on the continuum of other human evils, not in a realm of its own.

In somewhat the same spirit, there has been a general rejection of the corollary claim by Wiesel, Rubenstein, Fackenheim, and others that the Holocaust must now become a second Sinai, the determining reality of contemporary Jewish existence. If by this they only mean that Jews should reject any interpretation of Judaism that has not been centrally shaped by the Holocaust, few would disagree. But since they have proposed that we should now view all of existence, human and Jewish, in terms of the Holocaust, their position has been rejected as disproportionate. Genocidal destruction has not been the common theme of many terrifying ills of late 20th-century history, which mostly have arisen from a doleful continuation of the human failings so often seen in history: inaction, ignorance, mindlessness, venality, perversity, and mendaciousness. Little seems new except the scale of our malefaction, the education and efficiency we bring to it, and the immediacy with which the world gets to know about it. Moreover, a Holocaust-centered view of life might easily obscure how much goodness people do day by day. Our people is a case in point for, despite our troubles, we do not spend our days desperately fending off extinction. While the Holocaust must fundamentally figure in our view of Jewish identity, it does not faithfully teach us the reality of Jewish existence.

Our Good God, Limited or Inscrutable?

When the thinkers turned directly to the issue of theodicy, they mostly followed two lines of interpretation. Jews who above all sought clarity in their beliefs and wanted good reasons for believing, argued that rather than being omnipotent, God has but limited power. God may be as powerful as anything can be and supremely good; God does all the good that God can do. Occasionally that will not be sufficient to counteract an eruption of the evil latent in nature or caused by human freedom. This very human freedom to do good or evil, and thus to affirm or defy our most intimate knowledge of God's will, decisively proves God's finitude and rationally explains why evil, slight or gruesome, can occur.

This theodicy was not the esoteric possession of a Jewish elite but had been widely disseminated among American Jews by the many disciples of a number of influential teachers. Thus, Mordecai Kaplan, echoing the thought of American religious liberals like William James, taught his students at the Jewish Theological Seminary the concept of such a finite God already in the 1930s and then wrote a book elucidating it. Henry Slonimsky, the inspiration and spiritual guide of two generations of rabbis trained at Stephen Wise's Jewish Institute of Religion, taught a similar doctrine in the same period. Utilizing European philosophical trends, he intriguingly suggested that the limited God "grows" as does everything else alive, in God's case through human partnership in completing creation.

The more philosophical rationalists and their followers took an oblique approach to limiting God, developing their theodicy in terms of reason's proper power rather than by speculation on God's nature. They generally followed Hermann Cohen's neo-Kantianism, which maintained that a properly rational mind cannot logically deal with questions about ultimate reality, i.e., metaphysics—in this case, whether God's power is finite or infinite. Thoughtful people should therefore base their religious belief on what the mature mind can know with certainty, namely, one's ethical obligations. So the main stream of American non-Orthodoxy communicated a "God-idea" whose religious function essentially was to ground its ethics. But its concept of God had nothing to do with "explaining" the reality of evil, a metaphysical problem that transcends the powers of reason. Instead of worrying about meaningless because unanswerable questions, a rational person would "answer" evil by ethics, that is, by preventive or remedial action. This pragmatic, anti-speculative response to evil has so spoken to the American Jewish soul that it has become a major aspect of every variety of theodicy among us.

Theories of God's finitude are appealing because they clarify how one can intelligently believe in a good God without denying the reality of evil. They also have won wide acceptance because they motivate moral responsibility by their conclusion that human ethics must complete what God's limited power leaves undone. But they generate a sufficient number of new religious problems, logical and spiritual, that many Jews have rejected them. (I shall return to this issue in chapter 10.)

These more traditional believers reaffirm the view commonly considered characteristic of rabbinic Judaism: Though we know much about God, we also know that God far transcends what we can know about God. We do not know why the good God permits the evils of this world but we trust God anyway. We do so out of gratitude and awe. Each day, rising up and lying down, if we can say the hundred blessings required of a Jew, we are reminded of God's continual gifts. Our observance teaches a piety of the ordinary, a hallowing of the many gifts we might otherwise arrogantly consider ours by right. This daily thanksgiving sets the context for facing the evils beyond our control or understanding; it enables many people to accept the unexplainable. For few of us are Job and most of us would acknowledge that God gives us very much more than we deserve or could claim. Of course, the Jobian exceptions are real and they deeply disrupt everyone's relationship with God. In the hideous evil of the Holocaust, the exceptional threatened to become the norm. No wonder many people spoke of the death of God, and no wonder limited-God theologies gained great currency. Yet large numbers of Jews also took the classic path of Jewish faith: they affirmed God even though they did not understand God. They may have done so with trembling, but as in their experience of human love, they knew that some mysteries require us to give the heart priority over the mind.

Both these post-Holocaust positions regarding God and evil had been widely known in the Jewish community before Hitler. Astonishingly, for all that the death-of-God debates centered on theodicy, they produced no new theory or doctrine of God but only some linguistic variations of the old ones. Let me compensate for this sweeping generalization by immediately indicating how our sense of God's unfathomable absence during the Holocaust did intensify our two pre-Holocaust theodicies. Few thinkers had imagined before Hitler that God was so limited or so utterly inscrutable. No one had ever considered before that God could be so withdrawn. And this awesome sense of God's potential unavailability gave a terrifying new reality to the best defense that can be offered for God's tolerance of evil: that goodness is so central to God that God never violates humankind's freedom to do good or evil—not even in the face of enormities as great as those of the Nazis.

The Latent Content of the Holocaust Debates

Yet even after noting this radicalization of theological tone, the enigma persists. If our community had not seriously believed in the God whose demise had been announced, if our years of intellectual debate left us with largely the same understandings of God and evil known before the Holocaust, why did these religious debates so trouble our spirits?

For one thing, some Jews had never become as modern in their thought as in their life-style and their beliefs never progressed beyond the literalistic notions acquired as children. For another, the trauma of the Nazi barbarity made some Jews regress to their childhood notions of God as the all-nurturing Mama-Papa. All such images of God would be under severe stress as a result of the Holocaust debates. But these suppositions hardly explain why the spiritual dislocation we experienced in those days was so widely and deeply felt. We must seek our understanding elsewhere and we will find it by following up an observation of Elie Wiesel that the death camps, rather than shattering the faith of the traditionalists, most fully undid the worldview of the intellectuals and liberals.

This explanation, I am convinced, derives as much from our general cultural situation as it does from our frightful particular experience. With the inner life of modern Jews dominated more by Western civilization than by a distinctive Judaism, the general retreat from messianic modernism could not but deeply affect Jews. To explain how this manifested itself in our community, let me proceed by means of a theory of the mid-19th-century German theologian Ludwig Feuerbach. Seeking to reestablish religion's relevance to sophisticates giddy over the advances in human thought and technology, he suggested that, at its core, religion grows from human aspiration, not God's revelation. In creating our various concepts of God, we are, he argued, really specifying our highest, most ideal human values. Under cover of our God-talk we are celebrating the human potential, projecting the self we desire to be to a transcendent level and, by calling it "God," investing it with commanding power (a theological notion Freud later adopted and gave rich psychological content).

While I do not accept Feuerbach's insight as anything like the whole truth about our views of God, I believe what he taught us about projection powerfully explains a major part of our response to the Holocaust. If God-talk mostly discloses our human ideals, then our post-Holocaust theological distress was a classic instance of Freudian displacement, of substituting a less emotional topic for a highly disturbing one. Not having believed much in God, we modern Jews could not be deeply troubled by God's death. But if God-talk projects beliefs about humanity, "the death of God" shielded us from the tragic loss of the one "god" in whom we moderns had avidly trusted—ourselves, humankind. We had expected no other to save us from all our human ills. Our operative faith had been "the perfectibility of man [sic]" which culminated, through our ethical action, in "the Messianic Age." In high statistical disproportion, Jews had served as the prophets of this humanism and taught the secular salvation of politics, intellect, and high culture.

Then we saw Germany Nazified and our people become Nazi Germany's special victims. This "transvaluation of all values" turned out to be more seismic than any imagined by Nietzsche, who late in the 19th century proclaimed the death of religion's God and became the darling of optimistic Jewish secularizers. The Holocaust refuted everything we had identified with modernity, so much so that, before the evidence of what had occurred become incontrovertible, it was not deemed possible. Trusting human progress as we did, we could give as little credence to the early reports of the mass murder as the hindsight historians now can give to our blindness then.

A corollary psychic denial of Western culture's spiritual bankruptcy operated for years after World War II as American Jews basked in unprecedented social acceptance and economic success. Only America's own self-doubt brought on by racial conflict and the Vietnam War made it possible for Jews, like others, to begin to face the clash between their experience and their functional optimism. Even then, our psyches could not stand so direct an attack on the faith on which we had staked our lives. Instead of facing up to the loss of our messianic self-image, we found it easier to agonize about the death of the traditional God we had not really believed in.

Human *Tzimtzum* Makes a Place for God

Not the least irony in this ongoing development has been its eventual reversal of course. The Jewish death-of-God movement heralded itself as the triumph of modernity. By ending our dependency on a revealing, saving God it liberated us for maturely independent responsibility. The result, however, has not been the proliferation of socially concerned ethical activists but a radical loss of sure values that has sapped the moral energy of our society and thereby discredited modernity. Even more unanticipated was the unwitting role of the death-of-God debates in bringing our community, or a critical portion of it, back to God. The Holocaust discussions began with many people denying God's existence out of simple moral indignation. Some, asserting their credo as moderns, believed that human rationality itself mandated ethics. Others claimed human nature was intrinsically good so that once we made society less malignant human evil would disappear. In either case, why should rational people mourn the passing of the God of synagogue and church?

But where else shall we gain such secular moral certainty after the Holocaust? Surely not from the old assumptions about human rationality and goodness. German culture and intellectuality abetted more than it challenged the Nazi madness and the democratic, liberal ethos of the Allies did not motivate them to disrupt the Nazi murder. With this dismal record before us, with our continuing exposure to the evil done everywhere by people in places high and low, only a minority of Jews can still unhesitatingly assert that human beings are primarily rational or inherently good. Contemporary philosophy does nothing to refute these practical conclusions. Academics once made what appeared to be a convincing case for considering ethics an essential component of human reason; today's thinkers regularly restrict rationality to logical reasoning, relegating the motive and content of ethics to less compelling aspects of our being or social life. Thus, the commanding sense of rational moral law, which we once took so for granted that it justified our denying God's value and reality, has been repudiated by history, experience, and intellect. We Jews have not been exceptions to Western civilization's disillusionment with modernity. If anything, our experience has been a major factor in bringing it to its postmodern turn.

For decent human beings, the loss of a sure ground of human values must be traumatic. For Jews, it is utterly intolerable, for it blurs the qualitative difference between the Nazis and their victims. *Regardless of what the world knows or cares, anything that mitigates the categorical distinction between the S. S. death camp operators and their Jewish victims violates our most fundamental contemporary experience and contravenes a central mandate of our tradition.* One need not be a philosopher or intellectual to know this truth; one only needs still to be human. Against all our modern expectations, the Holocaust showed us evil, real and unrelieved, and taught us that, against all our yearning to be tolerant and pluralistic, utter evil must be opposed absolutely. And that mandate makes sense only if we can still honestly affirm the reality of unqualified good.

The experience of primal evil, confronting us with its thoroughgoing negativity, has forced us to affirm an equally elemental good. But pure secularity no longer knows so categorical, so definitive a good and our moral indignation therefore forces us to move in an opposite direction. If we insist that our intuition of a commanding goodness is not an illusion, then, as thinking people, we must search for its ground—and this has led the Jewish community, as so much of the rest of Western civilization, to a postsecular spiritual search. If we have even a dim, troubled, barely verbalizable acknowledgment of an unshakable demand for value at the heart of the universe, one that we must, to remain human, answer and exemplify, then we have found our personal way to what our tradition in various ways called "God." It is this postmodern recovery of spirituality that lies behind our community's general rejection of the death-of-God movement and a significant minority's involvement in Orthodoxy, *havurot*, mysticism, and other forms of religious search.

This experience of the absoluteness of the good has been critical to the spiritual change that has come over Western civilization and has, even more profoundly, affected the Jews. For the grisly evil of the Holocaust epitomizes all the vileness that, out of revulsion, has been the dominant motive bringing individuals and groups to search for a postmodern, realistic spirituality.

The Corollary Ethnic Turn of the Postmodern Sensibility

There is an important concomitant to postmodern spirituality: ethnic rootedness. Emil Fackenheim identified this post-Holocaust reality famously in postulating what he termed our 614th commandment: "The authentic Jew of today is not permitted to hand Hitler yet another, posthumous victory." A commanding if unidentifiable Voice from Auschwitz demanded that Jews do what they could to promote the survival and welfare of the people of Israel, and much of the positive tone of Jewish life in recent decades has been due to Jewish acceptance of this responsibility. I focus on two major aspects of this resurgent ethnicity, artificially separating them from one another: The more obvious renewal centered on the State of Israel; its companion development involved Diaspora Jewry in a more explicitly ethnicized—that is, particularistically Jewish—manner of observance and belief.

The State of Israel became a central concern of most of world Jewry only as a result of the Six Day War of 1967. Before then only ideological Zionists—a tiny minority among us—found the reality of their Jewish lives substantially altered by the establishment of the State of Israel or its early accomplishments. Few Jews immigrated there who did not have to; few learned Hebrew or involved themselves in political action on its behalf. Only in rhetoric did it serve as world Jewry's "spiritual center."

The circumstances of the Six Day War and its consequences radically raised our Jewish consciousness toward the State of Israel. The prior public discussion of the Holocaust had made us apprehensive that God would again be absent, and television pictures of demonstrators in various Arab capitals calling for the destruction of the State of Israel made the threat personal. The great Christian churches were silent, the leaders of the democracies noncommittal. The three-day news blackout after the war began was a time of hideous imagination, of deep soul-searching, of religious hope and consternation, and produced an overwhelming, voluntary outpouring of help, most notably from Jews who had never previously included themselves in the community. Then news came of the staggering Israeli victory. World Jewry experienced an elation that transcended relief from dread or rejoicing at Israeli prowess; the Bible calls it deliverance. Jews everywhere found themselves uncomprehendingly overwhelmed by the sight of soldiers converging on the Temple Mount's Western Wall; atheists, agnostics, and believers alike found themselves moved to prayer. I believed then and believe now that we had personally experienced God's saving power, something I can explain as little as I can God's absence during the Holocaust—but an experience I remain certain was not illusion, one real enough that it moved a critical mass of our people to rededicate themselves to Jewish existence.

Subsequently, the effect of this revelatory moment diminished, but it still powerfully shaped the ensuing ethnic-political struggle, particularly when the 1973 war with Egypt showed how vulnerable the State of Israel remained. Now proudly particularistic, Diaspora Jews demanded that their leaders unabashedly lobby their governments on the State of Israel's behalf so that this generation would never be accused of repeating the sins of the Holocaust.

World Jewry also had positive grounds for its new sense of identification of Jews with the State of Israel. Again and again Jews who visited there returned deeply affected by what they saw Jews achieving as a Jewish society. In what Koestler called "our political ice-age," the State of Israel appeared a model of moral politics; it also became the shining symbol of our people's transpolitical, instinctive, life-affirming answer to Hitler's nihilism, giving it a numinosity, a sacred aura that even a secularized generation could not ignore. Theologically put, it made evident what the Holocaust had made us doubt: that the Covenant between God and the people of Israel continues in full force. With this resurgence of particularity, self-deprecating universalism gave way to the postmodern query, "Is this good for the Jews?"

Does God Still Have a Role in Jewish Particularity?

I believe the roots of our intensified Jewishness go far deeper than national solidarity or group pride. In these years of danger and self-esteem, many of us partisans of human equality, who had eschewed making special claims for the Jewish people, found that we also believed an absoluteness attached to Jewish survival and flourishing. We had finally become conscious that for us the demise of the Jewish people would mean not merely a social trauma or broken emotional ties, but an irreparable human loss. Whether in response to danger or a result of love for this folk or both, many of us discovered that we believed the Jewish people to be indispensable, not merely to ourselves but to the universe and its scheme of things. We now knew there was something transcendent about Jewish continuity. I will dare the overstatement: We believe God "needs" Jews—or, if you prefer, God "wants" Jews to be Jews and not simply Noahides with a Hebraic ethnic coloration.

The unconventional Orthodox writer and community leader Irving ("Yitz") Greenberg has reached the opposite conclusion. His vision of post-Holocaust Jewishness rejects any more-than-human mandate for Jewish survival. He contends that the Holocaust teaches us not that God is dead but that God no longer has any right to command Israel, i.e., the Holocaust proclaims the death of *mitzvah*. Only the Jewish will to continue Jewish existence now keeps the Covenant and Jewish obligation alive.

I hear in this radicalism the anguished outcry of a traditional Jew who, for love of Jews and all human beings, cannot bear what the God of classic Jewish practice allowed to happen in the Holocaust. But denying any transcendent significance to Jewish duty raises the issue of how much importance we should attach to it and, more critically, what sacrifices we would make for it. Of course, as long as we find Jewish experience rewarding and have a Jewish memory rich with emotion and knowledge, Jewish life will continue. And as long as Western culture remains spiritually barren, the varied resources of Jewish culture will commend themselves. However, if

Jewish living is only a matter of choice, why should we take on its special burdens in the State of Israel or the Diaspora when we can do as much or more for ourselves and others through less troublesome social forms?

Greenberg apparently believes that we can count on the endurance of postmodern Jewish ethnicity and he seeks to insure this by educating for Jewish literacy and values. Where he and others believe we can separate the ethnic from the spiritual drives in the postmodern ethos, I believe this exclusively humanistic view of ethnicity returns us to the faulty premise of Jewish modernity, the humanization of Jewish obligation. And as we move toward the 21st century I see considerable evidence in the State of Israel that an increasing number of Jews who feel the extent of their Jewishness is essentially a matter of personal choice are giving it a considerably lower priority than it once generally had. If, on the other hand, we primarily know that Jewish discipline deserves more concern than this, that it has a certain commanding power to it, then we need a more adequate theory of Jewish duty than this. The conflict between these two interpretations of post-Holocaust Jewish particularity will have a considerable influence on the vitality of Jewish life in the generation or so ahead. I return to this issue frequently in the later chapters of this book.

The Postmodern Integrity of Folk and Faith

To some extent, the Jewish turn to religious particularity began as part of the late-1960s search for ethnic roots. Diaspora Jews frequently said they wanted to be "more Jewish," by which they generally meant more visibly and identifiably part of their folk. Despite their identification with the State of Israel, this led only a few to become dedicated nationalists or Hebraists, a development paralleled in the State of Israel where Zionism as an ideology motivating personal sacrifice evaporated. Significantly, Zionist idealism remained strong mainly when linked to religious belief, and the initial activities of the Orthodox Gush Emunim movement in the 1980s evoked the admiration of secular Israelis because of its adherents' uncommon willingness to sacrifice for the national good.

In the Diaspora, where Jews faced greater obstacles in asserting their Jewish particularity, the drive to be "more Jewish" mainly resulted in people adopting more traditional forms of Jewish observance. For the first time in modernity, a sizable number of young

American Jews insisted on being more visibly Jewish than their parents were. Reform Jews became more Hebraic, Zionistic, and ritualistic while Conservative Jews stressed the halakhic aspects of their movement. Responding to the lack of Jewish seriousness and the impersonality of the established institutions, *havurot* and *minyanim* burgeoned. Some modern Jews became visibly observant, *frum*, and many others adorned their life-styles with identifying practices selected from the neotraditionalistic *Jewish Catalog*—all of this a shock to the comfortably universalized.

The most unanticipated surge took place in Orthodoxy. In the decades after World War II, the most visible segment of the movement combined faithful halakhic observance with such cultural pursuits as the *halakhah* found acceptable and called itself "Modern Orthodoxy." Ironically, as this modernization reached maturity, fundamentalisms generally became appealing because their God-ordained particularity distanced their adherents from a failing modernity. By the late 1970s, Orthodoxy, once thought a doomed relic of the Middle Ages, began attracting many sophisticated Jews disenchanted with modernity. As the society's social conservatism grew, separatistic Orthodoxy took on a new self-confidence and challenged the non-Orthodox about the depth of their Jewishness and the grounds of their universalistic ethics.

In this shift to the right, Modern Orthodoxy found itself accused of being "too modern." Ultra-Orthodoxy, the Jewish equivalent of our civilization's fundamentalist movements, now demanded a Jewish life more absolute in tone and less "goyish" in demeanor. They argued that the Holocaust gave Jews every reason to put as much distance between themselves and the gentile world as was compatible with community security. Not seeing the broader context, most community observers were startled by the number of modernized Jews attracted to just those Orthodox communities that appeared to have compromised the least with modernity. Perhaps the most dramatic manifestation of this Jewish rejection of modernity may be seen in those *baalei teshuvah* who seek out *yeshivot* of such premodern piety that their leaders, right-wing adherents of Agudat Yisrael or various Hasidic sects, decry the State of Israel itself as un-Jewish.

A larger and more politically effective group united their ethnicity and religiosity in an activist Orthodox Zionism, esteeming the State of Israel for enabling Jews to live the fullest form of Torah-centered Judaism. Their Diaspora cohorts, unlike most secular Jews, found *aliyah*, immigration to the Holy Land, a compelling Jewish obligation while their Israeli compeers took action to fulfill God's injunction to take possession and settle the whole biblical land of Israel, most notably by settlements in Judea and Samaria. They believe that the laws of the Torah alone define the proper status of Palestinians in the Jewish land; and if this stance or their activism arouses an adverse world response, that is a gentile problem, an assertion of religio-ethnic self-respect that clearly exemplifies one form of the postmodern consciousness.

As We Move to a New Secular Millennium

Social conservatism and spiritual orthodoxies dominated the ethos of the 1980s, everywhere scoring impressive victories over liberalism. In so doing they also demonstrated the excesses to which they can lead and thereby caused many moderns, and certainly most Jews, to see the limits of their revisionism. I am not saying that the power of the right has so ebbed that it will have few future political victories and the old liberalism will regain dominance. Should antimodernity regain its messianic fervor and social sway, the Jewish spirituality I see arising may well die aborning—but I do not expect that to happen. Rather, in a manner more Hegelian than I am usually comfortable with, the modernist thesis having been succeeded by a conservative antithesis, what appears to be emerging is a spiritual synthesis that learns from yet transcends them both. My own Jewish theological program speaks to this new spiritual sensibility.

My analysis of the postconservative mood begins with noting how much those who fought modernity quietly coopted many of its concerns. We see this epitomized in the phenomenal burgeoning of right-wing Orthodox publishing, which has made available an extraordinary range of classic Jewish texts with commentary, halakhic literature, how-to books, and general spiritual inspiration. The characteristics of this literature are telling. For one thing, the authors typically keep the reader's personal interests before them rather than merely communicate their understanding of the tradition, as earlier Orthodox authors did. Moreover, the concerns they often seek to respond to turn out to be quite modern, like ethics, respect for people, and person-to-person relationships. Most important, these books are in English and fully Western in their idiom, making this the first generation of rabbinic Jews that has so substantially sought to communicate its message in what our tradition called *laaz*, a "foreign" language.

Orthodox Zionism furnishes another example. The Jews most resolutely opposed to Western culture became anti-Zionist, deeming political Zionism, as did much of European Orthodoxy, a heretical secularization of Judaism learned from gentiles. Orthodox Zionism itself results from a certain modernization. One sees this even more clearly in the contrast between the politically passive piety of the old Diaspora religious tradition and the contemporary activism of Gush Emunim and its offshoots. In this Orthodoxy, modern political activism has become a companion to the *mitzvot*.

Simply put, though many Jews now seek some distance between themselves and the culture, few of us indeed want to re-ghettoize. Overwhelmingly, world Jewry has rejected the two outstanding forms of intensified ethnicity and religiosity, living in the State of Israel and becoming Orthodox. Many have done so out of inertia, self-serving, or a bland refusal to take Jewish identity seriously. Yet assuming most Jews are not simply venal, we have a right to ask about the metaethic that makes them want to stay Jewish but not through such ethnic and religious transformation. In chapters 17 and 18 I argue that though Orthodoxy and the State of Israel have powerfully molded the postmodern Jewish consciousness, each has also given Jews reason to deny it Jewish primacy or ultimacy. Here I want only to indicate my conviction that the limits to our particularization come from our belief that much of the universal ethical message of modern Judaism remains true even in a post-modern era.

The Modern in the Postmodern

World Jewry's great pride in the State of Israel had largely been connected with its moral accomplishment. Few Jews expected that one could run a state and remain saintly, and for years whenever certain Israeli actions seemed morally questionable they overlooked them. But in the 1980s, with many Jews believing ethics to be central to Judaism and Jewish morality the key to Jewish continuity, the situation changed. The realization that much of Israel's citizenry and its leaders had a radically different view of Jewish obligation finally brought many of them and even some of their organizations to the point of public dissent and private dissociation from the State of Israel. From this experience I infer that, for all our intensified ethnicity, we so strongly retain a commitment to modern ethics that it can occasionally take precedence over the unique focus of our ethnic pride, the State of Israel.

Not the least evidence leading to this conclusion has been the parallel development in the State of Israel itself. The incursion into Lebanon and the response to the Intifada caused many Israelis such unsettling ethical distress that it has led to an unprecedented division over national purpose and character. In their exposed and dangerous situation, Israelis have very much more at stake in whatever decisions are made than anyone else. Nonetheless, they face the same conflict of values that confronts Diaspora Jews: To what extent should the universalistic ethics of Judaism espoused by us in our modernity influence our postmodern Jewish commitment to ethnic self-respect?

This same return of our repressed modernity emerges in our renewed spirituality. The attractive assets of contemporary orthodoxies, their certain standards and their close-knit communities, appeal greatly by contrast to liberalism's moral flabbiness and personal uncertainty. Yet these very strengths contain such potential dangers that they prevent most Jews from accepting our Orthodoxy. Those who truly know what God specifically wants of us can tolerate only quite limited dissent. Seeking or achieving political power, orthodoxies can channel their absoluteness into what most Jews would call extremism, zealotry, and fanaticism—we have seen too many examples of this phenomenon both in our community and without not to be disenchanted with claims to absolute truth. It seems far more reasonable to most Jews to affirm another motif of modern Judaism: that all human beings necessarily have a limited knowledge of God's will. Though we passionately stake our lives on such knowledge of God as we do possess, we think our limited understanding requires us to live in peaceful mutual regard with those whose faith radically disagrees with ours; our postmodern religiosity must foster pluralism and practice the spirituality of democracy.

The continuing modernity of our postmodern spirituality has been epitomized by the anomalous invocation of the concept of *tikkun olam* as a Jewish call to ethical action. This represents a remarkable transformation of the term, which was first used in the Talmud to provide a pragmatic justification for certain compromises the rabbis made between clashing values in the law. Thus, its earliest Jewish meaning was something like "good social policy." In the 16th century, the Lurianic *kabbalah* utilized the phrase to designate a human mystical task. Luria's cosmogony taught that God's act of creation resulted in a shattered material world, which the Jewish people was brought into being to "mend" (*tikkun*), thus, eventually, bringing the Messiah. We were to do this by meticulously observing the commandments, accompanying each deed by a mystical intention to restore the channels of grace between the upper and the lower worlds that were specific to this act. In particular, this system stressed the value of *kavvanot,* the mystic commentary-intentions that the adepts created for each required prayer. Today's *tikkun olam* has little or nothing to do with halakhic adjustments or mystical intentions. Rather, it summons us to Jewish ethical duty, most often of a universal cast—but in keeping with our intensified postmodern particularity, it legitimates this remnant of modernity by cloaking it in a classic Jewish term.

In sum, this dialectical postmodern evolution has brought much of world Jewry to a paradoxical spiritual situation. We are too realistic about humankind to return to the messianic modernism that once animated us. Instead we sense we derive our deepest understanding of what a person ought to be and humankind ought to become from participating in the Covenant, our people's historic relationship with God. But not exclusively. The Emancipation was not altogether a lie. It taught us something true about the dignity of each person and about the democracy and pluralism that make it effective, and this must be carried over into our postmodern Judaism. These affirmations—corporate Covenant and self-determination—can easily come into conflict, yet we propose to live our lives affirming both of them. I understand it to be the task of Jewish theology today to give a faithful, thoughtful explication of this paradox.

The Particular Self That Undertakes This Effort

I cannot bring this section to a close without an additional personal/professional observation. I do not mean by this Jewish historical/spiritual analysis to convey the impression that had these developments not occurred I would not have come to the theological position I detail in what follows. My concern with these issues and the earliest work drawn on for this book preceded most of the history I have been discussing.

My theology has evolved primarily from my ongoing personal effort to understand my Judaism. What began as a childhood interest in the ideas behind Jewish living took on intellectual form at the

university and led me to my anomalous concern with Jewish theology
at rabbinical school. This interest of mine seemed so odd to most
other Jews I knew that I was delighted at two discoveries I made
there and later. For one, I found a few friends who also wanted to
delineate the intellectual system undergirding a richly particular yet
universal modern Jewish belief; we were, I can now say, proto-
postmodern. We instructed each other by argument and proposal,
and perhaps more lastingly by calling attention to the contemporary
resources each of us discovered that might be of help to us. The
second happy revelation was that, though no one ever mentioned it
in class, there had been a century-long though limited tradition of
modern Jewish theology/philosophy. I found my place in American
Jewry as a member of the small subcommunity of abstract thinkers
still carrying on this activity. I discovered my compelling problem
and appropriate method by comparison and contrast with their ideas,
past and present. Dialogue with them, as the following pages testify,
remains central to my thought.

In the initial stages of groping with my problem and seeking a
way of responding to it, I did not anticipate that much of our
community would be moved by historic events to the religious
situation I was struggling to understand and articulate. I rather
thought that were I able to bring my thinking to systematic form—
an effort that, in the writing, has taken more than three decades—I
would be speaking only to that small minority of Jews interested in
thinking about their religion. It came as a special joy to me then
when, as postsecularity made its effect felt, the number of people
interested in Jewish theology increased. But I never imagined that
my thought would speak to the more general experience of less
abstractly inclined Jews, as I now think it does. In this experience of
being able to comprehend the spiritual depth of what our people has
been going through in recent decades, I have found both confirmation
of my basic position and much that caused me to refine and amplify
it. I still believe it independently persuasive because of its intellectual
merits, yet I now dare hope that, by the insight it gives into what
we have been living through, my theology may commend itself to
many Jews as a reasonable version of their hitherto unarticulated
faith.

A Postliberal Theology of Jewish Duty

I

God, the Ground of Our Values

יִתְבָּרַךְ וְיִשְׁתַּבַּח, וְיִתְפָּאַר וְיִתְרוֹמַם וְיִתְנַשֵּׂא וְיִתְהַדָּר,
וְיִתְעַלֶּה וְיִתְהַלָּל שְׁמֵהּ דְּקֻדְשָׁא, בְּרִיךְ הוּא, לְעֵלָּא
מִן כָּל בִּרְכָתָא וְשִׁירָתָא, תֻּשְׁבְּחָתָא וְנֶחֱמָתָא, דַּאֲמִירָן בְּעָלְמָא,

Though God is beyond the blessings and the hymns and the praises
and the consolations offered on earth,
blessed and praised and acclaimed and exalted
and extolled and honored and glorified and lauded
[by God] be the name of the Holy.

מַח נֹּאמַר לְפָנֶיךָ, יְיָ אֱלֹהֵינוּ וֵאלֹהֵי אֲבוֹתֵינוּ, הֲלֹא כָּל הַגִּבּוֹרִים
כְּאַיִן לְפָנֶיךָ, וְאַנְשֵׁי הַשֵּׁם כְּלֹא הָיוּ, וַחֲכָמִים כִּבְלִי מַדָּע,
וּנְבוֹנִים כִּבְלִי הַשְׂכֵּל,

What can we say in Your presence,
Adonai, our God and God of our ancestors?
Are not all victors as nothing before You,
those of great renown as though they had never been,
the wisest as if without knowledge,
and the most intelligent as if without understanding?

4 God-Israel-Torah: Our Holistic Context

A SIMPLISTIC distinction between philosophy and theology lauds the former for beginning without assumptions and asserting only what reason requires, hence yielding new truth. It belittles theology as proceeding from faith, containing its content in advance and using reason not to generate truth but to bolster its preconceptions. I would agree that systematic religious thought often exhibits a certain circularity so that its major conclusions echo its grounding premises. How could it be otherwise? When one seeks to probe the most fundamental issues of reality—as theology seeks to do—the results ought to tell us about what is utterly primary and, therefore, should remind us of the premises on which the work proceeded. Today, we see such methodological circularity not only in theology but in most other intellectual disciplines. The methods we employ for our investigations turn out to be decisive for our findings, which is one reason we argue so much over proper methodology. And, in theology as elsewhere, if too much dissonance arises between the results of our studies and the preliminary intuitions or other knowledge we brought to them, we will consider revising our method of procedure, even to the point of a Kuhnian "paradigm shift."

The generative vision I bring to this work is holistic, a vision of a Judaism in which God and the Jewish people stand in an ongoing relationship structured by Torah as record and mandate, and the background of whose practice is God's relationship with all humankind. I believe our tradition centrally transmitted this understanding to me though I have reinterpreted it in ways particularly appropriate to our time. From my postmodern perspective, universalism can be legitimated only from a particular base (see, especially, chapter 13). So I proceed more from my Judaism toward the culture than did the modernists, who thought society had the surer truth. Working this way, we cannot proceed with the doctrine of God alone—for it is universal—nor the doctrine of Israel alone—how will we transcend the particular?—nor from the doctrine of Torah alone—who authorizes and who lives it? We must intimately correlate God, Israel, and Torah, rendering our Jewish theology holistic.

Here, as elsewhere, holism means the field effect of each element—each major Jewish belief—on each other element and their combination with each other to constitute a patterned entity. Two formal considerations flow from this. First, only the interaction between beliefs, not some alleged discrete content of each of them, gives each notion its special character in a given belief structure. Second, the pattern of the relationships between the beliefs—that is, which are primary, which secondary, which held in dialectical tension—gives the theology or religion its distinctive spiritual cast. Let us explore these methodological guidelines before applying them. Since gaining greater understanding of our God supplies the foundation for all that follows, I use that topic as an example of the effects of employing a holistic approach to specific theological motifs.

What is the Characteristic Jewish Interest in God?

Historical Christianity concerned itself centrally about redeeming humankind from its sins. Not every faith in Jesus or the one God will do this, so Christianity devoted much of its intellectual energy in its first five hundred years to defining the idea of the God who saves. Christianity's very term for an exposition of faith, "theology," literally "the science of God," indicates the importance it attaches to the analysis and exposition of the doctrine of God. By contrast, the older Buddhism, that of the Theravadins, considers the notion of God irrelevant. Devoted to releasing humankind from suffering, it teaches the Buddha's way of achieving this by reorienting our consciousness. The task being a human one, the Buddha maintained a "noble silence" about "God."

What equally preoccupied traditional Judaism? I venture to suggest that most of us would say: the hearing and heeding of the old but continuing divine command to sanctify our lives as a people and as single selves. We call this living instruction—its holy history, its manifold amplifications, its study, and its faithful or creative practice—"Torah." Broadly, "Torah" refers to the substance of our ongoing Jewish religious experience, and I shall be using the term in this expansive sense.

Three facets of our tradition confirm the correctness of this surmise: our controversies, our literature, and our structure of authority. From the conflicts between prophets and priests down to the differences between Reform, Orthodox, Conservative, and other Jews, understandings of Torah have divided Jews. Our literature too has largely dedicated itself to defining with greater clarity and in changed circumstances how God would have us live. Furthermore, in the area of Torah-duty and there alone did classic Judaism provide for binding decisions and an officialdom to exercise religious discipline.

We can easily draw the intellectual implications of this distinctive religiosity: The *halakhah* details the actions that Judaism considers primary. It does not directly embrace the realm of religious thought, which must therefore be judged to be of secondary Jewish concern, and this it relegates to the Oral Law's subsidiary realm of discourse, the *aggadah*. Where the *halakhah* seeks to resolve opposing views, the *aggadah* grandly tolerates apparent contradictions, where the *halakhah* labors to fix the authoritative path for all to follow, the *aggadah* extends liberty to all to seek an ever more adequate expression of the meaning of their faith. As long as they are reasonably observant of the prescriptions of the *halakhah*, then, Jews may traditionally indulge their aggadic imaginations.

This arrangement begs for a theological interpretation. I see it as a creative outcome of the formative Jewish religious experience that duty is primary. Our sages developed the *aggadah* as the proper vehicle for Jewish religious ideas because their awe of God transcended their respect for reason, and their certainty about obligation exceeded their confidence in religious speculation. By making the *aggadah* the junior partner of the *halakhah*, the rabbis created an ingenious, bipartite conceptuality that allowed "theology" to continue searching for ever better symbols as long as practice remained faithful to the evolving law.

The First Criterion: Mandating Jewish Duty

An acknowledgment of the secondary significance of theology in Judaism seems to be a necessary preface to the chapters that follow. As *aggadah* helps us freely fill in the grounding suppositions of *halakhah*, Jewish theologies appear in our history to provide us with an intellectualized meta-*halakhah*, a theory of Jewish duty. Considering how lackadaisical Jewish observance has become in our time, the need to intellectually revalidate it now takes on special urgency.

With Judaism centering itself on Torah, the classic criterion of the Jewish authenticity of beliefs was functional, not intellectual. That approach still commends itself, for non-Orthodox Jews retain a surer intuition of what a good Jew must do than of necessary or impermissible beliefs. To gauge the Jewishness of a new theological idea, then, we can inquire: How would affirming this notion likely affect the behavior of the individual Jew and that of the community? Let me illustrate its use by applying it to an example, a conception of God.

To claim Jewish significance, a contemporary idea of God must first motivate and mandate the life of Torah. A Jew ought not simply think about or study Torah and then live as a pagan but, rather, should carry out the Torah's injunctions continually. A Jewishly adequate idea of God would move Jews to do this by indicating the cosmic authority behind the Torah life and thus the ultimate significance of its required acts. The more completely an idea of God commends Jewish duty, the greater the welcome it can be accorded by caring Jews. We reach our Jewish theological limits in the opposite direction: When thinking about God in a certain way devalues Jewish obligation, it cannot easily claim a place in a properly Jewish theology.

This standard finds support in the yardstick that Orthodox Jews use when chiding the non-Orthodox for following inauthentic versions of Judaism. Considering our Jewish observance inadequate, they infer—with Jewish logic—that our ideology must be faulty. We respond not by denying their canon of criticism but only by changing its substance. We say that though we have reinterpreted the traditional conception of Torah and, hence, of its entailments, we nonetheless consider modernized Jewish action our greatest religious concern. For us, as for every generation of Jews, the Jewishness of our lives best indicates the depth of our faith. An idea of God that kept us from ethics, ritual, prayer, study, love of Jews, and the rest of what we know Torah demands of us, would readily appear to have moved to the border of Judaism or beyond. This may explain the general preference among marginal Jews for political and cultural humanism rather than Unitarianism. The latter may teach ethical monotheism but our non-believers are willing to bracket the God-question so as to live what they consider, because of its utter ethical emphasis, a more recognizably Jewish life.

If this first part of the criterion seems vague, it is because we non-Orthodox Jews have done so little to detail and communicate just what we believe the Torah demands of Jews today. We do not hesitate to criticize the protagonists of the *halakhah* for failing to solve its pressing human issues and for refusing to accommodate more to modern life. Yet, having declared that changes in history validate changes in practice and that Jews ought to be ethical, we have done little to specify and educate for the acts we believe God wants us to do here and now. When we have made the life of Torah not only the obligation of rabbis and some few others but the effective standard of a critical minority in our community, then we will have a more effective standard by which to judge the Jewish authenticity of proposed Jewish God-ideas.

The Second Criterion: Shaping Sacred Community

Second, a Jewish idea of God must also be such as to mandate and motivate sufficient loyalty to the Jewish people that its vigorous continuity will be likely. For the Torah is not meant to be carried out by individuals in isolation but as part of a local community and worldwide folk, Israel.

Jewish secularists deny that the existence of the people of Israel has anything to do with God and merely ask for it the same natural right to life and self-expression we grant every folk. In most of the Diaspora, democracy and sociology have made this an unlikely mode of Jewish continuity. Secular Judaism's unwillingness to demand anything more than Jewish normalcy—an unquestioned desideratum for our long-troubled people—raises the troubling issue of whether most Israelis and Diaspora Jews would be satisfied to have their state, a Jewish state, operate at the ethical level, say, of Syria. This uncommon identification of social quality with corporate Jewishness bespeaks our people's ethos from its birth in the Exodus down to the present era. The Hebrews understood that they became Israel not as a result of ethnic virtuosity but because they lived by a national ideal, Torah, sanctioned by the holy God. And involvement with the Ground of all value, not a rich culture, motivated Jews to keep Israel alive, identifiable and indomitable, irrespective of history's blows.

Through the centuries, Israel ascribed its being a people of Torah to the mutual pledge, the Covenant, that made Israel God's people and God, as it were, their God. Despite secularization, some version of that alliance continues to move Jews so that they want to exist as Israel and not merely as the Hebrew or Israeli nation. As long as their God and ethnicity interweave in this classic pattern, these Jews cannot be satisfied with conceptualizing God in abstraction, essentially isolated from their people. A theology adequate to their religious experience must have an idea of God that makes possible some kind of Covenant between that God and Israel. The Jewish sufficiency of this concept will be determined by its ability to evoke Israel's continuing dedication to God's service; to make Israel's suffering, when we encounter it, a worthy burden; and to motivate and mandate individual Jews to entwine their destinies with that of their people. To the extent that an idea of God inspires Jews to be faithful to the Covenant among the historic Household of Israel, our community can embrace it. But should this idea of God be such that it negates the value or importance of Israel as a continuing folk bound to God, it makes itself Jewishly unacceptable.

The Third Criterion: Validating a Commanding Piety

There remains a third thing an idea of God must do for Jews—it must make life with God possible for them, not just in their lives as members of corporate Israel but as individual Jews and persons as well. Life with God means a life of personal piety, in which we see all our experiences, our failures as well as our activism, in divine perspective. It means a life of faith in which, despite the frustration of our plans and hopes, we remain confident that God's rule continues and we can therefore steadfastly hope for God's vindication of the good; a life of prayer, one in which we can speak to God out of the fullness of what we are and long for, expecting to be inspirited by God's own strength and trusting that, if not now, we shall soon know God's answering concern. A concept of God that makes direct address to God infantile or denies that God can be of help to us to meet the varied experiences of life stumbles against a theme of divine approachability unbroken in Jewish religious experience over the ages. But insofar as an idea mandates and motivates a rich and intimate relationship with God, it can begin to take its place among the many honored Jewish ways of thinking about God.

The Jewishness of an idea of God, then, ought to be judged by its capacity to empower the life of Torah within the Household of Israel in direct personal involvement with God. In accord with Judaism's classic undogmatic bent, this criterion does not imply a specific content for a Jewish idea of God. Its substance becomes a consideration only as it affects its ability to induce Jews to live the life of Torah (which includes, to be sure, life amid Israel with God). As long as it functions to this end, its elaboration may be naive or philosophic, simple or extensive, symbolic or discursive, without disturbing its claim to be another worthy Jewish effort to aggadize our faith. One need not be a philosopher to be a believing Jew, and the clashing ideas of different thinkers may be found equally valuable among us.

Of course, I think we should pay special attention to the thought of those Jews who find abstract reflection intrinsic to their piety. Their expertise helps every Jew whose education, experience, or simple curiosity prompts them to test calls to action by asking how they fit into an integrated view of reality. With self-determination so critical to our generation, enabling Jews to think through the meaning and entailments of their Jewish faith should help many Jews bring personal conviction to their and their community's ongoing life of Torah. For its part, the Jewish people needs its philosophers to give its ever-the-same-but-changing, ever-clear-but-mysterious faith new and better articulation, thereby enabling us to be truer to it in our lives. Thinking about our belief can guard us from turning religion into magic, superstition, or worse. It can make us more fully responsible to our God. In this role, reason serves religious integrity as a valuable counterbalance to religious experience.

Living Experience: The Ultimate Arbiter

The picture presented thus far suffers from one major flaw: it is static, as if Judaism existed essentially in the present. Yet little is more critical to Jewish faith than its forward thrust to the Days of the Messiah. In this dynamic context, history, Jewish history, finally determines the Jewish adequacy of a Jewish theological idea.

On the simplest level, we begin with a question about its relation to our tradition: How does this newly proposed idea of God relate to those that once enabled Jews to live the life of Torah? We have had such varied corporate experiences over the centuries, few ideas can now come before our community responding to human realities unknown to our ancestors. Often even the contemporary idiom that gives it fresh appeal or greater cognitive reach will have traditional analogs. Our doubts about its functional efficacy will be partially assuaged if we know something like it has had prior good effect among us. As fresh *aggadah*, it need not imitate the past and it will certainly have difficulty speaking to our present need if it does not do so in the idiom of our time; yet our evaluation of its Jewishness will depend upon our being able to recognize it as a meaningful continuation of our tradition.

For all our respect for the past, as long as our faith has a messianic goal the sternest test of Jewish ideas will always be history yet to be. The generations to come will determine the Jewish worth of a proposed theological idea by testing its truth in their lives over time. If it continues to appeal to the Jewish soul, they may live by it for some generations. Seeing what it makes of them and their communities, they may reject it as they did the idea of original sin, or make it their own, as they did with belief in resurrection, or continue to struggle with it if they find it meaningful though unresolvable, as with the problem of theodicy. History, then, becomes the ultimate proving ground of Jewish theological ideas, and our estimate of the ability of a given concept to survive over time will be one factor in our sense of its Jewish desirability.

Four Paradigms for Structuring Jewish Belief

We encounter another holistic issue when we expand our focus from single doctrines to take in the shape of the system of ideas as a whole: The form of the theological structure affects the meaning of its constituent beliefs. I detect four models of ordering the relationship between God, Israel, and Torah in contemporary Jewish thought, all of which seem inadequate to me and lead me to carry on my own work by a fifth one.

(1) The revelation-dominated paradigm of Heschel. Because he writes so evocatively about God's immediacy, readers often identify Abraham Heschel's thought as a variety of natural revelation. That holds true only of the introductory, apologetic level of his discussion; he considers natural religion only a prelude to the authoritative revelation at Sinai, the Written and Oral Torah. Arguing for the reliability of prophetic revelation, Heschel accepts the accuracy of the biblical record and with it the authority not only of the Written Torah but of the Oral Torah of the sages as well.

Making God's revelation—Torah—primary and deriving the rest of one's Judaism from it appears to be the most traditional pattern for a Jewish theology, at least until we inquire what has happened in this system to the people of Israel and, in particular, to its land. In his writing, Heschel barely discusses the folk as such, reducing its ethnicity to the social forms it has as the revelation's recipient. Not until prompted by the churches' silence during the Israeli Six Day War did Heschel give any theological attention to the role of the land of Israel in Judaism. Previously he had made a major statement that Judaism was a religion concerned with time, not space. Now he wrote another seeking to provide a theological justification for the Jewish claim to the land, especially for continuing Israeli sovereignty over the recently conquered old city of Jerusalem. I know of no more evocative description of the intimate relationship between the people of Israel's faith and its land.

What Heschel did not do in this presentation, what the preeminence of revelation in his system prevented him from doing, was to demonstrate the theological necessity of the land of Israel in his understanding of the faith of Israel. He could only refer to the Torah's promises, the people of Israel's living memories, and the paradox that the people of universal history should need one particular land as its own. But having previously argued that Judaism's Torah-centered spirituality enabled one to be a complete Jew anywhere, he could not find a theological way to clarify the religious value of just this land and just this city.

Franz Rosenzweig's theory of Judaism, completed nearly half a century earlier, utilized this same theological model, which led him to a similar indifference to ethnicity. He not only distrusted Zionism but looked askance at even its cultural aspirations, such as making Hebrew, the Holy Language, into the Jewish vernacular. One can understand Rosenzweig's non-Zionism in terms of his historic situation, one so different from ours. However, when we seek a statement of Jewish faith adequate to our religious experience we must ask what spiritual meaning we personally ascribe to the existence of the State of Israel and consider its central Jewish significance for almost everyone proud to bear the name Jew.

Some contemporary Jewish thinkers have agreed in principle with the Rosenzweig-Heschel depreciation of ethnicity and utilized their revelation-centered form for their theology. Jakob Petuchowski and Arthur Cohen immediately come to mind. Louis Jacobs's work with the same design provides an interesting contrast because he simultaneously arrives at a more traditional position on observance while pointing to a greater human role in revelation. This apparent anomaly may be explained by the different theological positions they pose themselves against: Jacobs takes pains to explain his differences with Orthodoxy while Petuchowski and Cohen want to remain at arm's length with liberalism.

Michael Wyschogrod also utilizes this model but applies it in strikingly original ways. To begin with, his is a unique effort to give a systematic presentation of Orthodox Jewish faith. More surprisingly because without precedent, Wyschogrod confines himself to the message of biblical revelation, interpreting the Written Torah while momentarily bracketing out the Oral Torah. Basing himself on the philosophy of Martin Heidegger (whose Nazism Wyschogrod believes can be separated from his philosophical ideas), he makes a case for accepting the God and legislation of the Torah as given there. Though the content of this system could not be confused with the theologies of Rosenzweig or Heschel, Wsychogrod's theology exhibits the same form, and it leads in a similar manner to his own version of non-Zionism.

(2) **The rationalistic model of Cohen and Baeck.** The thought of these two great pioneers of liberal Jewish thought, Hermann Cohen and Leo Baeck, initially exhibits a classic God-Torah centrality, but close examination reveals that both terms have been rationalized and universalized. God now becomes the underlying concept unifying a properly rationalistic worldview, and Torah, in turn, undergoes a metamorphosis into rational, universal ethics. Such revelation as remains no longer proceeds from God to humankind. Rather, it results from the ongoing human quest for an integrated, comprehensive worldview, one best furthered by utilizing reason, and, particularly, its critical component, ethics, what the laity denatures into "conscience."

This initial exposition already discloses the difficulty of grasping the nature of a rationalistic systematization of Judaism by utilizing traditional rubrics. A rationalistically ordered theology can tolerate only universally rational ideas. A rationalistic Jewish theology therefore makes human reason superordinate to God and Torah and, thence, to the people of Israel. This model commends itself to moderns as generating "religion of reason" and enabling its Jewish advocates to defend their faith as the most rational of all religions. It also has great appeal because the primacy it grants to the universal removes the barriers that separate Jews from other people. Many modern Jews, striving to legitimate their presence in the general society, have found this pattern of thought true to their experience and persuasive to their reason, giving this system its exceptional staying power.

This paradigm has been problematic to many Jews because, to begin with, asserting the dominance of human reason makes Judaism a hostage to whatever version of rationalism the thinker finds convincing. For years Jewish Marxists were only the most aggressive of the many Jews who believed that rigorous reason required atheism rather than a concept of God. In recent years, Alvin Reines, advocating a rationalism based on a Sartrean commitment to individual freedom, has denied that reason requires ethics or a concept of God, though he personally finds it existentially persuasive to have a concept of God as the possibility of being. Hermann Cohen's own variety of rationalism, neo-Kantianism, has fared badly in recent generations, finding only one direct advocate among contemporary Jewish thinkers, Steven S. Schwarzschild.

The other great complaint against this model is the inability of a stringent universalism to legitimate a substantial Jewish particularity. In neo-Kantian and similar systems, only ethics is directly required by the God-idea, which, itself being fully universal, has no special relation to any particular people or land. The Cohenians commended Judaism as the most rational of all religions but became anti-Zionists because Jewish nationalism embarrassingly constricted the universal horizon of rational ethics. Leo Baeck could become a non-Zionist only by qualifying his rationalism and asserting that the idea of ethical monotheism had become so identified with the Jews that if they died it would not survive in purity. Hence keeping ethical monotheism alive in history now mandates Jewish continuity.

A century earlier, another universalist, Nahman Krochmal, had argued along Hegelian lines that great ideas must have peoples as their historic carriers, that every notable people embodies such an idea, and that the people of Israel was an eternal people because its idea (of God) was infinite or absolute. But Baeck is a Kantian, not a Hegelian, and his desperate claim for Jewish particularity strikes an utterly discordant note in a system where universal reason always outranks religious consciousness.

In theologies structured by universalistic rationalisms, Jewish particularity can have little normative worth. We know this most commonly from systems founded on rational ethics, but even a nonethical universalism, like that of Alvin Reines, can at best support only an instrumentalist argument for particularity; we do such Jewish things as help us be more universal and all the rest become a matter of personal preference. More consistent than many rationalists, Reines empties all Jewish symbols, not excluding the word "Jew," of any particularistic significance and considers them meaningful only as they speak to the universal they exemplify, thus, in principle exchangeable.

Ironically, some contemporary mystics, most notably Arthur

Green, reach a similar impasse. Overwhelmed by the universality of God with whom they stand in communion, they do not go on, as classic *kabbalah* did, to assert the mystic uniqueness of Torah. Rather, while they happen to rejoice and be edified by what they frankly identify as Judaism's symbol system, they know it, like all other religions, to be only our fallible effort to speak of the ineffable. In principle, God considers no system better than another and we, should we find one speaking to us more richly, have every reason to adopt it.

This form of theologizing, then, dooms a minority, culturally idiosyncratic faith like Judaism to the Sisyphean task of seeking to demonstrate its particular worth by a standard that essentially undercuts it. Obviously, the value one attaches to Jewish particularity will critically influence one's decision about using this form to structure one's Jewish thought.

(3) Kaplan's socially based philosophy. Creating a new model based on social science, Mordecai Kaplan radically reversed the traditional ranking of Jewish beliefs. Instead of God giving Torah to a people thus transformed into Israel, Kaplan's sociological paradigm assigns preeminence to the Jewish folk. Its folk creativity, like that of all ethnic groups, produces a culture—"Torah"—including a religion, and thus, eventually, a notion of God. Kaplan justifies this humanization of Judaism on the grounds of the drastically changed Jewish social situation and its naturalistic ethos.

By making the Jewish people the creators of Judaism—our "evolving religious civilization"—he can rationalistically validate a robust particularity. Religion, as another product of normal ethnicity and not God's revelation, must be quite particular despite its air of transcendence and its universal reach. But insofar as it can claim some element of truth, it must have a universal substance, locally representing what any human spirit at its height would discern. Kaplan thus preserves the fundamental insight of rationalism, the universal availability of religious truth, but now has stringently linked it to the social particularity inevitably associated with human existence.

It should be noted that Kaplan follows the philosophic school of naturalism, which understands rationalism as limited to the functional realm: to accepting the dynamics of nature as a given, learning what we may do within them, and then pragmatically determining how best we can realize our values. If sociology indicates that all peoples naturally display the culture-to-religion pattern, we may conclude that it is simply a human given and we should normally behave this way. The term "natural" therefore takes on a quasi-normative status in such thinking.

Many problems have been raised with this construction; I limit this discussion to one stemming from the form of the theology: the attribution of primary authority to the group. The two previous theological models derived commandment from God, which seems reasonable if one believes in God. But why ought we follow a given cultural pattern or accept a folk value merely because we were socialized into a given group? Kaplan answers that people are by nature members of groups; to reject the group's forms of expression indicates a certain measure of self-hatred and is, thus, unhealthy. He agrees, however, that his theory can only speak to people already committed to their Jewish identity who are looking for a believable philosophy of group life. But groups have often badly betrayed their members; subordinating conscience to folk or nation or culture has proved to be particularly poor counsel in recent generations.

Mindful of the demonic possibilities of folk self-assertion, Kaplan denies the group supremacy when it violates what he takes to be universal ethics. He does not ever explain, however, on what basis he makes this one exception to his sociological frame of reference. Apparently he takes the truth of ethics for granted, as if no naturalistic thinker could doubt the notion and as if sociologists had never insisted that their science was value-free. Yet naturalism, following the scientific method, cannot mandate values, only ever-continuing, open-minded study. One can admire Kaplan's humanity and Jewish intuition in overlooking a bad inconsistency in his system, but until the issue of social relativism has been decisively settled, a group-centered paradigm for theology seems both humanly and Jewishly deficient.

The same problem surfaces in the Zionism of Jacob Klatzkin and, by extension, in the less intellectualized nationalism of many Israelis. Klatzkin was an intellectually sophisticated Jewish national-ist of the pre-State period and he defined Zionism in terms of the essentials of nationhood: to acquire our land and speak our language. He rejected as rationally unfounded any suggestion, such as that of Ahad Haam, that Jewish nationalism also involved a commitment to high culture and a stringent universal ethics. For Klatzkin, with the group primary, the Jews only need to be a nation like all other nations even if that meant mediocrity and amorality. Today the issue of the quality of a Jewish state continues to arise in relation to the standards by which one should properly judge it. Anyone seeking to utilize this model of structuring Jewish thought must then be willing to accept considerable potential clash between the demands of one's conscience and one's folk.

(4) The Buberian model of the mediating self. Shortly after World War I, Martin Buber transformed his early romantic Zionism into his mature theory of Jewishness founded on his notion of I–thou relationships, thereby creating a fourth distinctive paradigm for Jewish theology. For Buber, neither God alone—à la Cohen—nor Israel alone—à la Kaplan—can serve as the determining principle of Jewish thought but only God-and-Israel in Covenant. What we Jews know about God, we know only from our human and natural, albeit directly person-to-person, experience of God. Hence, for all Buber's emphasis on God, his thought does not lead to an orthodoxy. Yet because we enter into relationship with God as with persons, directly and intimately, what passes between us, like love, has a life-affecting authority.

Any person might come to know God in this manner and so true religion abounds. The children of Jacob became "Israel" as a consequence of their unique, folk-transforming, corporate relationship with God, which they termed "the Covenant." They remain fully ethnic, except that their ethnicity has no independent, "natural" validity but arises from the Covenant and is conditioned by it. In like manner, in response to their relationship with God, the Jewish folk produces the Jewish way called "Torah."

Buber's subordination of Torah to the God-Israel relationship has a strong initial appeal to many non-Orthodox Jews because it makes religion as much human as divine. Taking all sacred books as human records of encounters with God frees us from having to defend disturbing texts and submit to old laws and practices that seem unconscionable. Yet Buber teaches no single-minded humanism, as Kaplan appears to do, but the duality of the God-people relationship, so innovation has validity only as a response to intimacy with God.

Making relationship determinative renders Torah hostage to immediate experience and this evokes the major criticism of Buber's theological model: it encourages laissez-faire permissivism. Always awaiting the results of the next encounter with God seems most unlikely to produce patterns of folk practice or the accretion of tradition, much less adherence to Jewish law. This subordination of folk and law to the self cannot assure the long-range corporate stability necessary for the recognizable continuity of Israel.

Buber had an answer to this criticism, and my understanding of it requires me to make a critical revision of this fourth paradigm. Buber fully believed that God addressed nations I–thou and so addressed the Hebrews at Sinai and on later occasions elsewhere. But he always quickly made clear his opposition to any notion of a group spirit or a collective ego (as Ahad Haam taught). God's corporate encounters take place only with individuals of the group who, when they form a critical mass of the mutually involved, give the whole community a consciousness of being in a new relationship. Then, as they respond to their new insight in similar ways or through joint doing, rightful group duty arises.

Critical of what orthodoxies and institutionalization had done to living religiosity, Buber stressed that only the personal experience of God's commanding presence can justify duty. However, Buber's own nonobservance bolstered the criticism that this exaltation of the self leads to antinomianism and the loss of community and tradition. What appeared to be a theological model giving pride of place to God-Israel has turned out, upon examination, to be a priority of God-self-Israel. All efforts to bring existentialist personalism into a religion must run afoul of the difficulty created by giving selfhood such authority.

A case in point is the effort by the liberalistic Orthodox Jewish thinker David Hartman to Buberize the classic form of Jewish theology, paradigm (1). Hartman's reading of God's revelation of the Written and Oral Law emphasizes its personalistic aspect. Much in classic Judaism supports this interpretation, though other Orthodox thinkers have emphasized the law as obligation and discipline. Hartman criticizes two contemporary Orthodox theoreticians, Yeshaya Leibowitz, the most extreme Judaic behaviorist, and Joseph Baer Soloveitchik, who has emphasized its cerebral quality, for not giving adequate scope to the personal dimension. Hartman so stresses the capacity of individuals to have a relationship with God that he alone among Orthodox thinkers admits the possibility that, while God gave the Torah only to us, God may well have also revealed divine truth to other peoples.

But Hartman has not yet faced the critical problem engendered by an emphasis on personalism: What happens when individual conscience clashes with Torah law? How seriously can one take personalism in a religious system that requires, as Orthodoxy continues to do, that the *agunah* and *mamzer* must bend their personal wills to the regulations set by God's authority? Hartman cannot easily follow Buber's model in subordinating Torah to the God-Israel relationship lest the human input vitiate the authority of God's revelation. If, then, the self only takes its place after the divine gift of Torah, then why do the less personal approaches of Leibowitz and Soloveitchik not commend themselves as more authentic than that of Hartman? We shall not fully understand Hartman's Orthodox personalism until he clarifies its effect on the Torah as discipline.

The Key to a Fifth Model: The Notion of the Jewish Self

Having completed this survey of four major forms utilized in Jewish theological work today, it remains for me to indicate how I propose to carry out my work here. I now face a peculiarity entailed by my holistic commitment: Before beginning my exposition I must say enough about my conclusions to indicate why I structure my theology as I do. This nonlinear procedure has a stylistic corollary: Each central affirmation—God, Israel, and Torah—must be considered three times, once as primary topic and twice again in relation to the others; if mention here is added, four times. I have sought to counteract the potential tedium of this procedure by providing different emphases in each discussion. Here, I shall do so by taking the risk of condensation, hoping that what may be cryptic in this presentation will become clear and cogent elsewhere.

We need a Jewish theology for those believing non-Orthodox Jews who sense their Jewishness is neither incidental nor marginal to their existence but essential to it. The incredible Jewish saga of recent decades, its Jewish accomplishment as well as its ineffable tragedy, have made many in our community recognize how primarily Jewish they are. They cannot be satisfied with the common move from universality to particularity where selfhood comes first and Jewishness second, thereby dooming Jewish identity to what crumbs of utility it can claim from the table of universal humanhood. I utilize personalism's extraordinarily resonant term, "the self," and apply it to these Jews, enabling me to characterize them as having a Jewish self. As a member of this subcommunity, I seek to give a theological explanation of what it means to be a Jewish self and why I believe this understanding should commend itself to others.

These considerations bring me to a fifth paradigm, that of the holism of God, Israel/self, and Torah. God grounds the whole but must be understood (metaphorically) in the correlation of personal relationship, not in some splendid isolation. Most specifically, God has an ongoing, historic relationship with the Jewish people, one that Jewish practice rehearses and reinstantiates. The nature of peoplehood and Jewish selfhood emerge from this Covenantal relationship, not the one without the other. Against Buber, who subordinates peoplehood and Torah to self, the Jewish self stands in relationship with God not in bare individuality but as one of the Covenant people. It knows its most personal singularity stems largely from its people's corporate closeness to God and, therefore, that its very selfhood is substantially constituted by its participation in the Covenant. The "Torah" that results from this God-Israel/self relationship is more individualistic and pluralistic than Orthodoxy can tolerate, more particularistic than rationalists will find responsible, more theocentric than humanists can allow, more ethnic than personalists find congenial. Let me begin, now, to explain what that means.

5   Not Absolutely Absolute

HE GENIUS of religious modernism lay in disclosing humankind's creative role in shaping religion, the very insight that has now led to its deprecation for letting humanism replace reverence for God. However, in the struggle between modernism and religion, behavior, not theology, has been the critical battleground. I think the orthodoxies are generally correct in their criticism that liberalistic humanism too easily led on to permissiveness and thence to license. With personal freedom enshrined but the older rationalistic ethics no longer compelling, liberal religion appears to abet moral relativism. When does a liberal committed to tolerance and understanding ever say no?

Religious orthodoxies propose curing our moral crisis by giving us an Absolute that yields unequivocal standards. They know God's will for us and challenge the liberal religions to specify what independent role God has in their largely humanistic faiths. In response, what can we say about our belief in God that is spiritually responsive yet true to our insight that the orthodoxies claim to know far too much and the relativists far too little?

My answer begins with an exploration of one extreme of this issue: Just how absolute an Absolute is the God of the Covenant? I begin somewhat far afield. I often find that such confrontation with apparently uncongenial religious beliefs directs my attention to aspects of spirituality to which I should have been more open. When I find them still unconvincing, this often also gives me a fresh if indirect access to my own sense of religious truth—a method analogous to the logical procedure of definition by negation.

The perception of an Absolute that gives stability to an ever-changing world goes back to ancient times. Much of Hindu religion centers on attachment to Brahman, the one unconditioned ground of all existence. So too a major strand of Greek philosophy, initiated by Parmenides, concentrates on the nature of what truly exists and must therefore be permanent and beyond change. In Jewish terms, this widespread intuition of an Absolute testifies to humanity's universal response to God.

Yet the people of Israel's particular religious experience has given its understanding of the universal God a different slant. By contrast to the monistic philosophies of Hindus or Greeks, ancient Israel had a different kind of certainty and Absolute. Rather than move from the human psyche to the Ultimate, God's revelation so dominates biblical experience that the biblical authors regularly depict the Hebrew Absolute forcing itself upon resisting individuals or the community. Obviously, this Absolute, in its most primary manifestations, is relational. God creates a fully real, independent world and makes covenants with people free to accept or reject God's will, including a special Covenant with a single people, linking God's own historic destiny to that of the Jews.

The God of the Hebrews, then, can only be termed "an" Absolute, an oxymoron begging for explication. To the extent that biblical and rabbinic Judaism know no reality or rule equal to, much less greater than, that of God's, we may call God their Absolute. Yet this cannot be meant in its philosophic sense: a thoroughly self-contained, aloof, immovable reality. The most common Jewish practice relating to God nicely captures this ambivalence: We know God's personal, four-letter name, but we may never say it, keeping our proper distance by using only the euphemism *Adonai*. As it were, the special Jewish sense of God's absoluteness requires us to say that Judaism knows of an Absolute only in a weak, not a strong sense of that term.

The Weak Absolute in Modern Jewish Thought

The modern Jewish search for an "Absolute" and its postmodern successor, to be considered in turn, receive their characteristic form from their rejection of the traditional Jewish doctrine of revelation: *Torah mi-Sinai*, the self-disclosure of God's will, once and for all, in the Oral and the Written Law. To an emancipated Jewry the constraints that the *halakhah* imposed on change and innovation seemed religiously unwarranted, historically refuted, and intellectually self-serving. Convinced of humankind's spiritual power by their own liberation, they adopted their culture's confidence in the rectitude of self-legislation and therefore demanded greater scope for the human partners in God's Covenant.

Though they heartily espoused the right to change, no thinker who spurned assimilation and advocated a non-Orthodoxy radically shifted the locus of Jewish absoluteness from God to humankind. Even Samuel Holdheim, the most uninhibited pioneer of ghetto-less Judaism, espoused the glories of personal freedom in dialectical tension with the Jewish tradition and the demands of God. It has remained for Alvin Reines in our own time to explore this possibility and make an Absolute of freedom itself. He contends that a rational approach to religion yields neither a God who can make demands nor a tradition that can exert a legitimate claim upon us. Reason requires us only to be true to the givenness of our freedom. He does not shrink from the possible dissolution of Judaism as a consequence of this radicalism, though he personally finds Judaism a congenial means of living out his philosophy.

Even a century ago, non-Orthodox thinkers often rejected the sovereignty of the self, the regnant "Absolute" of modern secularism, because they knew that although the weak Absolute's relationship with humankind granted them full responsibility, this responsibility was grounded in God's own ultimacy. As against Ethical Culture and full-scale agnosticism, they found a principled humanism making too little of God, and they found Unitarianism denying the irreducible religious genius of Torah. Our tradition balanced the human and the Divine, classically envisioning God as self-conditioned by creation and Covenant and thereby dignifying human selfhood, a polarity the non-Orthodox intensified by strengthening the rights of the Covenant partner. Like prior Jewish generations, they found the life of Torah mediating God and so they celebrated an activist piety. Hence they correlated their quest for a freshly weakened Absolute with an effort to create a modern theory of non-Orthodox Jewish obligation.

Mostly they changed the classic Jewish balance between God and humankind by transferring the power of legislation from God to the human mind, a move we have met in the leading rationalists Hermann Cohen and Mordecai Kaplan. Less intellectually inclined Jews found their guiding *absolute* (as I shall style its metaphorical, secular correlate) in modern culture, specifically, in the university, the arts, and socially concerned politics, what modern Germans idealized as *Bildung*. Because this stance, the "best of the modern mind," authorized a dismissive attitude toward Jewish tradition, we shall not appreciate the grounds for the tradition's partial postmodern revalidation until we understand something of the academic downfall of the attempt to render mind our Absolute.

The Downward Philosophical Career of the Absolute

The term "the Absolute" became significant in Western philosophy in the early 1800s in response to the philosophical paradigm shift initiated by Kant. Kant had answered Hume's skepticism about the correspondence of human knowledge with reality by positing a necessary, reliable structure to all rational thought. But having distinguished between the way the mind works and what the world truly is, he had unwittingly opened up the possibility that our conceptions of reality say more about us than about it; unwittingly, he had become the progenitor of late modernity's radical relativity. This possibility contradicted a central thrust of Hellenic rationality—that mind gives us reliable access to reality in itself—and generated the subsequent philosophic quest for the Absolute.

A few decades later, Hegel gave what remains the most comprehensive solution to this problem. He dissolved the distinction between mind and nature, ingeniously reinterpreting the rational as a dynamic reality. This enabled him to give an extraordinarily synoptic account of reason's creative movement through the lives of individuals, society, and history. Allowing for no gap between spirit and reality, Hegel advocated a strong Absolute, one the philosopher brings to full self-consciousness. Should that be fully realized, he and Absolute Spirit would be one—a notion congenial to Christian theologians of the time. More troublingly, with humans obviously social, the good state, which incarnates the spirit of the nation, could even more fully exemplify such unity with the Absolute. In rightist and leftist transformation, Hegel's own humanistic hopes for the Prussian state became the absolutistic model for the Nazi government of Germany and the communist regimes of Lenin and Stalin. The alleged rationality of the ideas behind such states rendered them so strong an Absolute that individuals had no rights over against them but had to yield to their superior, because Absolute, will.

In the thinking of the apolitical British philosophic idealist, F. H. Bradley, this line of inquiry came to a striking climax. He argued that enduring reality must be utterly unconditioned, that anything less pristine would be unworthy of the title "Absolute." Two consequences flowed from this line of thought. First, if there were any change in the Absolute or it were involved in a relationship of any sort, it would not be truly Absolute. Hence Bradley insisted that the Absolute exists in utter solitariness, and rational people will therefore consider *Adonai*, the God of the Bible, only an appearance. Second, Bradley's Absolute has such independence that we can say very little indeed about it. As it were, Bradley's consistency about the absoluteness of reality left it an essentially empty category, something like the kabbalistic notion of the *En Sof*, the Limitless.

Nietzsche's somewhat earlier philosophic ruminations can easily be read as a passionate protest against the sacrifice of individuality demanded by the many absolutisms of his time, including philosophic rationalism. In reaction he made the self his *absolute* by denying that anything else, like conscience, reason, God, or institutions, had compelling power over persons. Only the single soul freely expressing the full range of its natural self-assertion made and transformed values, hence no inherited idea or established norm can rightfully stand against the will of the truly superior individual. By Nietzsche's standards, even the weak Absolute of the Bible must be judged far too strong and thus Nietzsche's prophetic madman proclaims the death of God.

Modern Jewish religious thinkers found themselves standing between Hegel's idolization of mind and Nietzsche's deification of self. The case of the mid-19th-century German thinker, Samuel Hirsch, is instructive. He sought to create a Hegelian reading of Judaism but found it necessary to break with the master's denial of the independent, autonomous worth of the individual. Without the benefit of Kierkegaard's later critique of Hegel on this point, yet presaging later Jewish thought, Hirsch refused to surrender the ethical dignity of persons by sublimating their self-determination to the good state or Absolute Spirit. With recognizable Jewish self-respect, this Jewish Hegelian could affirm only a weak Absolute. Later Jewish rationalists, almost without exception, similarly juxtaposed an autonomous individual to a weak Absolute, thereby endowing modern Jewish thought with its characteristically high ethical tone.

When nonrational Jewish thought arose it took a similar tack. Franz Rosenzweig opened his seminal work, *The Star of Redemption*, by announcing the human futility of rationalistic philosophy (thus anticipating our contemporary search for an *absolute*). He then posited the primal realities, Man [sic], the World, and, most unexpectedly, God. By specifying three brute givens, Rosenzweig limited the sway of each of them by the reality of the others. Hence none could now lay claim to be a strong Absolute, a stance he took in conscious opposition to Hegel and other German idealistic thinkers.

This survey indicates that though the modern non-Orthodox thinkers changed the balance of power in the Covenant, they did not change its essential form; they merely extended the weakness of the God who enters into covenants.

Secular Jewish Surrogates for a Religious Absolute

The postmodern search for a substitute *absolute* began as it became clear that modernity had betrayed our faith. Repelled by the social disarray and moral anarchy around us, we are attracted by systems—remarkably diverse ones abound—which provide clear cut, authoritative direction, in other words, which offer a strong, or at least strongish, Absolute. In religion, the turn to orthodoxies has also been prompted by the intuition that God did not create and then abandon the universe, but provided humankind with a sure revelation.

In our community, non-Orthodoxy has similarly found a resurgent spirituality arising out of opposition to contemporary pagans and nihilists. Our two religious wings differ radically only in the balance they make between revelation and autonomy, between the relative authority they ascribe to human will and God's instruction. The theological challenge to non-Orthodoxy, then, is to identify an Absolute (God) weak enough to allow for human self-determination yet absolute enough to set the standards for autonomy's rightful use. Let us first examine the secular responses to this postmodern loss of a ground of value.

The simplest alternative to religion has been a flight to ethnicity. We want more *Yiddishkayt*, or, more elegantly, "tradition," perhaps even *"halakhah,"* by which we mean not the law and its discipline, but only more Jewish doing. Anyone who attaches absoluteness to the people of Israel will applaud the desire for greater Jewish identification and activity, but not if it presumes that Jewish folk-life can itself become the arbiter of human and Jewish existence. Like every other ethnicity, Jewish folk practice is a grab-bag of values, vulgarity as well as sensibility, self-indulgence as well as philanthropy, smug ignorance as well as the admiration of intelligence. How can one make even a weakly commanding *absolute* out of the mass of contrarieties we call Jewish style? Even the most admirable product of the turn to *Yiddishkayt*, the guide to a richer Jewish life entitled *The Jewish Catalog*, merely set out options. The nagging question persists: On what basis shall we choose?

Many Jews accept one or the other, or a combination, of two further candidates for a postmodern Jewish *absolute*. One is the State of Israel: the other, the Holocaust. Obviously they bear a relation to one another.

Those who want to make the State of Israel our *absolute* regularly upbraid Diaspora Jews when they publicly criticize Israeli actions. They are anathema because "anti-Zionism is war against the Jews" or "threatens the survival" of the State of Israel. These usages have little to do with sober analysis indicating that a given public protest would decrease the chances of the State of Israel existing in reasonable health. Rather, in this context, the terms "war" and "survival" are a rhetorical signal that we have come to an *absolute* that should rightly override our conscience.

Despite all that the State of Israel means to us and has done for us, there is a compelling Jewish and human distinction between its claiming our deep devotion and serving as our actional *absolute*. As a matter of Jewish principle no political entity deserves being so exalted, not the kingdoms of Israel and Judah in biblical times; not the United States of America, where love of flag often serves to cover its failings; nor, either, the State of Israel. Consider a once hypothetical scenario. To solve the Palestinian problem, an Israeli administration imposes martial law, suppresses civil rights, forcibly expels Palestinians, and institutes one-man rule. I think most Jews (including many Israelis) would find such policies utterly intolerable in a Jewish state, our state. Simply because it is a nation with Jewish sovereignty, the State of Israel cannot serve as our ultimate Jewish source of value or standard of judgment.

I discern a similar judgment about ultimate criteria behind the subtle shift in recent years in Emil Fackenheim's thought on this topic. During the 1970s he wrote about the State of Israel as if it were the climactic fulfillment of his 614th commandment and thus beyond ethical critique. By the next decade and, to his credit, before the incursion into Lebanon, he responded to the criticism of his views by making spiritual resistance in the death camps his fundamental criterion of Jewish authenticity. He applied this new standard to the issue of publicly criticizing the State of Israel differently than I would, but by this turn in his thought he has acknowledged that the post-Holocaust Jewish search for an *absolute* must ultimately turn from the realm of politics to that of the spirit.

Can Our Reaction to the Holocaust Be Our *Absolute?*

No Jew should speak about the Holocaust so as in any way to diminish its pain; that cannot be overstated. But I now must say some troubling words about the proper implications to be drawn from the Holocaust, that is, about the way the Jewish community "uses" it. I want to object to one of these—seeking to make the Holocaust our community *absolute*—and this may lead some to think that I seek to mitigate the horror or its significance for our Jewish lives. As a responsible, believing Jew, I seek only to try to distinguish between a matter of extraordinarily great significance and an *absolute*. I therefore approach this discussion with a more than usual sense of standing under God and our community's judgment—but I do not believe I am disqualified from speaking about it because I did not suffer personally. I pray no words or acts of mine ever blaspheme the memory of the dead or wound the soul of any survivor.

Elie Wiesel, Richard Rubenstein, Emil Fackenheim, and others (perhaps including Irving Greenberg) have suggested that the Holocaust was a new "revelation"—one of God's utter absence—which equals or even supercedes Israel's receiving of the Torah. As a consequence, the Holocaust should now function as our *absolute*. I think we can reject this proposal by showing that it cannot support the two great consequences alleged to derive from it, that we must revise our faith and redirect our action.

Negatively, thinkers have asserted that we cannot any longer affirm the Deuteronomic God of retribution and providence. No new "revelation" was needed for this. By the early 20th century modern Jews had been thoroughly secularized and if they worshiped anything it was an enlightened humanity. This, our functioning deity, is the most realistic candidate for the "God" who died for us at Auschwitz. But for many Jews, traditional faith—in *Adonai*, or in *Adonai*'s working in history, or in the coming of the Messiah, or in the resurrection of the dead—survived the Holocaust as well as did liberalism. In recent years believing Orthodoxy, not messianic modernism, has been resurgent.

Positively, we are told, the Holocaust functions as an *absolute* by mandating loyalty to the Jewish people and the enhancement of its life. Michael Wyschogrod first pointed out the logical inadequacy of this contention. If the Holocaust becomes our *absolute* because of its consummate evil, why must its negativity lead us to positive duties? It would proscribe any repetition of its perverseness and prescribe opposition to anyone who pursued even vaguely similar evil goals—but for all its importance, that remains a highly limited commandment. To extend it to include every social evil, from the American exploitation of migrant labor to the world's refusal to immediately ban fluorocarbons, demeans the Holocaust unconscionably.

Wyschogrod has also convincingly argued that our people's loathing of the Nazi evil also cannot explain our spontaneous post-Holocaust commitment to the rebuilding of Jewish life. Such destruction should more logically have led to assimilation or indifference—and often did. That most Jews rejected such realism and took an opposite course makes no sense as a natural social phenomenon but only as an intuitive response to a Reality beyond us. Though every search for a contemporary Jewish "Absolute" must centrally confront the evil of the Holocaust, it cannot find its goal there.

Where Is the Ultimate Ground for Our Commitments?

If neither *Yiddishkayt*, nor the State of Israel, nor the Holocaust—the most commanding secular realities of present-day Jewish existence—can satisfy us, perhaps nothing can. We may be left only with the quest itself; can this alone serve as our *absolute*? Surely, it has the virtue of opposing the claims of the orthodoxies to final truth and of the new messianisms to transform history. Against all such finalities, moral skepticism asserts the virtue of further inquiry, judgment, and formulation—a pragmatism born of human freedom and the openness of history.

Yet for all the appeal of process over product, this restatement of the classic liberal strategy ignores the change in ethos that brought modernity down. When Lessing in the 18th century uttered his famous preference for the way rather than the arrival, he took it for granted that everyone agreed on which road to travel and the substantial baggage one might take along—the rationality, ethics, and aesthetics he assumed every person of good will acknowledged. But can we today be satisfied merely with journeying when we radically disagree on where to start, how to go, or even what constitutes going? We already have such an over-production of doubt that our problem is less in asserting our freedom than in how to stop generating options and make a responsible choice about the latest of life's demands. With freedom often within reach, our primary spiritual concern must be to define duty: How shall we exercise our autonomy most responsibly?

To begin answering this question positively we must move beyond our everyday, secular certainties and open ourselves to the weak Absolute I believe our postmodern turn has enabled us to allow into the fringes of our consciousness. If we acknowledge it as One—without equals or partners—and thus sufficiently ultimate to be the universal criterion of quality, then we must know any lingering hint of idolatry will keep us from it. We discover that idol worship remains a cardinal Jewish sin when we honestly acknowledge how often we allow things to function in our lives as only God should—

we make them our *absolute* and serve them "religiously." In existential reinterpretation, the old truths remain: People already committed to another "god" must deny *Adonai*, who is nothing if not unique. So the shattering of the inward idols must precede any effort to point truly toward *Adonai*.

I think we can engage in this self-scrutiny best by abandoning this cerebral talk of *absolutes* and utilizing a formulation of the mid-century Protestant theologian Paul Tillich. He suggested we will best understand our effective faith if we ask ourselves what in fact is our ultimate concern—in the Torah's language, what it is that we "love with all our heart, with all our soul, and with all our might" (and thus our existential *absolute*). As we make our most fateful decisions, sacrificing lesser for greater goals, what does our most basic concern turn out to be? For many of us it will be trying to create faithful marriages, close families, compassionate communities, a caring society, a livable world, all founded on healthy selves exhibiting high human excellence. If we know these goals rightly demand unremitting, lifelong dedication of us, then we cannot be satisifed to speak to them as commandments we alone have laid upon ourselves. Too much is being demanded of us here for that; rather, something ultimate is at stake in our response to these ideals. We know this because we sense that our obligation to them arises from an elemental standard of quality fundamental to the universe, one modernity taught us to censor from consciousness. The postmodern spiritual turn begins as we become aware of a Reality that qualitatively transcends us, one that nonetheless impinges upon us by its commanding presence. Universally, "it" arouses us human animals to our unique capacity to exemplify its superlative value and thus rightfully use our freedom.

Perhaps the reality to which I have so gingerly begun to direct our attention seems so weak that it cannot hope to serve as our non-Orthodox Absolute. We can only make that judgment as our exploration proceeds, but I believe that we should evaluate the adequacy of any suggested weak Absolute in terms of our present situation. We stand bereft of our old confidence in our familiar proximate ultimates: democracy, knowledge, psychotherapy, love, or the self, the biggest problem of all. In this context, it is an accomplishment indeed for an open-eyed person to believe in even a weakened Absolute. To do so not out of panic but in the ancient intuition that ultimately despair is false and hope real, continues Judaism's redemptive faith.

6   More than Immanent

F WE ASSERT a very strong Absolute, we demean our non-Orthodox appreciation of human religious creativity; yet, to move to the other extreme, if we substantially weaken our Absolute by equating it with some aspect of human existence, we deny ourselves a firm ground of values. A survey of eight contemporary strategies that Jews have used to reduce God to utter immanence—identified with some aspect of creation—will show them to be self-defeating and in need of supplementation. Two terminological understandings will help in this enterprise.

Any discussion of God's nearness and availability quickly brings us to the word "spirituality," which easily brings to mind unctuous and self-righteous souls or, in our day of proliferating faiths, gullible and other-worldly types. Nonetheless, I use the term in a positive sense, not only because of its currency but because its experiential connotations have a valuable therapeutic function. Against all theologies that know God only in abstraction and distance, talk of spirituality reminds us that religion is more a matter of personal piety than rarified ratiocination. And against a Jewish concentration on observance and community, the calls for Jewish spirituality renew the classic Jewish instruction that God is close enough to be addressed as "You"—in the singular—and is best served in fervent love.

I also want to continue minimizing the use of the term "God" so as not to let its many troubling associations distract us from our subtle task: to allow into consciousness the two-sidedness of our experience of the ground of our values, its intimate nearness and its qualitative distinctiveness. We have no metaphor that smoothly signals this duality. The familiarity of religious immanence increases the difficulty of speaking of what lies beyond immanence yet accompanies it. When we come to this issue in the analysis, I shall employ two terms to this end, "otherness" and "transcendence." The former points to the One sufficiently different from us as to rightly be able to set our standards—what I have heretofore been calling our weak Absolute—who is also the close-enough-Other to stand in intimate relationship with us. (As a non-rationalist, I do not find the similar phenomenological language of Emanuel Levinas, the French Jewish philosopher, directly helpful here.) However, when immanence threatens to dissolve distinctions of worth and I need to

highlight that which gives our values an utterly imperative quality,
I shall use the relational, dimensional metaphor "transcendent," or
as an entity, the Transcendent.

Rationalism's Strategy: God as Logically Necessary Idea

We have already encountered one of the eight modes of reinterpreting classic Jewish faith as essentially personal experience: the
rational approach to existence, a notion our intellectuals understood
as creating a philosophic *Weltanschauung,* a coherent worldview.
Today it seems odd to call this devotion to cerebration a form of
spirituality, but its advocates enthusiastically built their lives on it.
Moreover, their neo-Kantian view of mind included aesthetics and
ethics as well as logic.

In most respects philosophy makes religiosity radically immanent by shifting the source of Torah from God in heaven to thinkers
on earth. Yet the leading Jewish rationalists never limited God to the
human level alone, Cohen insisting on God's logical transcendence,
Kaplan limiting the notion to the unique authority of ethics. Thus,
Cohen argued that the endlessly disparate phenomena of nature
could not, as such, ever yield the notion of an encompassing unity.
Monotheism requires an analysis that rises above the fragmentariness
of experience and the creative, rational assertion of reality's ideal
nature. The same is true in grounding ethics, for only by virtue of
its logical transcendence of any situation can rational religion teach
a moral law that is universally compelling.

Kaplan's unwitting bow to transcendence arose despite his
rigorous effort to confine Judaism to the natural, specifically, to folk
creativity. But he mystifyingly invoked one limit to this authority:
universal ethics. The moral law, he contended, inhered in the universe
in the same manner as does physical law, an idea contradicted by
science's empiricism, the usual source of his worldview. He sought
to remedy this systemic fault by suggesting that rational religion
extended science by faith but never contradicted it. In his later
thought he sought a better approach to this difficulty by seeking to
identify what he called the "trans-natural," hoping via holism to find
the compelling standard of quality that strict immanence could not
yield. His perplexity is telling evidence of what happens to the
problem of value when we limit ourselves solely to what we know
from nature.

I do not see how postmoderns can be satisfied with either

of these views of the balance between the immanent and the transcendent. While they have the virtue of securing the individual will in a universal order, and thus checking its potential arbitrariness, they also confine the scope of transcendence to what our minds consider rational. One can only justify this restriction of the spirit by assuming that humanhood can be equated with being rational. A more realistic analysis of the human situation and much experience make us doubtful of the primacy of reason in life and skeptical of which of its forms we should employ when we seek its second-level guidance in reaching important decisions. Moreover, if the proper rational control of the human will derives from a transcendent level, why should we not make it, rather than our mental versions of it, the basis of our existence?

We will find similarly valuable yet limited insight in each of the seven other ways non-Orthodox Jews have sought to develop the human side of their religious sensitivity.

Feeling and Ethnicity as Surrogates for Faith

Few Jews were able to be as strictly rationalistic as the ideal of religion of reason required. Eventually, most Jews, including some philosophers such as Leo Baeck and Mordecai Kaplan, began emphasizing the role of feeling and emotion in religious living. Without denying the importance of rationality, these Jews pointed out that most of us are primarily motivated by affect and sensibility. We rightly ascribe a certain power to our feelings and say that they command us. The great emotions, like patriotism and love, regularly move us to devotion and sacrifice. When, then, we face an important decision, we hope to be mature enough to bring our rationality to bear upon it but we know that an extraordinary complex of factors will affect us and we will determine what to do as much by emotion as by reason.

Religiously, that induces our generation to give very much more attention to the feeling tone of our religious practice than to its ideational content. When people attending services and life-cycle events feel warm and embraced, when they leave with a sense of well-being and connectedness, we consider the experience another indication of the worthwhileness of Judaism. In large part we cherish such experiences because they remind us of the fuller selves we know ourselves to be but so rarely feel in the rest of our lives. At their best, when they couple mind and heart in us and others, realizing self and community as one, we can be most deeply moved for we have in a simple human activity been taken far beyond ourselves to know the reality of our ideals.

Can we, then, be satisfied to equate our spirituality with heightened affect? Not if we are among the many disturbed by the high personal and social cost regularly paid by people seeking to live by their feelings. The virtue of increasing our emotional well-being by getting in touch with our feelings soon gives way to the nontherapeutic issue of how we should then act on them. In themselves, as counselors have taught us, our aggressive and pleasure-seeking drives are amoral; they therefore might lead us to do anything. That which simply gives us the most intense feeling can often be personally destructive, something that our ancestors apparently felt in steadily opposing Dionysian religiosity and that we face most painfully in the drug culture. The gap between heightened sensuality and worthy living points to our need for a criterion of value that transcends the realm of our feelings.

The third of our eight modes of reinterpretation suggests that we let our people's folk culture become a secular equivalent to religion. When decisions perplex us, our people's heritage, rich in the human insight it has refined over the centuries, can give us worthy guidance. Group loyalty generally leads people to rise above their personal interests for the common weal, even risking their lives or endangering those they love for the sake of folk, nation or humankind. We Jews celebrate an awesome record of idealism triumphing over circumstance in our people's history, and its enno-bling view of humanhood has been captured in its folk life in manifold ways. So we still devote much of our community energy to heightening each Jew's sense of ethnicity, hoping thereby to impart standards as well as joy, vision as well as pleasure, all without revelation or theology.

When I come to discuss the people of Israel in chapters 11 to 16 I shall amplify this case for the sociality of the self, but here I wish to indicate something of why we cannot be satisfied with folk consciousness as the principal guide to life. We have often felt betrayed by institutions as diverse as governments, philanthropies, political parties, universities, and religions. Even groups as small as families can be pathogenic, with husbands and wives destroying each other, or parents badly traumatizing children, or children injuring parents or siblings. How, then, can we be asked simply to rely on group wisdom? And the Jewish people, like all groups, often exploits our loyalty for its own ends, even to the point of subverting its own vaunted ideals. Our folk more frequently reflects the appetites of its masses than the ideals of its sages, and Jewish nationalism often demands that our state be an exception to the standards of moral behavior we commonly demand of all other nations. The tensions that these clashes have aroused should be sufficient evidence of the need for a sense of duty that transcends folk wisdom.

Religiosity as Aesthetics or Behavioral Patterns

Fourth, some have suggested that the one effective element in our religious lives is its aesthetic appeal. For them, Jewish religiosity is an art form and insofar as Judaism appeals to their higher sensibilities they find it valuable. In fact, the modernization of Judaism early manifested itself as a revolution in Jewish taste. By reshaping the ghettoized style of Jewish living to their newly acquired Western sensibilities, the non-Orthodox hoped to make the old tradition freshly effective in the lives of emancipated Jews. Their hope of high culture as character-shaping arises from the common experience of being exalted by certain works of music, art, or literature in a manner we otherwise rarely experience. By calling such experiences elevating we mean to convey that the beauty of the work had an effect on us as persons, going far beyond refined pleasure to humanize us entirely.

A moment's reflection quickly indicates that beauty does not obligate and elegant sensibility can be characterologically inconsequential. Anthony Blunt could simultaneously be the Queen of England's art historian and a traitor. Isaac Bashevis Singer's fiction may deserve the Nobel prize for literature, but for all the skill with which he has created Jewish types, some quite learned, they can rarely be recommended as models of Jewish responsibility. Indeed, many modern artists have insisted on the autonomy of the aesthetic impulse and its independence of other value considerations, thereby justifying in the name of art their disdain for the common entailments of personal relationship. Without denying the ability of beauty to transport us to a level of heightened significance, we nevertheless cannot reasonably expect a cultivated taste to remedy our culture's loss of a ground of value.

Fifth, a kind of Jewish behaviorism contends that Jewish doing yields its own validation. This view finds some substantiation in thinkers as notable as Franz Rosenzweig and Abraham Heschel.

Though Rosenzweig reserved a place in his theory of Jewish obligation for personal exception, he declared that during actual observance what had previously been an impersonal, inherited rule suddenly became a personal obligation, that observance itself demonstrated its commanding power. Similarly, Heschel called for a Jewish leap of action in contrast to Kierkegaard's Lutheran demand for a leap of faith. And Heschel enhanced his theology of *mitzvah* by writing memorably about Jewish observance as the traditional locus of a Jew's personal encounter with God. Many of us know this pragmatism of the deed from our own experience of the *simḥah shel mitzvah*, the joy of Jewish doing that climaxes in bonding us so intimately with other Jews present and past that we feel in miniature the reality of "Israel."

According to this theory, habitual action itself seems to mandate living in a Jewish manner. But it has two fundamental flaws. First, our practice does not, by and large, bear it out; if it did, Jews would be more observant. To the contrary, from immigrant times on, familiarity has not bred discipline. Second, this theory leaves us passive before the law. Both Rosenzweig and Heschel accepted the binding character of the received *halakhah*. Most non-Orthodox Jews find this neotraditionalism too great an infringement on their most intimate intuition of their Jewish obligation. Thus, against a substantial body of Jewish teaching, they find Jewish law on menstruation and *mikveh* not a *mitzvah* but an impediment to creating the kind of family life that they understand Judaism to be mandating. In these matters and others, Jewish behaviorism has the reverse effect: Seeking to do what the tradition dictates generates a compelling sense that our authoritative teaching must be transformed. Fundamentally, we believe we personally have access to a standard that sometimes transcends the received Jewish law and becomes our basis for judging what in it remains Jewishly compelling and what must be abandoned or revised. It will not do to seek to save this theory by saying that when these changes have been made then the behavioristic effect will be manifest; at that point our sense of obligation will derive from the criterion of Jewish validity that we utilized to make the adaptation. Of course, I have been unfair to both Rosenzweig and Heschel in this discussion by extracting their descriptions of Jewish doing from the context of their theology. Both believed Jewish deeds had their effect because God had ordained them. They knew quite well that immanence cannot have its salutary effect without a complementary transcendence.

Is Piety Good Relationships or Deep Self-Knowledge?

Sixth, some Jews, in a practice related to Martin Buber's teaching about the I–thou relationship, have argued that the act of helping people, particularly one-to-one, furnishes all the spiritual experience anyone needs. The flood of Jews into the helping professions and the increasing pastoral emphasis in the rabbinate testify to the appeal of this idea. One need not be a professional to know the rare satisfaction of having personally helped someone in a time of tragic or joyous need. Surprisingly, though others greatly appreciate what we tried to do for them, it is often we who find ourselves immeasurably enriched by the experience. In helping them, we find we have confirmed what we most deeply believe. Hence, personal helpfulness suggests itself as a surrogate for religion.

All that may well happen but, like Jewish behaviorism, it hardly does so often enough to constitute a normative way of life. That the opposite experience often arises must be taken into account. Many people to whom we reach out helpfully respond by being indifferent, resistive, difficult, or nasty. Not knowing what the response will be, why ought we build our lives on the risk of extending ourselves to large numbers of people? Moreover, should we establish a personal relationship with them, we would not only receive certain personal gains but would also add to our responsibilities and further inhibit our freedom. Why, then, should people who complain fervently about being overburdened take on ever more social responsibility? Not, surely, from gains derived from the usual helpfulness, which often requires great discipline and self-sacrifice, but because we know we must do so in order to retain and fulfill our humanness. This principle may be reinforced by the joy that sometimes comes in the experience of lending a hand, but it cannot be established thereby.

Seventh, rather than reach out to others, some spiritual guides urge us to go beyond mundane existence and our humdrum self by learning how to plumb it to its utter depth. The strategy for this delving within takes many forms. The most exoteric of these teaches us to know our body and integrate our physicality into our sense of self. More subjectively, one seeks "to get in touch" with one's feelings or unconscious and be liberated by psychotherapy from one's inner compulsions. Either process can prove revelatory as we discover how much our lives have been dominated by processes of which we had hitherto been unaware. Bringing them into our felt, conscious life exposes us more fully to our selves, empowering us to be more truly ourselves.

In a more radical move, we seek to transform the level of consciousness so as to attain a higher plane of reality. An ever-deepening/heightening search within begins, arduous enough to demand discipline and dangerous enough to require an experienced guide, yet fascinating and exciting as it liberates us from the prosaic and introduces us to reality's underlying spirituality. As we become adept at going through the self to what lies beyond it, we discover its ultimate truth to be the One, embracing and utterly undifferentiated—and all else is ephemeral. This enlightenment can result in an infinitely expanded sense of self, leading us to be serenely patient with every ordinary experience of life because each one is both nothing in itself and also another way to reality's pervading Unity.

This inquiry into the varieties of immanent spirituality among Jews has now begun to take us beyond immanence, for the human level can only proffer alternatives but not itself direct an elemental choice between them. Thus, seeking to make the whole self, or an aspect of it, the measure of all things confronts us with a wondrous, hazardous freedom that can lead as easily to arbitrary or self-centered acts as to ones considerate of others. (Our Jewish concern, the life of Torah, redoubles this sense of inadequacy, for how can a tradition-laden life be derived from a standard like the self, which is indifferent to history, community, and messianic endurance?) Recognizing this difficulty, many spiritualities that stress immanence complement it by reaching toward a transcending Otherness which, by virtue of its superior level of quality, can give us the stability and sociality that we associate with human fulfillment.

Mysticism, the Communion of the Self and the One

The fullest identification of immanence and transcendence arises in the eighth path of personal religious experience, mysticism, a spirituality that brings the self beyond itself and into contact or union with ultimate Oneness. Against everything modernist Jews anticipated, a sizable minority of our community today knows the reality of such experience. They turn to the burgeoning literature on *kabbalah* and books of contemporary Jewish spiritual guidance to learn how to make past practice contemporary technique. The postmodern search for a personally felt religiosity makes itself clearly evident here.

Unfortunately, this immanent piety cannot be of much help with our immediate theological agenda. Most of those who write for this subcommunity find their spiritual experience reinforcing their

Orthodoxy, a spirituality that would leave us more subject to the law and less free. A few teachers combine their mysticism with a non-Orthodox pattern of observance. Arthur Green, for example, makes a clear distinction between the universal, ineffable essence of religion—the One God—and the ephemeral social forms through which finite beings seek locally to express their relationship to it. Such mysticism yields only God and a sense of values but not an equivalent mandate for the life of Torah; another symbol system could conceivably function as well or better. This brings us back to the corrosive effect of universalisms reducing Jewishness to a means rather than something of an end. Theoretically, it should be possible to have a non-Orthodox mysticism that taught some absoluteness attached to Jewish particularity, thus mandating Jewish obligation, but in the absence of any statement of this kind I must leave the matter here.

Two factors prevent my pursuing this option further. If by mysticism we mean reaching a special state of consciousness where one achieves union with the Transcendent, I have not yet experienced it. My Jewish thought and practice has been nonrationalist, but without any intimate involvement with God in which I transcended my individuality through communion with the now-not-simply-Other-but-also-deepest-Self. Since the teachings of our Jewish mystics derive from an experience I have not shared, I cannot empathically amplify or extend their interpretations of Judaism.

Moreover, I remain troubled by a major religious difficulty engendered by the ultimate loss of self in mysticism. When self and God unite, personal will and God's will become one, giving the resulting command absolute authority. Mystics can allow for pluralism only as some adepts have fuller experience than others, but when they have equal experience the only way to settle a difference is for one to leave and start another community. All the problems created by orthodoxies that know just what God wanted resurface here more intensely, not the least being the surrender of our critical faculty, limited though its value be.

For the non-Orthodox this raises a particularly critical issue. Classic Jewish mysticism, by linking the personal will to that of God, gave cosmic weight to every aspect of the life of Torah, including obscure customs and individual stringencies. The mystic must accept everything from God. Where, then, can contemporary non-Orthodox Jewish mysticism find independent grounds for abandoning anything in our Jewish tradition, e.g., its sexism? It might do so if it posits a self with sufficient independent authority to occasionally act as a guide or brake on our mystic experience. But if its standard of value remains what transpires in the *unio mystica* I, as an outsider to the experience, exercising the same critical judgment here as elsewhere, do not see how it can do more than ground a non-Orthodoxy arbitrarily.

Words and Symbols for the Ineffable

I have tried in this survey of the virtues and limits of the various kinds of spiritualities manifest in our community today to indicate why our pursuit of immanence cannot yield a satisfactory ground for our general moral and particular Jewish existence. Defining my own position by these negations makes plain my affirmation of an Absolute that is stronger than that called for in the first seven paths but far weaker than that of mysticism. Or, to put it more directly, my religious response to the culture's question of the ground of our values is the reality of an Immanent Reality that is also transcendent, one that grounds my self yet validates its independence.

I do not mean by emphasizing the transcendent quality of God to negate the accompanying reality and virtue of God's immediate availability in personal religious experience. I believe God is immanent and that this conditions the tone of Jewish religious life. But when God becomes virtually only what can be identified on the human level, then we have an imbalance that demands correction. The critical issue is the authorization of duty: a merely immanent God cannot command for it has no status greater than anything else in nature. And it is this issue—of how we shall choose one rather than another among the possibilities that the natural sets before us— that has surfaced in each of the non-mystic immanentist approaches to Judaism we have studied. We must, then, investigate what it can mean to us to call God transcendent.

Before doing so, I want to explicate five spiritual difficulties that arise from this paradoxical assertion that God is both immanent and transcendent, intimately available yet always utterly beyond us.

First, to ground values so that nothing can supersede them or vitiate their claim on us, their Ground must be utterly primary; it must be, so to speak, the Ground of all grounds. This unique transcendence makes it prior to everything, including logic and language. Then how can we talk about it? The rabbis said that only silence fitly praises God, for saying nothing does not, at least, diminish the divine ultimacy.

Yet the rabbis also multiplied comments about God and put many words about God in the mouth of every observant Jew. They could do so because they had God's revelation, the Bible, and it provided them with a human vocabulary that avoided blasphemy and was "acceptable" to God. The philosophers like Maimonides who relentlessly pursued abstraction and the mystics with their doctrine of God as *En Sof*, Without Limit, agreed as to the inadequacy of human language, yet wrote theologically almost to the point of garrulousness. Contemporary Jews, lacking the assurance of a symbol system authorized by God or reason, have given new currency to silent prayer and meditation, as well as wordless music. Yet we, like our forebears, cannot deny the legitimacy of reflection and the greater responsibility that verbalization makes possible. So we break silence and speak, hoping that our necessarily inadequate symbols will be useful in pointing beyond themselves to the Ineffable.

Second, once committed to religious symbol making, we go far afield to devise rites and acts and *realia sacra* of uncatalogable diversity. Seeking ever less inadequate personal access to this Otherness, we wonder what might now best serve us as its living symbol. Yet, what could not so serve as long as we did not turn it into an idol by fully identifying it with the Transcendent? For in "Its" utter primacy It is implicated in every thing. We might therefore conceivably find anything an effective means for coming in touch with It—one reason we partially find It even in our eight different immanentist spiritualities.

Yet most things do not point far beyond themselves; as we say, "They leave us flat." And new insight often negates once effective symbols, as the feminist critique has done to male metaphors for God. Religiosity means seeing the numinous in the ordinary, the sacred in the commonplace. But if we always need new living symbols, how can we find the genius to see in the continuingly ordinary the way to the extra-ordinary?

Of Continuity, Duty, and Serenity, and Shaping a Life

Third, Jewish spirituality requires regularity. We do not aim at the kind of life-changing conversion experiences cherished by some

Christian churches. In Judaism, as in some other Christian churches, a personal relationship to the Transcendent is less event than continuity, something that we must work at rather than entirely receive. Our tradition overflows with rules and counsel for building a continuing association with the transcendent Other.

Yet despite need and practice, the sages of every era testify that genuine spiritual experience occurs sporadically, more often than not coming more as a surprise than as a result. Few people—at least, few not encapsulated by secularity—have not at some moment been deeply touched by an unexpected experience of the Transcendent. So although we must make religious practice a regular part of our lives to keep them firmly grounded, the occasional rather than the steady will more likely sustain our personal sense of contact with the Transcendent.

The soul's inconstancy dooms us to vacillate between seeking the special only to then seek its regularization. Yesterday's certainty—or perplexity, for that matter—often does not define this moment's reality. Faith needs to be regained and strengthened all the time; it helps to build from the experiences and habits of a lifetime but they guarantee nothing. We often feel that, no matter how far we have already come, we must once again start at the beginning. Spirituality knows little stasis but shuttles restlessly between evanescent reconfirmation and the steady domestication by which we seek to hallow our existence.

Fourth, religion often commends itself as a respite from daily perplexities and burdens. By keeping us in touch with the sacred Other, it contrasts the ultimate with the transient, giving us the special peace of broader vision. In relation to transcendent value, what overwhelmed us with its urgency can now easily be seen as only serious or even far less than that.

Yet if everything we do should reflect our involvement with the Transcendent, then every act becomes an occasion for duty and judgment because we know Its high quality demands manifestation in our lives and in the world. It gives us no rest, then, the command to be holy being insatiable, and we not only tire, we ignore, deny, or pervert it as we careen between the extremes of scrupulosity and morbid guilt.

What a joy, then, to discover that transcendence also implies generosity, what the greater freely does for the lesser. Being limited, we cannot be expected to realize the abundant value of the Transcendent but only what we might do as particular selves here and now.

And when we do not do even that, the One who transcends us does not abandon us. If we do our best to make amends and start afresh, we discover Its otherness enables It to see further than our failure. For our limited malfeasance does not end Its transcendence. It always remains the qualitative reality beyond all particular existence and though we momentarily despair, Its relentless call for realization will not forever be denied.

Fifth, this dialectical spirituality needs to integrate our passing years. The religious accomplishments of one stage of life do not always carry over to another. Worse, only as we meet the new spiritual challenges maturity and age bring can the prior years find their proper realization. Only the mean-hearted will not celebrate the idealism of the young, but Judaism from its historical perspective teaches that only if it becomes life-long commitment and action will it create a religious self. Until we have confirmed our integrity in face of all the unknowns that yet await us, we shall not know how faithful we have been.

How odd that we must live in the present and yet be largely judged by what is yet to be, that as our biological vitality begins to ebb we should still be expected to rise to our best. And yet just this ongoing press for spiritual fulfillment allows us at any moment to turn from continuing to live as we should not have and now, at this new moment, begin to be the self we ought always to have been. For the Transcendent makes Its claim anew at every instant and waits for us to seize the moment to make the past right and culminate our lives in faithfulness to It.

7   Reaching for Transcendence

ANY JEWS are inhibited from seeking a theological position between the absolutism of Orthodoxy and the modernist immanentism of the non-Orthodoxies by Mordecai Kaplan's insistence that we must make a stark choice between naturalism and supernaturalism in religion. Since Kaplan considered supernaturalism incompatible with modern culture, he assumed that Jews confronted by this dichotomy would adopt naturalism. In the postmodern ethos, with Kaplan's naturalism another discredited humanism, his forced choice has led many Jews to supernaturalisms. Is there not a third possibility that eluded Kaplan but that we find true?

Moving Back from a Functional God to a Real God

The differing views of two of Kaplan's disciples, Harold Schulweis and William Kaufman, should help us better understand the religious values at stake in seeking this different theological path. Schulweis has revitalized Kaplan's humanocentric religiosity by his "predicate theology." Schulweis proposes that we give up thinking of God as something other than ourselves, for that inevitably entangles us in the insolubilities of theodicy. Instead, he wants us to use the term "God" as a collective symbol for all that we find highest in human existence, particularly morality. Thus, we should begin our theologizing with those human acts or demeanors that we consider "Godly" and have them in mind when we say "God." This would give God the reality of observable behaviors and the relevance of our ideals— but not the substance that would allow God to be blamed for evil occurring or justice not done.

This view not only shares Kaplan's anthropocentricity but his confidence that what constitutes human fulfillment and moral obligation are self-evident. But once we move beyond ethical platitudes and in-group expectations to face personal or social issues, little could be more problematic in our time of radical ethical pluralism and doubt. Schulweis, for all his acuity, has not thus far addressed the problem perplexing contemporary ethical philosophers: the foundations of our ethics. He provides no argument for their commonality other than their usefulness. Kaplan, acknowledging this difficulty, claimed that there was a scientific basis for this moral view of human nature, that studying behavior showed that people naturally seek to develop their potential to the fullest. Religious thinkers extend this finding with merely their healthy-minded faith that morality inheres in the universe itself. Schulweis does not reiterate this argument of Kaplan's to bolster his own redefinition of "God," almost certainly because he knows it to be intellectually untenable. Without it, however, we have nothing but our optimism about persons to make us believe that the human moral sense alone can be the sure foundation for all we will say about God.

William Kaufman, by contrast, concedes the philosophic charge that functionalisms—which confine our discourse to behaviors and consider questions about the reality underlying them irrelevant— illegitimately convert caused effects into self-substantiating activities. He agrees with Schulweis that a contemporary Judaism must be a rationalism, particularly to provide a satisfactory resolution of the problem of theodicy. Nonetheless he argues that the problem of authority must be faced. When the rationale that had previously produced a social effect collapses, people gradually lose the urgency for the old behavior. Only by providing a new "cause"—a view of reality that will prompt the life-style—will the "effect," the way of life, be restored. Modernity once made ethics seem rationally self-evident, but our changed conceptions of rationality and of human nature have made ethics itself in need of substantiation.

Kaufman therefore believes that a religious philosophy like Kaplan's requires a metaphysics to retain its plausibility. Kaplan had denied this in his early writings, agreeing with the neo-Kantians that issues of ultimate reality exceed our rational capacities and inevitably run afoul of the problem of evil. Kaufman, however, has pointed to certain motifs in Kaplan's later thought that the disciple believes show the master's grudging recognition that his system required a more secure foundation, perhaps even a metaphysics. Kaufman believes that Whitehead's process philosophy, which has a scientific context and a high regard for value, can provide this, a topic I will return to in chapter 9.

I shall let the historians of ideas decide about the accuracy of Kaufman's reading of the "trans-naturalism" passages in Kaplan. Here I only wish to state my agreement with Kaufman's analysis of the intellectual inadequacy of functionalisms and extend it with an argument of my own. If function is all we need to concern ourselves with philosophically, then does it self-referentially prove we ought to be functionalists? Can we give a functional validation of functionalism? Consider a not uncommon case: Because believing would produce a desired action or attitude, we try to act as if we believed in order to get its effect—but to no avail. We know we don't really believe it and all our desire to get the effect cannot remedy our unbelief except if we can delude ourselves. We will only return to something like the old vigor of Jewish practice if we can find ourselves believing something that empowers it. In the recent Reconstructionist involvement with mysticism—which Kaplan would have denounced as supernaturalism—I see a more typically postmodern effort than Kaufman's to provide a plausibility structure for Kaplan's esteem of culture.

The Rationality of the Concept of Transcendence

Whether we agree to undertake the metaphysical project or not, the issue of a foundation or ground for a system of obligation cannot be ignored without turning duty into option and thus vitiating the system's effect. The way out of Kaplan's dilemma lies in identifying a level of reality that does not share the disabilities of the clashing alternatives, namely, transcendence. I will momentarily leave the term undefined so as not to eliminate from consideration any of the numerous ways thinkers use it. Yet even allowing this ambiguity to remain, I think enough can be said about the nature of transcendence to indicate why I find it the preferable metaphor in speaking about our ground of value.

As against supernaturalistic theology, what transcends us need not be thought of as a person or a being; moreover, asserting the existence of such a realm does not contradict the general scientific view of nature, though it obviously points to a nonempirical level of reality. Two examples of such thinking may readily be adduced, Hermann Cohen and Alfred North Whitehead.

No modern Jewish thinker has more emphatically insisted upon the notion of transcendence in relation to God than did Hermann Cohen. The strictest of our Jewish rationalists, he construed transcendence in terms of logic, that is, it is the chief characteristic of the God-idea, the major premise of his system. This idea is so fundamental that it cannot be equated with any subsequent idea of the philosophy—scientific, ethical, or aesthetic—though they all originate in it. Even without a metaphysics, Cohen's view of the rational as ethical and lawful provide him with the basis for his strong notion of duty.

Where Cohen effectively subordinates the scientific to the ethical aspect of rationality, Whitehead makes it the major determinant of his religious metaphysics. Science itself operates on a level transcending nature as we ordinarily experience it—extraordinarily so, for instance, in the realms of particle theory, astrophysics, and grand unified theories. Whitehead's metaphysics arises by his inquiring what structure of reality would be logically necessary for our science and, with it, for our rounded human experience. This important latter consideration leads him to a consideration of the metaphysics of value and enriches his understanding of God, making God not only the enabler of the process we call nature but also the lure and conserver of value.

Thus, rationalists as diverse as Cohen and Whitehead can envision God as transcending nature—logically or metaphysically—without making God supernaturalistic, Kaplan's theological either/ or notwithstanding.

Authorizing Duty without Debasing Anyone

What I find critically at stake between a consistent immanentism and one that holds immanence in tension with transcendence is the problem of command or authority. Are there, despite our difficulty in giving them precise articulation, things we simply *must not* do or only various patterns of behaving that, for whatever reason, we might decide to follow? Though defining God—and thus our standard of value—as something immanent in nature makes Divinity thoroughly accessible, it generates the problem of why we identify one feature of creation—like mother love—rather than another—like survival of the fittest—as good. Nature itself does not so discriminate. One solution would be to assert that whatever occurs in nature is good—but that means child abuse as well as parental love, murderous aggression as well as nurturing affection, rape as well as self-giving—a fearful positivism indeed. If, then, we must make choices about that which we find in nature, including what we discover in our own human nature, on what immanentist basis shall we do so? There is hardly one motif that has not found someone to provide a rationale for seeing it as the key to human fulfillment. Or, more positively, why should strict immanentists continue doing what Jewish teachers have immemorially done, insist that some behaviors make more valid claims on us than do others and that some acts must not be performed, even if that means repressing certain aspects of our human nature?

Many feminist thinkers have carried on a strong moral polemic against theological efforts to retain notions of difference of status in relation to Divinity. They have cogently argued that the hierarchical distance between God and humankind has been the ultimate model for some humans degrading other humans, especially in male dominance and female debasement. They argue that only when we eliminate superiors and inferiors from our worldview and take our values from the same human level on which we all find ourselves can we rid ourselves of the ground of such anti-human personal relationships.

I am moved by the ethics of this argument but not by its logic, and thus venture this one discussion of feminist theology despite the great risks involved. I have been taught that my "logic" with its sharp distinctions manifests all the failings of an experience that has been too exclusively masculine. No rejoinder is possible against this charge, but I hope I may be allowed to follow a pattern often used by feminist thinkers, who regularly want to know about the political effect of the argument being employed. I note that the political effect of saying males argue from limited experience makes it possible to nullify the worth of whatever they have to say on topics related to women and perhaps on other human concerns as well. I am willing to be instructed but, like most feminists, I am not willing to be entirely silenced. Hence this statement.

If we derive our values from nature and male dominance regularly predominates there, on what grounds can immanentists reject that dominance in favor of egalitarianism? A contrary feminine experience of acceptance may direct us to do so, but how can the feelings of one group of people have moral priority over those of another group, since both occur naturally? I agree that we should make it a major ethical priority to replace sexism with as much human equality as we can create, but I do not see how we can derive that imperative as long as we remain strictly within the realm of the natural. Only a hierarchy of reality yields the hierarchy of value that makes sexism immoral or, in more precise religious language, sinful.

By my understanding of transcendence, the feminist ethical point has compelling urgency. Whatever theological hierarchy the notion of transcendence introduces must be guided by our compelling intuition that we must not join in the debasement of persons, females being the immediate test case. In my view, this only returns us to the critical postmodern religious-theological insight: The ground of value we intuit has sufficient beyondness to authorize values yet allows sufficient otherness in persons, all persons, regardless of sex, to accord them all unalienable dignity.

We can generalize. Thinkers who deny transcendence, transposing hierarchy into the breadth of the plane on which we function, give us no compelling basis for choosing among nature's plethora of possibilities or remaining steadfast about our choices when they prove demanding. We can see this issue in Hermann Cohen's unrelenting polemic against the prenaturalist thought of Baruch Spinoza, whose virtual identification of nature and God produced an ethics that does not seek to transform the world but to adjust one's intellect to it. All who hold messianism dear must reject such refusal to act against the world's evils.

What Do We Mean by "Transcendence"?

I can identify three significant characteristics of transcendence that make it an attractive theological metaphor.

First, our religious experience teaches us that another dimension of reality intersects with that of our customary existence. It manifests a distinctive beyondness. We sense its complete independence of us though we mysteriously have a most intimate consciousness of its reality and presence, one that allows us to recognize an ennobling sameness between it and our most essential being.

This farness amid nearness produces the phenomenon of religious awe with its broad range of human effects. It can so over-awe us that it produces fear and trembling, something like the response that may have occasioned the Torah's reference to God as *paḥad yitzhak*, the Fear[ful one] of Isaac. The Torah more commonly refers to our appropriate reaction with the ambiguous root *y-r-'* whose English equivalents hover between a figurative "fear" and an intense "revere."

A distinction of power already makes itself felt here. Where that which transcends us originates, orders, and sustains, we are only subsequent entrants into the process called existence and can do comparatively little to alter or extend the given terms of our participation in it. Fortunately, these include our genuine strengths, and when we unite them with those of others, we can accomplish the human works we rightly call marvels. Human genius being given its due, the Transcendent has power so exponentially greater than ours that its operation from the subatomic to the intergalactic beggars our imagination and excites our wonder. That is why we use metaphors in our attempt to give some intellectual content to our experience of it. They provide a device for allowing the near at hand to point beyond itself to that which eludes direct specification. Religious practice and community life come into being not only to raise and strengthen our consciousness of this numinous Otherness that everyday life normally obscures but to transmit the old great metaphors and make possible the creation of freshly effective ones.

Second, the otherness of the Transcendent confronts us not only with rightful authority but with exalted quality as well. Much of what we have recognized as most worthwhile in ourselves we discover raised to a superlative level in the Transcendent; what remains fragmentary, conflicted, and unrealized in us, we intuit has complete integration in its oneness. Though this qualitative aspect of transcendence also exceeds our ability to plumb or articulate it, it lures us via our qualitative likeness to realize our humanhood most fully by seeking to emulate its character. Thus its rightful authority arises not only from its transcendent power and status but also from a realized quality that, in itself, draws us toward it. Our amazement at this astonishing connectedness enables us to overcome the awe, fear, and hesitation that transcendent power and status awaken in the reverent, and it arouses its spiritual twin, love—and does so even when one, like Spinoza, has an impersonal, rationalistic understanding of God.

The authors of the Bible and Talmud, as I read them, sought to give priority to this qualitative attractiveness of the Transcendent. They did so by their preference for the king metaphor—which depicts not only the one whose throne concretizes "his" superior status but one to whom we look to instantiate our human ideals—over the creator metaphor—which depicts the awesomely powerful Cause of which we are an effect.

Our more impersonal ethos leads many people today to prefer spatial metaphors, such as levels, planes, and dimensions. While this circumvents the problems of anthropomorphism and sexism, it exposes us to the danger of appreciating only the hierarchial aspect of transcendence and not Judaism's classic celebration of its quality. Early in this century, the German theologian Rudolf Otto sought to surmount this difficulty by identifying our consciousness of the Holy as an inevitably twofold experience of awe and fascination. A more determined rationalist like Hermann Cohen called it "spirit," thereby integrating with its logical/mathematical aspect its ethical and aesthetic coordinates. Alfred North Whitehead's metaphysics describes the Transcendent not only as the process by which potential can be concretized but equally as the lure and conserver of values. We may not conclude, then, that the abstruseness of the notion of transcendence necessarily strips ultimacy of its qualitative character.

Third, brought together, the foregoing elements of transcendence indicate why it properly sets the standards for our existence—in more personalistic language, why it rightly commands us. The distance between the realms of being explains our vaunted human independence. We therefore remain free to ignore or reject the claims we find made on us by our contact with the Transcendent, a self-assertion modern religiosity vigorously expanded, not infrequently to the point of collapsing transcendence into humanism. Postmoderns have once again become open to the reality of transcendence amid immanence. Because we find it manifesting supreme quality, we cannot be satisfied with the relativism that pure immanence would impose upon us. Its superlative quality also gives us the confidence that, despite our limited ability to specify its nature or its exact entailments (as the orthodoxies can do), we gain from exposure to it the criterion for the rightful exercise of our freedom. Should we then defy the standards it enjoins on us, we do so at the cost of rejecting the source of our own unimpeachable dignity and thus our very own worth.

The Varieties of Experiencing the Transcendent

This transcendence-with-likeness lies behind human religion generally—a truth Jewish tradition recognizes in its concept of God's covenant with the children of Noah. Believing Jews can evaluate various religious views of the Transcendent by inquiring whether or not they lead to such covenantal religiosity. For example, some understandings of the Transcendent do not include this primary sense of quality-to-be-reflected-in-acts but set forth a compelling life goal in which good deeds are only a secondary means to attain the highest piety. Thus the common sense of Atman in Vedanta Hinduism and of Sunyata in Zen Buddhism indicates that both have a transcendent, integrating oneness, in the former case one of ultimate being, in the latter one of dynamic no-thing-ness. However, in these cases the oneness of both so transcends all else that it allows for no ultimate distinctions, such as that between good and evil. As a result, both faiths raise insight into unity to a far higher level of value than acts of righteousness, though both consider right living a preparation for true understanding. In Judaism, God's goodness has always been an essential characteristic of God's holiness and thus it has always been a primary duty for Jews to do good, at first largely to other Jews but, since the Emancipation, to all humankind as well. I will return to this theme in later chapters.

Thus far I have limited this discussion of the idea of transcendence to rationalistic, impersonal models. In principle, as long as a conception of the Transcendent vitalizes the life of Torah, I believe Judaism open to either impersonal or personal understandings of it. I myself have found that a personalistic version conveys a fuller metaphoric sense of the religious reality I know (and also shows greater continuity with the images utilized by our prophets and sages). I therefore have personal as well as theoretical reasons for turning now to personalistic symbolizations of transcendence.

Milton Steinberg, an early disciple, championed Mordecai Kaplan's theory of Judaism as a religious civilization but rejected Kaplan's impersonal concept of God. He did so because he thought it reductionistic to base our theology on science; he remained open to what the human spirit entire, and not just the mind, might find in its experience of likeness with the Transcendent. In his later years, as he grappled with the problem of human evil, he sought to move beyond the simple trust in human goodness on which he had modeled his prior thought. He might well have become one of the pioneers of postmodern Jewish thought but his early death prevented him from pursuing his personalistic, nonrational approach.

Some decades earlier, in Germany, Franz Rosenzweig and Martin Buber had pursued this necessarily elusive trail. In Rosenzweig's influential book, *The Star of Redemption*, he diagrams the three primal realities in a triangle having God at the apex—and thus transcendent—and Man and the World at the base. In the unequal interaction of the three givens, God relates to the World by creation, to Man by revelation, and through Man to the World by redemption— thus becoming immanent in three modes. When the triangle of active relationships is superimposed and inverted on the triangle of the independent realities, we have the six-pointed Star of Redemption, the standard of all true religion—with God at the highest point.

Though Rosenzweig displays a typical nonrationalist's reticence about making discursive, as it were, "objective" statements about God, he plainly characterizes the personal quality of the Transcenent–Immanent One by the metaphor he utilizes to speak about revelation: love. Nothing could be more personal, and it is this sense of personal relationship that enables Rosenzweig to replace God's revelation as verbal communication—and thus Orthodoxy—with what passes between friends or lovers: not words but presence. He reminds us of the commanding power of the beloved even in the absence of verbal interchange. Love issues imperatives without denying the beloved's independence and dignity but, in the loving, rather affirming them. And love can respect yet vault differences in stature as we know from our experience of truly loving those who, by reason of age, attainment, office, or person, might be far above or far below us.

Buber's Version of Transcendence in Relationships

Much in Rosenzweig's thought remains obscure, largely because of its fragmentariness and declaratory tone. Martin Buber's thought of the same period provides a fuller if somewhat different understanding of our relationship with God. Note the critical shift of terminology. Where rationalists thought the critical religious issue was to have a proper *idea* of God. Buber called for us to enter the kind of *relationship* he explored in his famous discussions of the I–thou encounter. We ordinarily know this relationship best from our experience with people and so gain our clearest insight into his meaning by thinking of it by analogy to interpersonal intimacy.

We can gain considerable insight into Buber's sense of transcendence–immanence by considering the ambivalent functioning of the hyphen in the term I–thou. It both unites and separates. In the former role, it establishes relationship, linking the I and the thou intimately. Yet it also keeps them apart, thereby preserving their personal singularity (which he claims arises in optimal fullness only in such mutuality). By contrast, if either of us, as the romantics and mystics advise, surrendered self to the relationship and merged into the other, we would surrender our individuality and thus our personhood.

Two aspects of transcendence stand out in this quite human situation. First, we meet a certain transcendence of the other in his/her irreducible reality and over-againstness in our relationship. Second, the relationship itself, in summoning the true selves into being through the I–thou, exercises a commanding power over us unseen in our individuality or impersonal interchanges.

However, Buber does not believe this relatively horizontal "transcendence" can be separated from what he takes to be its necessary dimensional otherness. He points to another I–thou relationship whose special quality lies in having an uncommon Other, one who never becomes an it for us as all other thous do. For us it is always thou; hence Buber calls it, with a measure of awe, the Eternal Thou.

Reflecting later about such an encounter, we realize that it involved us with the fullest quality we can know. Though all true relationships ennoble us, direct intimacy with the Eternal Thou does this most fully, for it not only draws us fully to what we ought to be but does so in personal involvement with the source and sustainer of all that is. We also can become sensitive to its far more common if penumbral presence. Buber points to the Eternal Thou's shadowy participation in every other I–thou relationship as its context and third partner. In genuinely knowing any other we momentarily find/become our true selves and brush up against the Divine Presence. Buber is saying that amid the ephemerality of existence, the Eternal makes itself readily available; it is an extraordinary restatement of the Jewish folk wisdom that one finds God best with people and in community.

Transcendence takes a special form here. In the special quality of the Eternal Thou, Buber gives some assent to the hierarchical aspect of transcendence; yet it is one that we paradoxically gain some indication of through its partnering with-ness. Buber does not assert that the Eternal Thou is a person or even personal; such categorization would impermissibly objectify what is Eternal[ly a] Thou. He says only that, so to speak, we find God present to us in the same way we find that persons truly encounter us. And even the hierarchically superior God respects the hyphen when establishing the commanding relationship, for God never violates the hyphen's limits but allows and endorses our individuality on its other side. I should think Rosenzweig meant something like this in his less detailed, more metaphoric account of revelation as love.

I find Buber's metaphoric description of our involvement with the Transcendent evocative of my religious experience but inadequate to its conferring a certain absoluteness on Jewishness. I shall therefore return to this issue of generating a more-than-personalistic life of Torah from a personal relationship with God when delineating my own theory of Jewish duty in chapter 20.

The Lesson of Heschel's Strong Teaching of Transcendence

Abraham Heschel's appreciation of God's transcendence challenges contemporary Jews to reevaluate their religious assumptions. He boldly proclaimed the root error of non-Orthodox Judaism to be its enslavement to the liberal paradigm of making human experience our standard for God's reality. Ungratefully, we never ask who made possible our experiencing, including our prideful doubt and skepticism. Heschel, by contrast, took God's transcendence so seriously that he daringly described God as an "ontological presupposition," the Granter of all that we customarily take "for granted."

One might fruitfully interpret all of Heschel's thought as an effort to restore God's proper transcendence to modern Jewish belief and to elicit the consequences of this fresh theocentrism. His incomparably evocative style sought to bypass the censorious rationality to which secularity had conditioned us and to reawaken our natural human sensitivity to transcendence. Thus, once we reestablish the reality of God's incomparable greatness we can see how meaningless because humanocentric are most of the theological questions we take so seriously. For example, when God stands before us in utterly transcendent greatness, prayer, even praise, seem simply God's due, not the problematic activity they inevitably seem when we begin by asking what they do for us.

By his uncommon evocation of God's transcendence Heschel brings us to a problematic point. His God so transcends the human situation that it makes possible a return to the classic paradigm of revelation, with God giving and people essentially receiving—that is, to a variety of Orthodoxy. Because his God is so awesomely other, no other pattern of revelation would be appropriate, and we, far less spiritually gifted than the prophets, have no independent basis for questioning the content of what God has been willing to disclose. And he grants the sages' rulings the same status as the words of the prophets.

This strong affirmation of transcendence would indeed serve to ground our values but identifies them as essentially those prescribed by Jewish law, without reference to individual judgment. It therefore forces reflective Jews to determine just how serious a religious commitment they have to self-determination and, as a corollary, whether they find truth in so strong a notion of transcendence as Heschel's.

All these theories of transcendence, whether rationalistic or non-rational, leave us with a more realistic view of human potentiality than that of humanistic modern Judaism. Restoring a significant independence and qualitative over-againstness to God frees us of the false optimism of belief in human perfectibility without taking away a strong sense of our being commanded to improve the world.

Our tradition supplies us with a most evocative metaphor for this awesome tie between the Transcendent and the human: *brit*, covenant. The Torah daringly asserts that, despite the disparity between them, the one God of all the universe enters into intimate partnerships with humankind. It understood God's covenants with the Children of Noah—humankind—and with the Children of Israel as contracts between partners mutually bound by the stipulations of their agreement. Non-Orthodox postmoderns find the term congenial to their mix of transcendence and self by reinterpreting covenant as relationship rather than contract. This shift enhances the human role beyond what our tradition could grant yet acknowledges God's independence in ways unknown to modernistic religions of immanence. As we shall see, it also makes the Jewish people central, not peripheral, to our Judaism, for our historic Covenant was not made with individuals but with our folk corporately. And thus to share in the Covenant immediately involves us in the God-grounded, community-directed, personally appropriated sense of responsibility that creates the life of Torah.

8   Sparks: The Transcendent in the Everyday

ELIGIONS glory in celebrating their cycle of sacred moments even as individuals rejoice in the great transitions in their lives. Mystics extend this capacity for greeting the Sacred by their genius for making the exceptional the stuff of everyday, the most dedicated among them seeking to live in communion with the Holy—what the kabbalists called *devekut*, clinging. Most of us, however, have no special spiritual talent and we spend our lives in routines punctuated by sporadic bursts of creativity and individuality. Knowing this, religions institutionalize, seeking by the rites they devise to help us to a steadier awareness of the Numinous.

The Lurianic mystics had a metaphor for this process so compelling that many of us, who do not share the myth that they took as fact, still find it evocative. They spoke about the divine sparks that remained embedded in nature after the creation and they envisioned daily religiosity as the mystic elevation of these sparks to their proper, redemptive unity with God. In our time the sociologist Peter Berger has given this old intuition new and appealing form.

Berger, a devout Lutheran layman, employs his academic expertise to expose a curious aspect of modernity. It is common for us to strike a posture of suspicion for the sake of sophistication, habitually censoring from consciousness any sense of ultimacy that may arise in daily experience. While the attitude reflects the values of only a small group in our society, many others adopt it because they think it culturally advanced. In contrast, Berger points to five ordinary experiences in which we can detect what, utilizing a medieval Christian phrase, he charmingly calls "a rumor of angels." In the face of life's confusion we assert that there is order; despite our seriousness, particularly as regards time, we insist on play; against life's continual disappointments and tragedy, we hope; in the face of the utterly despicable—here Eichmann is the chief example—we insist upon damnation; and in the most demanding circumstances, some people manage to manifest a sense of humor. There is nothing particularly spiritual, one might think, about these attitudes. Yet they make sense only as testimony to a reality that transcends the visible. These and other experiences demonstrate that, in fact, awareness of a higher quality regularly punctuates our customarily flat existence.

In Search of a Jewish "Rumor of Angels"

I find much in Berger's description convincing but I also adduce it here for what it indicates about our Jewish bent in apprehending the Transcendent. Berger takes his five examples from individual experience and focuses more on worthy feelings than on good deeds, a concentration that I believe stems from his Lutheran sensibility. Jewish spirituality, despite our religious diversity, almost universally denies Alfred North Whitehead's definition of religion as what one does with one's solitariness. With rare exception, we evaluate Jewish piety more by one's acts than by one's inner life, more by what one does in community with others than alone, though both aspects are comprised in the Jewish whole.

As my test case for Jewish "signals of transcendence" amid the humdrum realities of contemporary life I have chosen the experience of chairing a section of a federation campaign. On the surface, little connects this no-nonsense, bottom-line oriented activity with spirituality. But I maintain that the involvement has notably affected many Jews precisely because it brought a touch of transcendence into their otherwise secularized existence. I begin my analysis with what is usually the most moving of such experiences, a mission to the State of Israel.

Mostly we explain its extraordinary impact in terms of the strong emotions it produces. We are powerfully moved by a land reclaimed, industry thriving, a language and culture reborn, a people inexperienced at statecraft operating a new nation well, a citizenry passionate about democracy despite intense differences, a recently battered folk proudly asserting its will to survive, a maligned, besieged, and harassed community courageously striving to live with the high human dignity we associate with our people. Jews who might easily be us startle us by their refusal to give up idealism, and in their spiritual stubbornness bear testimony to a reality far greater than themselves.

But a few of us would be so deeply affected if this were only an intense experience of tears or laughter or both at once. For despite having been deeply touched we generally remain as hard-headed and skeptical as ever, complaining volubly about the accommodations, the food, the poor briefings, the boring speakers, the important people who say nothing and do so at great length, the unbearable over-scheduling, and the consequent utter exhaustion. Nevertheless, we have been moved at so primal a level that attributing it to mere feeling or ethnic solidarity robs it, and thus ourselves, of its full depth.

I suggest that on such occasions we have simply heard a Jewish "rumor of angels," that is, a signal of the reality of the Covenant that binds all Jews to one another and to the Transcendent. For we have seen our people engaged in Jewish action, building a modern Jewish way of life and doing so on Jewish soil, on the Land tradition tells us we were promised when we were called to the Covenant and was given to us on condition that we live up to the Covenant's demands. These ancient concepts sound odd to modern ears and yet they say far more about what can happen to us visiting the State of Israel than all the smart talk that reduces devotion to sentiment. If we could stop insisting that we can no longer have such experiences of Ultimacy, we would, as Buber and Heschel taught, become aware of how often they impinge upon us and live more steadily as a result.

The same phenomenon occurs locally as our *tzedakah* campaigns evidence the true Jewish ties that bind our community. Momentarily, Jewish duty unites us with neighbors we otherwise do not often see or regularly avoid. Through this work of charity we reach across the world to Jewish migrants or refugees, to those who need sustenance, defense, or education, to kin we do not know and may never visit. So the most satisfying moments of a drive are not limited to our successful management, the tough prospects cracked, the critical pledges gained, the improbable goals surpassed. They come rather in all those fleeting intimations that by our efforts we have fulfilled something elemental about being a human being and a Jew.

This subterranean revalidation alone explains why otherwise rational, loving people regularly deny their families' justified pleas for more attention and take on another campaign. And that entails considerable punishment: innumerable meetings of intolerable length and dubious accomplishment, suffocating detail and indigest-ible amounts of information, coworkers of maddening temperament and undependable reliability, anticlimactic dinners, empty awards and disappointing speakers, and most distasteful of all, the important donors who are monumentally selfish, purposefully impolite, or personally abusive. Why then do we come back for more? To be sure, as with childbirth, the memory of pain recedes with time. But that explains little. We take up the onerous burden again because of our dim intuition that in this grinding effort, prospect by prospect and dollar by dollar, we connect with what is Eternally True about Jewish life and hence about ourselves.

Only these personal intimations of transcendence, I believe, explain what must be called the ongoing miracle of American Jewish *tzedakah*. The wonder is not that we raise so much money but that decade after decade this old duty elicits an incredible outpouring of Jewish creativity, intelligence, and energy. That we give so generously of our money is impressive—that we give so unstintingly of ourselves is, literally, awesome.

Brushing up against the Sacred in Ordinary Life

Let me also provide two more private examples of finding the sparks. First is the commonplace Jewish duty of saying a *berakhah* as a way of regularly opening us up to the Transcendent.

This scenario should have its analog in many lives: I dash out between classes to grab a fried-fish sandwich at McDonald's. As I find a seat in the crowded, semi-greasy table area, I am quite preoccupied. I have to get back to class early because someone wanted to see me and I'm troubled because I'm not sure I prepared adequately for the meeting I'm later leading. As I hastily unwrap the sandwich I remember—this time—my Jewish duty to say a *motzi* before I eat. Something inhibits me from doing that in McDonald's. Even elsewhere, I don't quite know how to handle the situation when I lunch with another Jew who does not say the *berakhah*. In either case, if I say the *berakhah* out loud, other people will feel uncomfortable. So, not wishing to be a public nuisance or because of my inhibitions, I say it to myself, silently—which, because of the tumult, isn't always easy. If I let all this overwhelm me, I know that saying the *motzi* will not be very meaningful. So, hoping to let its spiritual purpose work, I must stop dead still, take control of my frazzled self, center my soul for a precious minute, and only then say the *berakhah*.

If I am to find the Transcendent even in McDonald's, I must do my part seeking it—in this case by fighting cultural norms and my personal drive to get on with my work. Yet if I ignored my Jewish duty, I would come to most meals mired in the muck of using and being used. I make no claim that every time I follow this ritual I encounter the Transcendent. Judaism rejects automatic means of summoning up God, as in magical religion, but that it does not happen every time does not mean it never happens. Though I have no special gift for spirituality, something does occasionally happen. Saying my *motzi* amid the city rush, I sometimes again fleetingly but truly touch the Ultimate, reaffirming in this instant what I believe and must yet do. For all that these slight, intangible experiences pass so quickly, few things are as precious for they momentarily restore to me everything the metropolis seems organized to take from me.

My other personal experience is quite specific. I was once in the hospital for a torn kidney and was very grateful when it began to heal. As a sophisticated modern who felt refined by high culture, I had thought it rather crude, even vulgar, for the rabbis to have prescribed a *berakhah* after urination and defecation. In the hospital I discovered that urination was an extraordinary gift. In deep appreciation of the wonder and grace of my body's functioning, I taught myself to say that *berakhah*. Saying it in innumerable repetitions over the years has taught me a good deal about the physicality of my spirituality and of the intimate depths of my dependence on God.

In such ordinary experiences as these—which vary as do our temperaments and situations—we personally make our contact with God and regain our people's millennial assurance that the Covenant-relationship abides.

Recognize the Signals amid the Static

Can we say much more? Can we put into words something of what we have experienced? Let me try by starting with one by-product: our occasional sense of certainty that some act we have been doing is right, truly and ultimately right. For an instant, all our usual ambivalence vanishes. We "know" its value, though it is surely an odd form of understanding. It cannot be merely an overflow of emotion or we would quickly write off its depth of significance. Moreover, we generally describe it as quiet rather than intense, calm rather than sensate, though if it has deeply moved us, a certain afterglow may come over us. In large part we trust it because it does not so much give us a self-satisfied certainty as it imparts a renewed, even purified sense of what we must now turn and do. Often that means the reimposition of a wearisome burden, so our response may be a heavy sigh: like it or not, this we must do. Paradoxically, we also can accept the veracity of such moments because, most of the time, our old doubts and questions speedily return, perhaps accompanied by new ones. We recognize ourselves in this familiar conflictedness and take a certain pride in testing experience with skepticism to make it properly responsible. It is not an easy way to live—but it is a most mature one.

The process also conveys a sense of personal confirmation. All the pestiferous questions about who I am and what I am living for momentarily fall away. For all my weakness and failings, I know that I have created true worth and may do so yet again. This is what I can do—and be—and thus, who I truly am. Such insights, great or small, barely felt or utterly memorable, ground a Jewish life. If I can build on them and reinforce them, I may be able to resist the world's insidious efforts to shrivel my soul and my psyche's continual threats to engulf me in despair.

Many people with whom I have discussed these matters cannot remember having had the positive experiences I have been describing. They suggest that what I have been pointing to, rather inadequately I admit, has less to do with reality than with my imagination, perhaps in response to an unconscious need of mine. They may be right—as may many other possible, quite unreligious motives for my taking these notions so seriously. These days we have no dearth of reasons for religious skepticism and I think it a major responsibility of theologians to expose themselves to them (as well as to the claims of religions other than their own). If the day comes when I cease entertaining such self-critical notions I hope I will recognize such complacency or defensiveness as a symptom of fading certainty.

I think it only proper, however, to ask critics to engage in similar self-examination. Modern education often demands that analysis occupy the place where awe once dwelt. One sad consequence of this ruthlessness has been that many of us cannot easily give or accept love. We may be productive but we may also not be very human. To people who insist no breath of transcendence has ever blown through their everyday life I suggest the possibility that they have shut it out. Our society being what it is, the suggestion is at least worth some exploration.

Dogmatism from all of us having been set aside, I want to press my analysis one step further. What we gain from brushing up against the Transcendent conveys a significance we could never bestow upon ourselves. No welcome release from a punishing inner restraint or conflict, no liberating welling up of self-confidence or vital energy, could ever affect us so deeply. Happily we all know such buoyant moods but we also recall that for all their confirming power they may well be succeeded by equally intense waves of self-doubt, meaninglessness, and depression. What may at one stage of our lives have been mandated by a peak experience can years later make us wonder at our earlier judgment. The spirituality I am pointing to offers no tight answer to the problem of reliability. Only an orthodoxy could do that. But when we have retained the checks of mind, community, and tradition (to be explored later), it conveys the assurance and empowerment that our lives and acts are linked to an axial reality far more elemental than mind or feeling or unconscious or self but one undergirding them and thereby endowing them with unique worth.

Jewish tradition calls this reality God, but that word is so heavy with question and misconception that I have mostly avoided using it. I am far more concerned about the nature of the encounter than I am about the term we use for its referent, though how we allow ourselves to identify it and thus the mandates that can arise from it will largely determine our human and Jewish ideals. In any case, I do not see that we can long speak of the depth we find in Jewish acts, of our sense of the absoluteness connected with the Jewish people and personal Jewishness, without acknowledging God or, if you wish, the Transcendent. Because of our personal experience of Ultimate Worth we know how we must respond to the root question of modern (Jewish) life: Why do you care so much about the good that you do and give and serve with messianic stubbornness? I am not saying that I or other theologians know very much about God and I am not arguing that to be a good Jew or a loyal Jewish folk we must accept a certain specific modern or ancient understanding of God. Instead I have spoken directly about our commonplace experiences of transcendent reality because I think we are more certain of them than of any theologian's conceptualization of God. Such personal insight also gives us an initial autonomous standard for judging the Jewish adequacy of any religious idea, another manifestation of individual dignity in a religiosity grounded substantially in Otherness.

Evading the Transcendent via Jewish Education

Two desiderata would result from clarifying this critical aspect of Jewish religious experience. If we had some idea of what personal Jewish religiosity involves today and, perhaps more crucially, what it does not directly entail, we would probably find ourselves less inhibited about receiving the signals of transcendence that beam through our lives. And that would make possible a growing Jewish subcommunity who shared a common religious quest and not only could amplify each other's fleeting intuitions but by empathic dialectic refine our belief and its responsible consequences, that is, what constitutes an authentic life of Torah today.

Let us consider an alternative proposal. Surely the easiest way today of avoiding religious belief as the personal foundation of Jewish living lies in the hope that Jewish education will, on its own, provide this foundation. I want to pursue my theological point by analyzing the relationship between Jewish education and transcendence.

We Jews have valued education highly because our Jewishness derives from a long historical experience that has left a continuous trail of text and commentary. We continue to believe with prior Jewish generations that the early founders and shapers of our people's relationship with God remain our best guide to its character and exemplification. As moderns we read these sacred records as accounts of our people's continual modification of the life of Torah in order to keep it authentic and relevant in shifting social circumstances. Being an ethnic group, they did not limit it to what Western civilization calls religion but articulated it in lore as in metaphysics, in music as in responsa, in cuisine as in liturgy. And where they did not utilize their national tongue, Hebrew, they often created new Jewish languages like Yiddish and Ladino.

This vast ethnic-spiritual inheritance succors each generation as it enters upon conscious Jewish existence. Because no single Jew can master this precious legacy, our community has created and maintained a scholar class and institutions of higher learning. Today, as the university has opened up new methods of study, we require a far more ramified and advanced Jewish scholarship than anything we have ever known.

After a slow and dispiriting start, the education of American Jewish youth has made notable progress. On the simplest level, the current generation of *bar* and *bat mitzvahs* regularly delights us with its competence. That does not make them scholars of Judaica, but our people survives not primarily because of its geniuses but because of the devotion, practice, and knowledge of ordinary Jews. Moreover, a sizable minority of our adults is increasingly well educated by day schools, university courses in Judaism, great academic centers for Jewish research and *kollelim* for advanced Talmud study, erudite journals, recondite books, and Jewish scholarly associations. Anyone with some decades of experience in Jewish affairs cannot help but be struck by the accomplishment.

I have made the positive case not only because I believe it to be true but because I want my appreciation of what we have done and may yet well do to set the context of my judgment concerning its limits: No amount of Jewish knowledge, even of the classic texts in the original languages, can by itself secure Jewish survival. For knowing does not necessarily produce caring (though it can help and Judaism has made it a *mitzvah*). University professors of religion and philosophy are the most obvious example. They may be highly acclaimed experts in a religion or in ethics but not personally practice the faith or exemplify the morality they teach. The same is true of students in their courses, as I have often seen when teaching Jewish studies at a university. Some admirable students turn out to be otherwise uninvolved Jews, or Christians seeking information about their savior's people.

We can easily be misled as to the effects of education. Those who pursue it in depth generally do so because they care about it. The critical issue then becomes what causes a student to care in the first place, for in the long run, only that devotion might then lead us to transform knowledge into responsibility. It may also happen that the material we study itself touches us so deeply that we know we must shape our lives by it. Exposure to texts and concepts can give us intimations of transcendence, and Jewish study at its best gives us just such a "rumor of angels." But like most other activities, education is not magic. Sometimes it exalts us; mostly it is a discipline to be followed. We surely ought not expect Jewish education to make us dedicated Jews if we persist in secularizing or academicizing it, concentrating so on textual mastery that we filter out the signals of transcendence in its subject matter. Education that stresses the creation of a feelingful experience will touch us more deeply, at least for the moment, but, if it only gives us pleasant associations with Jewish data it will not mandate and motivate dedication to Jewish living. When we can shuck off the secular training that has conditioned us to turn from intimations of the Transcendent and instead be sensitive to the Other who pervades our texts, rites, and study halls, Jewish education can be a powerful means for creating this generation's version of the life of Torah.

Ultimately, What Else Powers Jewish Duty?

Every other Jewish activity raises the same challenge about its empowering basis. When we ask why, in our already overburdened lives, we ought to devote a major share of our energies to Jewish duty, what answer can we finally give? Only that in some rightfully compelling way we know we must do so. And that "must" cannot be merely a pragmatic term to have any significant efficacy in our harried lives. Any realistic audit reveals the cost/benefit ratio of satisfaction to aggravation in Jewish life to be small. But when an occasional spark of transcendence illumines an activity, then we know why we "had to" do this. And in the last, realistic analysis, that alone ultimately compels us to take up old or new burdens. Then Jewish duty arises as the behest of that Other at the heart of the universe that rightly lays Its demand of quality upon us. We may freely reject the injunctions that arise from our touching up against transcendence but only by not being true to ourselves as people and as Jews.

Were this a less determinedly irreligious time, I would put it more simply: We must undertake our Jewish responsibilities because, somehow, we know God wants us to do so. Today such words sound strange. Talk of God "wanting" conjures up childhood images of a powerful old man seated on a throne in a place called heaven. Because we are so sophisticated in many areas of our lives, we know we cannot believe so infantile a notion and therefore conclude that we cannot believe in God at all. But nothing in Jewish teaching—including classic rabbinic teaching—requires Jews to take the prayerbook and biblical images of God literally. Even in the Bible some authors reinterpret what other Bible writers had said; *midrash* goes back that far. We have a long, active tradition of seeking to find less inadequate language for the God whom all Jews have agreed is ultimately ineffable. My effort here to speak of God in terms of the experience of transcendence and to personalize it as relationship merely continues the Jewish devotion to interpretation. I think my theological *midrash* the best way of mandating and motivating a life of Torah. But whatever language a Jew uses to speak of God, the communication needs to make God sufficiently real that "commandment" results and energizes a Jewish life that deserves to be associated with the term "Torah."

9   The Who/What of God

N THIS and the following chapter I want to broaden our theological reach by considering the best way to talk about what God "is" and what God does.

I use quotation marks about the word "is" to signal the special difficulty we face when we attempt to verbalize about God's nature. Contemporary Jewish thinkers, reflecting a major theme in classic Judaism, show rare unanimity in acknowledging that human beings cannot hope to know fully "what God is like." One can reach this conclusion either by what we already know about God or what we understand about ourselves. At the one pole, one would have to be as great as God—be God—to truly comprehend God. At the other role, our mystics, today as in the past, teach us that despite the greatest intimacy with God, human language remains utterly inadequate to truly tell us about God. Our religious philosophers agree, for ever since Kant they have tried not to confuse the way disciplined minds function with what is in fact reality, a conclusion most of them believe debars us from doing metaphysics. Even those who have sought to do so—I shall consider an example below—do not equate their intellectual construction of God's being with its actuality.

Even the assertion that God is One involves us in this problem. Though contemporary Jewish thinkers differ substantially about much else concerning God's nature, they all affirm God's unity. Their views of science and ethics as well as their religious experience make this belief almost self-evident. Scientists seek ever more comprehensive unities of explanation while ethicists critically identify the good with its universality, its moral inclusiveness. We can work at either only if we have an initial sense of a unity that transcends the immediate data of either field. Here Judaism's revolutionary religious insight finds strong reinforcement in two of our major cultural activities.

Asserting God's unity, however, puts us in a logical loop that turns back on itself and creates a paradox. If God is truly One then there is nothing to compare God with and we cannot know literally what God is "like." But we know so certainly that God "is" One that we consider that affirmation basic to our Jewish identity and faith. Maimonides was so taken with this difficulty that his rationalism required him to deny that we could say anything positive about God's nature (though we could speak positively about what God did), a resignation that caused Thomas Aquinas, also for philosophic reasons, to term Maimonides an agnostic. Contemporary Jewish thinkers agree that they cannot say all that ought to be said about God but generally believe silence would create greater problems. Saying what we can as best we can makes it possible for us to be more responsible about our religion, at the very least by providing us with a working standard for judging which suggested beliefs are inadequate or even pernicious.

Since Evil Is Real, God Cannot Be Good

Today, two intertwining concerns largely determine the diverse images of God presented by our thinkers. One is methodological, the other is the problem of evil.

In the former instance, intellectual integrity requires the thinkers to exercise extreme vigilance about what they can and cannot rightly assert about God. Their standards of what people can truly know or of what constitutes meaningful statement become a channel and a filter determining which aspects of their religious intuition can enter into their view of God's nature. Since on these critical issues they divide radically into rational and nonrational methodologies, their understandings of God significantly diverge.

The problem of evil has been in the background of every modern Jewish conception of God but, since the Holocaust, it has more commonly occupied the foreground. No critical thinker wants to make pronouncements about God that contradict our experience of nature's moral indifference and humankind's tolerance, and even encouragement, of evildoing. Those realities already led some of our medieval thinkers to modify or denature the classic Jewish teaching about the dependability and reach of God's retributive justice; no modern thinker, rational or nonrational, has given the doctrine of retribution even that much defense. Instead, they construe God's nature in such a way that it obviates what they consider the crux of the problem of evil, as, for example, by asserting God's finitude or inscrutability.

Richard L. Rubenstein's writings starkly demonstrate how a religious response to the Holocaust becomes determinative for one's view of God's nature. He declares that after Auschwitz we ought, realistically, to envision the Sacred as the Holy Nothing. Though our spiritual sensibility must now be primarily negative, we know it to be religious because of our awe and appreciation of the ground of being from which all existents emerge and to which they return. He finds echoes of this negative intuition of Divinity in the mystic disclosure that, at the height of one's "cleaving" to God, one knows precisely No-thing, in *kabbalah*, the *En Sof*.

Rubenstein resolves the problem of theodicy by breaking with classic and most modern Jewish thought and teaching that "God," the Holy Nothing, is not good or determinative of value. Religion has no role in validating ethics and no special insight into the quality our lives should manifest. Rather we utilize religion and ethnicity as social instrumentalities useful for coping with the harshness of human existence. Consequently, we must work out our destiny utterly on our own, unblinkingly recognizing that social life and human history result from the jostling of political and economic power blocs. He therefore calls death, in which all beings return to the Ground of Being and find such peace as they can, the only Messiah there now is.

As I have argued above, I find this view of God self-refuting for it "explains" evil by the neutrality of reality and thus denies that there is any reason for our moral indignation at the Holocaust. Rubenstein tacitly admitted this problem by later seeking to create a theory of value based on our bodily nature and our capacity to love, but this immanentism persuaded few readers.

Another Approach to a Neutral God

Rubenstein's concept of God as Holy Nothing also challenges believers to probe their own religious experience. It certainly reflects what we may have known in times of personal despair as well as in the experience or recollection of the Holocaust. But if the context of our inquiry becomes our ongoing, everyday intuition of the Sacred, then I find that this view overextends one aspect of my awareness of God, unfathomable distance, at the expense of another of its qualities that I find more commonly manifest, namely, benevolence. I also do not see how this theology can respond to the other absoluteness in Jewish experience, that validity to Jewish identity which requires a theory of steadfast loyalty to the people of Israel and the practice of a vigorous life of Torah.

Alvin Reines, for methodological reasons, has similarly presented us with a value-free God-idea. Committed to philosophic rationalism as the only worthy foundation for religious belief, he seeks to delineate Divinity so that it will have cognitive validity or, more simply, so that it will not be falsifiable by analytic philosophic standards. Since his rationalism includes facing facts, he also seeks a rational solution to the problem of evil.

Like Rubenstein, Reines begins his religious thought from our experience of personal existence. (Both worked on doctorates at Harvard when Paul Tillich expounded his highly influential philosophical existentialism there.) Calling attention to the difference between existents and their ground, he acknowledges an element of transcendence in God, but connects it with being rather than with goodness and speaks of a God who is amoral. Since existence has a forward thrust, he identifies this transcendence with the possibility of new things coming into being. Our awed appreciation of existence and its dynamic continuity gives this religiosity a positive tone. On this basis he defines God as the enduring possibility of being and thereby fulfills his two critical conditions. One cannot empirically refute a "possibility of being," particularly as things continue to be and come to be, and one cannot be asked to provide a rational theodicy for a God indifferent to goodness or justice.

I do not find these arguments persuasive on their own terms, let alone on mine. For all his realism, Reines assumes but never makes a case for employing a rigorous rationalism to speak of human existence and the nature of being. That a rigorous rationalist can coherently speak of matters such as "self," "existence," "being," and "possibility" is a position widely abandoned in the academy and in our culture. In my own religious experience God is sometimes quite distant, perhaps withdrawn, and in that sense has aspects of neutrality, but I do not find the God I more commonly encounter to be less than good. Moreover, where Rubenstein made a case for Jewish ethnicity, Reines's theology has no direct connection with Jewish peoplehood. Again the methodology is determinative. Rigorous rationalism ascribes truth only to what has universal scope. As a consequence he denies that any Jewish (or other) particular experience can have any *claim* on a properly rational person, though it may be of some interest as an example of human nature. He therefore regularly empties Jewish symbols of their particularistic content and finds them valuable only for what they can universally signify.

God, the Grounding Premise of Goodness

For much of the modern period, when Jews referred to Judaism's "idea of God," they were utilizing a religious language derived from Hermann Cohen. As the only academic philosopher among our systematic thinkers, Cohen thought of humans as rational beings who sought to create a systematic understanding of the world. For methodological reasons, then, he conceives of God not as an entity or other existent "out there"—he does not think a rational person can know any such thing—but as the only reality we can rationally know, a true idea. Cohen's God is the generating premise of a rational person's coherent view of the world.

This God-concept eludes neutrality because in neo-Kantian thought the ethical aspect of rationality takes priority, thereby tightly linking God and the good to yield ethical monotheism. Cohen's emphasis on ethics also preserves the individual human freedom the Kantians identified as the heart of morality. If God is an idea rather than an entity operative in nature, then creation carries on value-free and it remains for human beings to bring moral value into it. Why reality has just this rather than another form is beyond rationality's competence and hence as good as meaningless. However, when we relocate the problem of evil from one of God's justice to one of human choice, we can stop uselessly speculating about the nature of reality and accept the inexplicable evil as a challenge demanding our moral response. This Cohenian activism about evil remains, in my experience, the "theodicy" most commonly spoken of in our community today.

In Cohen's neo-Kantian Judaism, it is rationality that determines just what we can say about God. But should we give any human intellectual system such imperial status in our belief? If rationality ought to be so utterly decisive about basic human matters, why cannot philosophers decide rationally which of the presently competing forms of rationality is most rational? I think the choice that makes us a pragmatist or phenomenologist, say, is made on a prerational level. If so, then our religion, which concerns itself with ultimates, ought to be derived from this more primal ground. This prompts me to identify the nonrational basis of my faith and then use an appreciative/critical rationality to explicate its implications.

My other major difficulty with Cohen's idea of God arises from its consequences for the people of Israel and the life of Torah. A stringently universal God-idea cannot have any special connection to a particular people and can only "command" ethics. It cannot give primary validity to Jewish identity since any rational mind can know all the essentials of religion of reason. Compensating inducements to particularity can now enter the system only on a derivative level of authority, and they must inevitably validate themselves in terms of universal ethics. Anyone who considers Jewishness more significant than that, and certainly those who connect absoluteness with it, must be troubled by this and other such stringent universalistic views of God.

Radically Limiting God's Power

Mordecai Kaplan tried to respond to Cohen's disdain of ethnicity by adopting a different rationalism, naturalism. This allowed him to think of people in their living context, their social situation. Sociologically, religion provides a culture's plausibility structure, so Kaplan rounded out his social theory with a concept of God sufficiently believable that it could drive Jewish civilization. As a naturalist, that meant God had to be rigorously immanent and he therefore defined God as "the power that makes for salvation." This parses as: When we say "God" we mean all the processes of nature whose operation enables persons to fulfill themselves as human beings. This God is as real as nature is real and we cannot deny such a God without denying the reason we can rationally dedicate ourselves to self-development.

Moreover, by this definition, Kaplan has eliminated the major impediment to rational belief, the problem of evil. With God limited to only that in nature which aids us, evil can no longer come as a challenge to God's omnipotence but, as with the Cohenians, only to our moral creativity. This notion of God as finite has had great appeal to Jews as providing the only rational explanation for the existence of evil. In a way, Cohen had already pioneered the limitation of God's power by categorizing God as an idea. Kaplan carried this much further by his ingenious dichotomy between God's unity and reality. For him, God's oneness is essentially nominal; "God" is a singular term we use for what in reality are disparate natural processes. As a unity, God has only verbal reality, though great cultural significance, and this clear delimitation of God's power fully frees the Kaplanian God of any involvement with real evil.

My difficulties with Kaplan's construal of God's nature arise from its substance and effect. He has so tightly defined God in terms of the human—what contributes to our growth—that he understands prayer as essentially communion with oneself at one's best. The optimism about human nature which grounds this humanocentrism seems unwarranted in the light of recent experience. Today one finds wide differences of opinion as to which of the clashing urges of the self we should heed to find fulfillment rather than narcissistic gratification. I doubt that our culture so requires us to have a religion that a nominal God can elicit devotion and vitalize our way of life. Rather, I associate myself with the many who believe our moral gropings testify to a reality that so transcends us in stature and quality that it rightly sets an independent standard for our behavior. I shall shortly continue this line of thought in my discussion of Whitehead's metaphysics.

Before doing so, I want to explain why I find the doctrine of a limited God ultimately unacceptable despite its great initial appeal. It does allow one intelligently to believe in a good God without denying the reality and intolerableness of evil. It powerfully motivates morality by demanding that human ethics complete what the God of limited power cannot do. But it also generates new, very serious religious difficulties. Emphasizing God's finitude easily becomes simple humanism in which we put our real trust in people and their goodness, a confidence made dubious by the Holocaust and much else in human conduct. Spiritually, many find it difficult to worship a finite God, one limited precisely in that aspect of God's nature that most impinges on our humanity, effective goodness. Pastorally, too, just when we need God most, when we are hurt and despairing, we cannot turn to this God for explanation or solace; God has apparently done all that God can do and only human power can now help us.

Our ultimate hopes are also thrown in doubt. On what rational basis do we now maintain that our limited God retains sufficient power to bring the Messianic Day? And if God does not lend the decisive power, will our post-Holocaust realism allow us to count on people to do what God now cannot, deny evil ultimate victory in history? These questions climax in a most troublesome ultimate one about all the evil in nature that is presently beyond God's power: In Whose control is it and by what Order does it exist? Is reality not, then, finally one? For me as for many Jews, to assert the Jewish centrality of God's Oneness and then limit its scope in this way creates even more difficulties than living with the problem of evil.

So, in the face of the Holocaust and in a paradoxical way because of it, I reject the description of God as finite.

The Limited, Real God of Process Thought

I now want to return to the issue of God's independent reality, specifically to the proposal of William Kaufman and others that Judaism would benefit from thinking about God's nature in terms of the process metaphysics of Alfred North Whitehead. His rationalism analyzes what structure reality logically requires to warrant our confidence in science. This leads him to conceive of reality as an organically interrelated and self-contained process in which God also participates, though in a most crucial way. For God is that utterly fundamental aspect of the dynamism that makes possible the individuation of things out of the infinite possibilities of being and also supremely localizes all human value, thereby serving as a lure for human action. As another participant in the reality process, though an unusually steady and constant one, God changes as things change since, as the structuring foundation of natural continuity (in which effects become conditions and causes), God never "forgets" anything. Most importantly, as the conserver of value, God "suffers" with every negation or loss of value while also remembering every good deed, thus giving the righteous immortality in God's unforgetfulness.

Whitehead's thought appeals to religious philosophers because it rationally integrates science and value, providing a rational ground for ethics and other humane values and preserving individual self-determination. Moreover, no contemporary philosophy offers a fuller, more rational response to the problem of theodicy than it does by limiting God's power to the ordering of the reality process and removing God as an efficient agent in nature—all this while maintaining God's goodness as the conserver and lure of value. It also sets out contemporary theology's only rational theory of immortality, one which makes this metaphysics an even more effective response to evil.

Nonetheless, process thought impresses me as intellectually unpersuasive and Jewishly unacceptable. As to the former, I wish to add only a postmodernist accent to the general philosophic literature critical of this school of thought. At the time when Whitehead wrote, one still could have great confidence in science as a picture of reality and in the mind's capability of unveiling reality itself. Today the reach of reason seems far more limited, the legitimacy of generalizations being limited to given contexts. Science and mathematics alike now present themselves only as possible constructions of the world. To build a metaphysics on them produces only a possible construction of a construction, not a compelling picture of an objective, independent reality.

My special difficulties with process thought arise from the particular implications of its universalism. Consider, to begin with, the consequences of its otherwise praiseworthy reinterpretation of immortality. Because God loses nothing of the past but remembers everything, the Nazi murderers have the same immortality as their victims. I think such evenhandedness begins to impeach this God as the standard of our values.

Even more disturbing is the universality of the process God's relation to the future. God lures us to increase value in the universe and any way we do that, Jewish or otherwise, will satisfy the system. This neutrality to Jewish particularity becomes more troublesome when we realize that process thought deems novelty to create greater value than does continuity. Thus, had Hitler killed all the Jews, the process God would have suffered badly at the terrible loss in value and would forget nothing of that calamity. But, like a natural force, God would also simply move on, processing process. Or, if all the Jewish survivors had deserted Judaism and become process Buddhists or humanists, God might have been pained at the loss of Jewish particularity but that would speedily have been compensated for by the increment of new value. Any God who cares only about value in general will find the Jewish people or any other particularity quite dispensable. Thus, process thought's initially appealing answer to theodicy carries with it a benign indifference to the Jewish future and thus seems to me a paradoxical way of dealing with the Holocaust. Those who believe that the particular existence of the Jewish people has ultimate significance cannot accept such a God. To be sure, without a counterbalancing universalism, this affirmation of the absoluteness of Jewishness could render Judaism an immorally parochial faith. But this is a danger our thorough secularization severely limits.

From Rational to Nonrational Notions of God's Nature

Henry Slonimsky added a significant nuance to the theory of God's limited power, forging a theology that straddled rationalism and nonrationalism. He suggested that we take the classic description of God, "living," as a hint that God, like all things alive, grows. God's limited power to deal with evil results from God's present incomplete development, a deficiency that humankind can rectify by serving as God's partner in completing creation. Furthermore, in this relationship Slonimsky boldly pictured God as dependent upon humankind and thus suffering when we do not live up to our moral and spiritual responsibilities.

Though he lectured on this theology with great effect for half a century, he never gave it detailed exposition. From his fragmentary essays we cannot tell whether he came to his denial of God's omnipotence because his rationalistic methodology required it or from a romantically defiant assertion of humankind's dignity in the face of God's greatness. Whatever the case, he disdained functionalism and attributed metaphysical reality and personal presence to God.

Were it possible to overcome the incompleteness and incoherence of this theology, it would likely appeal to those who, in order to believe, must have a rational understanding of God's relation to evil. This God, being a real and living presence, could inspire a vigorous spirituality and an activist piety. Moreover, this God seems good enough to worship and powerful enough to help us in our weakness, yet not so competent as to eliminate evil or disdain human initiative. Above all, this God has such involvement in history as to understand our sufferings and participate in them. But this theology survives only in tantalizing fragments because, I believe, Slonimsky could not intellectually meet the needs of both the critical mind and the sensitive spirit. I also cannot judge from his concern with theodicy how his view of God would affect the life of Torah.

I recognize, of course, that my judgment of all these rationalists has largely been determined by my own differing faith, which is the very reason I followed this procedure. I wanted to explain why I find contemporary rationalisms unsatisfactory even in terms of their greatest appeal, namely, the forthright resolution of the problem of evil. I also remain unpersuaded that unrelievedly universalistic conceptions of God, particularly ones that can only ascribe a mental reality to God, can satisfactorily ground our values, most particularly the life of Torah. I therefore take a nonrational approach to Jewish theology and, in particular, to its foundation, our understanding of God. I am not arguing that no future rationalism can suitably undertake what I believe to be the critical agenda for contemporary Jewish theology. I only know it to be true of our present rationalisms.

Before turning to nonrational discussions of God's nature, I wish to make some general observations about nonrational Jewish theology. It involves giving primacy to a nonrational religious intuition and bringing it sufficiently to consciousness that reason can be employed in the secondary role of helping us discern what our insight does and does not imply. Perhaps the root religious perception of the nonrationalists can be put this way: That we do not, cannot, know a lot about God is a constant accompaniment of the wonder of knowing even this much about God, particularly about what God wants us to do.

Beyond this stance, the theological positions diversify. Some thinkers perceive God to be impersonal. I rather know God in personal encounter and then curiously discover that my rationality confirms this by balking at the incoherence of persons being created in the image of an impersonal God. Some nonrationalists find the problem of evil to disclose God's finitude. I find that assertion to generate such serious problems that I normally live in acceptance of the mystery that God's good nature somehow allows for evil. I say "normally" because I reject the passivity an unconditional acceptance of God's inscrutability can bring on. When I sense my pietism immobilizing me, I remind myself of God's limits, if only the self-imposed ones of calling me to Covenant-responsibility. Nonetheless, though knowing how much God counts on me keeps me faithfully active, I try never to forget whose unique power rules creation.

Rationalists criticize the nonrational approach to theology for excepting itself from reason's critical judgment, all the while demanding that reason subordinate itself to a mysteriously superior wisdom. This kind of "thinking" makes possible all sorts of self-delusion and chicanery. I cannot deny the special risks of proceeding nonrationally. Still, these can be limited by vigorously employing reason as far as one can, particularly by close attention to the human entailments of one's faith, and doing this in community and with regard for tradition. To my mind there is even greater risk today in working at theology as a rigorous rationalist, most notably the inability of rationalism to provide more than a shaky validation of value and of the life of Torah.

Rosenzweig and Buber's Personalistic Views of God

Franz Rosenzweig deserves first place in the discussion of nonrationalist views of God's nature, for though he wrote little about

this topic his work constituted a decisive change in the way recent
Jewish thinkers have spoken of God. He began his theology with the
understanding that God is a simple given of existence, a reality
independent of yet involved with both the World and Man, the other
independent given realities. He holds all this to be true regardless of
what human reason wishes to be the case. We then properly respond
to God not by analysis or definition—which now must follow
reality, not construct it—but by grateful service. Rosenzweig, a most
sophisticated thinker, quite self-consciously left little theoretical
room in his new thinking for the kind of assertive theodicy so
common among rationalists. As it turned out, Rosenzweig's later
years of progressive paralysis put his theology to a test perhaps no
other Jewish thinker has ever faced, but he did not find this a reason
to repudiate his early insight. So to speak, experience, like reason,
could not alter reality.

What Rosenzweig taught largely by assertion and allusion Martin
Buber sought to give fuller articulation—only what he wished to say
prevented him from doing so directly. Consider Buber's problem. The
clarity we commonly seek requires a statement "about" something, a
procedure appropriate to objects. To gain clarity "about" God would
thus involve us in two enormities. On the human side it suggests
that our minds can comprehend God, and on the Divine side it treats
God like an object, an idol. Buber provides us with a new analogy
and fresh metaphors for our knowing God and thus, by implication,
some insight into "what" God is. Our knowledge of God arises
as does our knowledge of persons, by genuine encounter. (More
accurately, it arises in all I–thou address, which includes the spiritual
experience of artists and nature lovers. Dialogue cannot yield descriptive data since withdrawal to the position of observer instantiates
I–it exchange. Yet if we beg for description, Buber suggests that, so
to speak, God is personal enough to meet us as persons normally
meet, I–thou. God, we reflectively discover, is the "greatest" of all
thous and not only because God never becomes an it for us. Rather,
we have a sense that God is the Thou behind all thous—if you wish,
the Person behind all persons, an odd presentness we sense as we
intuit God's participation as a third partner in all I–thou meetings.

Buber's personalistic way of talking about God changes the way
we must approach the problem of evil for he rules out such standard
I–it observations about God as that God is omnipotent or infinite.
While rationalists treat theodicy as a problem of coherent intellectual
formulation, Buber thinks of it as one of maintaining a close

personal relationship. This different approach arises because of his understanding of our two-level way of addressing the world. It indicates that we cannot expect to encounter the Eternal Thou as long as we look about us with I–it eyes and therefore cannot say anything about God's relation to the evil we find in "nature," a thoroughly desacralized, I–it "reality." When we think of interpersonal evil, we quickly realize that most of it occurs not as God's judgment but as a result of our refusal to relate to others as "thous" and effectively rendering them "its," thus opening them to our indifference or malevolence. Very much of the problem of evil is human hardness, not God's faulty retribution system.

After the Holocaust, Buber could no longer make people the exclusive source of interpersonal evil. He now daringly suggested that there are some terrifying times when God, as it were, withdraws from us despite our seeking God. Absence is the worst evil. For Buber, the problem of theodicy then becomes not understanding "how" or "why" our good God ever countenances our suffering or "hides his face" from us, but contemplating how we might still maintain or regain a loving relationship with God despite our anguish. He suggests we do so by the same process we have found operating in any great friendship or love. We often do not understand why those most dear to us occasionally hurt us, sometimes very deeply. Little injures us more than parents, children, friends, lovers, or spouses not being there when we need them; should they withdraw willfully, we will suffer most intensely. Yet, miraculously, love often survives such traumas. Every relationship lives out of the faith that the meaning we once knew together might at any moment return and thereby be renewed—and that is as true of religion as it is of the love of persons. Though we cannot make sense of their acting this way, we may be willing to "bear" with them, to accept the burden of the pain they have caused us—not the least by showing themselves capable of this betrayal—and to forgive them. Sometimes we can do that because of what we have meant to one another; sometimes we do it freely, staking our lives on what this torment has taught us about the depth of our love. Buber says God does something like that for us when we sin. Similarly, we try to respond to God in love though evil overwhelms us, caring despite not understanding. The religious life involves building a relationship with God of such binding power.

Buber's view of God has been faulted for its inability to generate a life structured by Jewish law. But in this position he follows the religious intuition of most modern Jews who deny the disciplinary authority of *halakhah* and esteem it only as guidance. Hence I criticize Buber's understanding of God, not because I do not think the relating God incapable of authorizing a rich life of Torah, but because he so universalized the relationship between God and Israel that autonomy overwhelms tradition. I hope to substantiate this thesis in the last section of this book. Here I only wish to record my opinion that Buber's understanding of God otherwise substantially communicates what I take to be the core postmodern Jewish religious experience: The God whom we encounter is real, and great enough to ground our values, and yet respects us enough to give us personal freedom in our relationship with God, the Covenant. Nurtured by that love, we pray to be able to go on trusting God even when we are wounded and do not understand our momentarily unrecognizable Lover.

The Exalted, before Whom Questions Become Silence

I am confirmed in this judgment by the contrast between Buber's God of relationship and Heschel's polemic against theologies that approach God via human sensibility rather than God's revelation. Heschel, though appreciative of the religious experience he describes so well as wonder, awe, and the sublime, wants us to go beyond them to the full biblical vision of God's distance from us. In classic Judaism, God defines us, not we God, and all its fulsome praise of God as Creator and King seeks to instruct us in God's transcendent otherness. God's oneness entails God's absolute primacy, making God the necessary presupposition of everything. How, then, can human experience or questioning or doubt or reasoning ever properly set a standard for God, when God precedes them and they all should be thought of as God's gift? Only in the prophets' reliable depiction of God's pathos do we find a language enabling us to speak about God without blasphemy. By contrast, even our grandest human superlatives understate God's supernal reality. In consequence, we cannot hope to say anything on our own about God's nature but instead ought to devote ourselves to what we owe God: obedience, worship, and piety, the faithful service that includes what moderns call ethics.

With God so utterly beyond us, how can humans challenge God?

For all his personal exposure to the Nazis in the years before the death camps, and despite the loss of many members of his family in the Holocaust, Heschel rarely complained publicly about God's inaction during this evil. In the few instances where his writing touches on theodicy, he follows the classic rationalist tack of ascribing evil to people's failure to be ethical. When, most rarely, he turned to God directly, he could only allow himself some poignant questions about why God permits it to be so easy for people to do evil. Yet his great humanity shows in another aspect of his relative silence: He never points to God's infinite otherness to justify the God who permitted the Holocaust.

Of all the views of God we have considered, Heschel's has the least difficulty in grounding a robust life of Torah. God's utter preeminence allows Heschel to reassert a traditionalistic doctrine of revelation that validates both the Written and Oral Torah. But this also requires that conscience be subordinated to the law, a difficulty Heschel seeks to remedy by stressing the role of interpretation and the passion for ethics in the Torah tradition. Heschel's depiction of God, therefore, demands we take a stand on the independent religious worth of the autonomy God has granted human beings. All those who believe that it must be given greater scope in our Judaism than our tradition allowed it will find Heschel's God overbearing. His theology also minimizes the independent significance of the people of Israel, limiting our significant communal life to the activities specified in revelation and the law.

This shift from envisioning God as a result of human experience to doing so through God-given revelation has been most fully worked out in the thought of Michael Wyschogrod. Where Buber claims God never becomes an it for us and Heschel contends that prophetic revelation mainly clarifies God's feelings, Wyschogrod argues that the Bible gives us quite explicit information about God's nature. While making plain that we can never know God as God really is, it objectifies God sufficiently that we can confidently say God is a Person, one with a definite character and psychology. The most important revelation of the Bible is of the God-Person's name; uttering it would be such a presumption of intimacy that no human should ever dare do so.

God being a Person, the Bible indicates what God wants us to do. While much of God's will immediately commends itself to us, the biblical depiction of God's will makes plain that it functions on an utterly higher level than anything we might hope to understand.

Wsychogrod, giving a biblical motif a Hegelian exegesis, understands God as the Master and we as God's slaves. Of course, as Judaism has long emphasized, humans are free and therefore responsible creatures. But ours is an enslaved freedom and such autonomy as the Master has granted us must be used only within the scope the Master allows us by His legislated will and commanding presence. Of all the contemporary Jewish views of God we have examined, this one ascribes the greatest transcendence to God and gives the most minimal scope to human freedom. With such a theology, there will be little difficulty in authorizing a rich life of Torah—though Wyschogrod is surprisingly unconcerned about rabbinic Judaism— and a strong religious, if not ethnic, Jewish corporate existence.

With God so exalted and humankind without any legitimate, independent standpoint over against God, the problem of evil disappears. Not only does God know best but only God can truly know the ultimate explanation of why the righteous suffer. No human should ever presume to inquire about the Master's nature, reasons, or deeds. Our role rather is to do what we have been commanded, to accept sacrifice as a necessary if regrettable aspect of the service of God, and to be grateful for every good the Master gives us.

More silent on the topic even than Heschel, Wyschogrod makes almost no explicit reference in his work to the issue of theodicy or to the Holocaust. Yet he clearly alludes to both when, in terms echoing medieval Jewish poetry, he describes the people of Israel as having corporately taken Isaac's role on the altar of history. If sacrifice turns out to be what God demands of a given generation of Jews, the Master has every right to ask for it and we must find a way, in faithfulness, freely to accept God's will.

I detect one remnant of modernism in a significant omission from Wyschogrod's depiction of the biblical God. He does not discuss its central motif of God the judge who faithfully rewards the righteous and punishes the guilty. Considering his determined effort to be faithful to the biblical view of God, his silence concerning retribution is telling. At the least, it testifies to his compassion for what our people as a whole and Jews individually have suffered in our time. But I cannot help but see it as more than that. Realism has prevented any modern Jewish thinker from affirming anything like the strong view of retribution that the Bible continually sets before us. Not even Wyschogrod, for all his biblical positivism, can honor the Master on this point.

Of course, I may be saying more about my own faith here than about Wyschogrod's, but that is the point of working at theology in this comparative fashion. Confronting the thought of Michael Wyschogrod, who is in many ways the most implacable theological opponent of the modern impulse in religious belief, requires us to ask just how strong an Absolute and how weak a version of autonomy we find true of our postmodern God. In similar fashion, each of the many thinkers surveyed here instructs us by challenging us with their special visions. Not the least of what they have to teach us as they prod us on our individual ways is that, despite the Holocaust, their thought and lives center about God, often doing so in substantial continuity with pre-Holocaust modern Jewish thought.

10   What Does God Still Do?

F THEODICY has been the major human problem requiring us to rethink our images of God, science has been its intellectual counterpart. The Bible and Talmud unhesitatingly describe what God did, does, and will yet do. Modern science, by its mathematical descriptions of nature's operation, explains why things work and even why they "must" do so. It depicts creation as a self-contained, lawful process and thereby dispenses with the need for God as a causal factor in nature; why should we multiply causes beyond the minimum necessary for explanation? But if God really does nothing, God is nothing, and if God does very little, then God deserves scant attention, so atheism and religion's irrelevance have become common among us.

Liberal understandings of religion came into being partly as the response of believers to the scientific worldview. Almost all began by abandoning efforts to establish God's metaphysical role in a strictly causal world, process thought being the great exception. Rather, the liberal theologians commonly coupled an acceptance of the scientific worldview with a denial of positivism's capacity to plumb the richness of human experience. They created a hermeneutic that translated traditional depictions of what God does into *human* action or experience. Revelation became discovery, sin became error, judgment became self-criticism, atonement became self-acceptance, and so forth. This humanocentric piety had the virtue of making believers radically less passive before God and their clergy and empowering them with personal responsibility for their spiritual welfare and their society's betterment. Self-reliance, individual or humanity-wide, became the supreme virtue, making God a marginal figure in this theology.

Demythologizing Science as True Explanation

Time and experience have thrown increasing doubt on the two assumptions of this modern demotion of God. The idea that mature people can assume most of the functions God once performed reflects an optimism that seems illusory today. And the faith that the Western physical sciences and mathematics as good as describe nature's reality has lost both its social and intellectual credibility. One sees the postmodern reaction against scientism most spectacularly in the vogue of New Age speculation and experience. In the multifarious groups that eclectically blend ancient and contemporary spiritual practices to open us to truth and power, beliefs and rites often acquire virtue in proportion to their divergence from scientific explanation. Less extremely, science has been thoroughly discredited as our savior because the aftereffects of many of its technical triumphs now threaten our existence and well-being.

Academically, a newly critical view of the nature of scientific explanation denies that it provides us with the only rational worldview. If mathematics, the foundation of scientific explanation, might be done in any one of a number of different ways; if what one studies empirically arises not sensually but out of what interests the researchers; if the studying itself often influences the data and thus what one might know; if alternate explanations might equally "explain" the data but we prefer the simple and elegant to the complicated and ungainly; in short, if science is only one possible construction of reality, though a phenomenally useful one for many purposes, then it does not present us with a picture of the world as it "really" is. When, then, appreciators of science insist that God cannot have a role in nature rather than specifying that in their preferred view of nature God has no place, they become dogmatists.

In this changed intellectual situation, theologians, particularly rationalists, face the methodological issue of the extent to which the positivistic, scientific worldview should serve as the determining background of their thought. To be sure, no other contemporary worldview matches its ability to integrate and explain natural events. However, knowing it to be a limited and provisional guide to understanding reality requires postmoderns to reconsider its authority in our religious thought.

We find ourselves in the untidy intellectual situation where neither religion nor science can claim a very full knowledge of what reality is and how it works. I do not know of a philosophy that could presently resolve the clashing insights of both realms and fill out each of their lacks in a coherent system acceptable to both groups. Accepting this uncertainty, I propose to reduce the anxiety connected with it by teasing out what a postmodern Jew like myself believes about what our tradition has said God does.

God, the Agent of Creation

For example, the *keriat shema*, our classic liturgical statement of faith, rehearses five such activities: God creates (the world), reveals (Torah), chooses (Israel), rewards (observance) and punishes (sin), and redeems (Israel). What have my theological teachers and colleagues made of these central affirmations and how does their thought help me clarify my own beliefs?

(1) God creates (the world). The use of the present tense "creates," may startle those who know the Bible and the medieval philosophical importance of creation out of nothing. The liturgy of the *keriat shema* refers repeatedly to God as "renewing daily the work of creation." Apparently the situation of worship makes it more appropriate to concentrate on what God does now rather than on what God once did, though the latter is certainly taken for granted. Modern Jewish thinkers have fastened on this focus as the most congenial way for them to speak of God as creator. They do not want to have to defend the accuracy of the Genesis account of creation against the scientific explanation of the available data. Moreover, how the creating actually went on "in the beginning" seems more usefully treated by scientific explanation than by the religious imagination.

This reticence has carried over despite the present flurry of interest in the way God might again be "scientifically" relevant as the agent behind the Big Bang Theory and the (potential) Grand Unified Theory of the four fundamental natural forces. There are many reasons why Jewish thinkers have not rushed to fill this beckoning theological gap. One cannot have any confidence that the current theories will last long; already theorists working with the notion of "fluctuations" have argued that even in a "perfect" vacuum matter would come to be, hence there would be creation without a divine act. Moreover, all scientific cosmogonies rest on such a tissue of daring hypothesis and creative mathematics that a serious challenge to any one of them would negate the model. Better to profess a certain agnosticism about the past than stake a significant aspect of one's faith on issues like the neutrino's mass, the unobservable "cold dark matter" largely filling the cosmos, the appearance of voids and clumps in the post-bang smooth expansion of the cosmos, or whether "tunneling" satisfactorily explains certain bizarre behaviors of subatomic particles. Besides, establishing such a God only leaves us with all the religious problems of 17th-century Deism, namely, of an Initiator who is irrelevant to the system's subsequent mathematical functioning. Since I believe that the normative function of the doctrine of creation—establishing God's right to command—can be established more convincingly by the experience of transcendence, I join in the pious contemporary agnosticism about what it means to say that God created.

Cohen and Rosenzweig: Two Philosophical Approaches

The paradigmatic modern strategy for speaking of God as creator derives from the thought of Hermann Cohen. As an antimetaphysical neo-Kantian, he transforms creation from an actual event to a logical observation: that our idea of God generates all the other concepts in our worldview. Since the task of being rational—and therefore of creating a cogent worldview—cannot be a temporary one (lest we lose our humanhood by not thinking) but must go on each day, Cohen considers creation a continual event. And it was he who, in this intellectual context, called attention to the prayerbook's reference to God "renewing the creation-work continuously each day." Though few Jews today know Cohen's logicization of creation, this text remains our favorite for such discussions for, whatever scientific theory of creation becomes current, it will attest to the order and underlying unity of the cosmos.

Ironically, while most Jewish thinkers today identify more with Franz Rosenzweig than Hermann Cohen, the younger man's extensive treatment of creation has had less resonance, almost certainly because his concern is the doctrine's intellectual role in the complex system of *The Star of Redemption*.

The three irreducible realities—God, the World, and Man—when first identified as "elements" do not yet "exist" but can only be discussed as, respectively, meta-physics, meta-logic, and meta-ethics. The world as we know it emerges only as the relationships between them are brought into the system, creation being the manner in which God relates to the world. It moves the elements from the shadowy, indistinct realm of the proto-cosmos into existence where they become transformed through "action" and transparent to human understanding (within limits). This enables Rosenzweig, for example, to resolve the debate about whether God created out of caprice or necessity by mediating between the ideas. God creates because creating is central to God's essence, hence necessary—but since God's essence finally is utter freedom, what might be "caprice" in others becomes in God a testimony to God's very nature.

Having been created out of nothing by God, the world and all its creatures remain, in some significant sense, "naughts"; incomplete and on the way, they are pointed toward the completion called redemption (the relationship between Man and the World), which is activated by revelation (the relationship between God and Man). Rosenzweig indicts Islam and philosophy as misled in their approach to the world because they only partially understand the holism of the three relationships integrating the elements. He climaxes his disquisition with a treatment of some key terms in the Torah's story of creation.

I do not know how Rosenzweig knows what he so confidently asserts, nor why he proclaims it has these rather than other outcomes. What I can understand of his concept of God's creating is so foreign to my experience of and reflection on this topic that I do not find him instructive, even by creative opposition. Norbert Samuelson, however, has undertaken a major Rosenzweigan effort to rehabilitate what he calls the Jewish "dogma" that God created the universe. His effort, thus far, continues the modern practice of not directly treating God's creating. Instead, Samuelson adds to the millennial chain of Jewish interpretations of the creation story, in his case by analyzing its philosophical assumptions somewhat in the fashion of Franz Rosenzweig. Samuelson's undertaking acquires particular interest because of its comparative method, his juxtaposition of Greek and quantum models of creation with what he sees as the main lines of Jewish theorizing. Nonetheless, he remains largely agnostic concerning what God did/does, concentrating his attention on the rational preconditions for thinking about these matters.

Two Experiential Approaches to Creation

To carry the irony one step further, Abraham Heschel, normally associated with Jewish mysticism because of his Hasidic background, seems far less "mystical" and more existential in his treatment of creation than Rosenzweig. Heschel does not directly treat *maaseh vereshit*, the creation-work, but, seeking a common ground with his reader, attacks the flatness of the secularist view of nature and seeks to return us to "radical amazement." Brainwashed by secularization, we take all existence for granted, transmuting our yearnings about "Whence?" into the mechanical "How?" This deprives us of the wonder and awe that would direct us beyond the creation to its creator. Particularly by his affecting prose, Heschel tries to recapture those moments when the sublime has broken through our agnostic armor and a sense of the glory in the universe has brought us into the presence of God.

In fact, all this evocation tells us nothing about why or how God created or how one is to reconcile these intuitions with scientific data—but Heschel believes this is all we can usefully know. Such experience, however, only prepares us to move beyond the spirituality common to all humankind to the reality of God's revelation, namely, the Hebrew Bible. It tells us what God deems important for our spiritual welfare, and thus all we can properly know about creation. Yet, to conclude this trail of theological ironies, it is only Rosenzweig, not Heschel, who seeks to provide a theological commentary to Genesis 1.

Like Heschel, I feel I must leave it to others to speculate about creation, not because I share his certainties about the reliability and sufficiency of the Torah account but because my spiritual certainties arise from my own experience—and who among us has had personal experience of God's creating heaven and earth? Yet I can emulate Heschel by trying to raise our consciousness of our createdness and thus bring us to an appreciation of our creator. In a word, I am concerned with gratitude. Our regnant secularity deifies the self, teaching it to face the world in terms of what it "has coming to it." So we take nature and existence for granted, never asking Who does the granting. Yet we have no claim on life, reality, or continuity, not even for an instant—but there they are. We cannot give any part of this bounty to ourselves when it is taken from us and yet, most "amazingly," an abundance of goodness is ordinarily handed us.

Mostly, we appreciate life's givenness only at emotional peaks: a birth, love, delivery from danger, a death—but Judaism hopes to habituate us to a consciousness of what we receive each moment. It teaches us thanks for the ordinary, like the bread God "brings forth," or the kidneys and colon that void our bodies of their wastes. In some sense, nothing just is, everything is created and a gift, even the power we have to work and achieve. The piety of everyday gratitude does not tell us much directly about the process of creation but, by sensitizing us to a universe not simply there, it opens us to the One who "renews each day the work of creating."

Cohen and Kaplan: God's Revelation as Human Insight

(2) God reveals (Torah). Non-Orthodox Judaisms distinguish themselves most characteristically from Orthodoxy by their revisionist theories of revelation. The divergence arose as a consequence of a dispute over the proper effect of modernity on the life of Torah: Could substantial changes in Jewish practice be authentic when they violated explicit or inferred provisions of the Oral Law? Non-Orthodoxies validated themselves by the religious intuition that change was inherent to the tradition as well as by their subsequent critique of the traditional doctrine of revelation and its reinterpretation as human discovery.

Hermann Cohen, as always, provided the most fully rationalistic interpretation of God's revelation. In his writings, what prephilosophic minds envisaged mythologically as events of God's disclosure became moments of human understanding, the times when someone's mind broke through conceptually to a more fully comprehensive truth. He envisioned his philosophical equivalent of the *ruah ha-kodesh*, the Holy Spirit, operating in every ethical decision as people rationally directed their freedom to greater concern for ends than for means. This philosophical idealism eventually filtered its way into the liberal Jewish consciousness as the notion that we hear God's voice in our conscience and reason.

Cohen's theory of God's revelation yields a "Torah" that is philosophical, hence utterly universal. This notion enshrined the modern Jewish insight that Judaism itself directed Jews to leave the ghetto and participate as equals in Western civilization. It also created the besetting problem of modern Judaisms: If we can observe the Torah by being ethically rational people, why should we be concerned about Jewish particularity? We shall see Cohen's response to this question when we consider his notion of God's choosing.

Mordecai Kaplan, eager to avoid anthropomorphism and other supernaturalisms, eschewed the term "revelation" and simply spoke of human spiritual growth. God, understood as the natural forces conducive to human fulfillment, enters our lives disclosively in those moments when we emerge from a developmental state or surmount a racking crisis and attain greater maturity. Analogously, we can speak of this happening to social groups as peoples have acquired spiritual insight and transmitted it to succeeding generations.

In both rationalistic theories, God is identified with the human process by which the new religious understanding is attained. In Cohen's case, God is the integrating intellectual link between the individual mind and the creative rational idea that now adds to the wholeness of the person's scientific-ethical-aesthetic worldview. In Kaplan's case, we identify as God that property of natural forces that enables us to flourish as human beings and develop to ever more mature persons. Both views are humanisms to the extent that God has no reality other than that which we discover in our experience, but both are highly spiritual in identifying these moments as the apex of our existence.

Presaging the later postmodern dissatisfaction with Cohen's rigid rationalism, his disciple Leo Baeck broke with the master's system and added religious consciousness to reason as a formative element in his theology. Calling attention to our experience of a mysterious depth to existence, one he intimately associated with God, Baeck argued that we learn as much about our duties from it as from our minds. But Baeck did not follow up on this expansion of the experiential base of our belief to revise Cohen's rationalistic conception of revelation. It remained for Rosenzweig and Buber to do this and in a most radical way.

What Does an Independent God Reveal?

In the existentialistic theologies of Rosenzweig and Buber, God has independent reality and can therefore provide something to human beings that they cannot acquire on their own. Yet both thinkers so respect science that they seek to explain the divine input as not blatantly clashing with its findings. They do this by reinterpreting God's revelation by analogy with interpersonal communication.

The shortness of Rosenzweig's life prevented his taking this analogy much beyond a description of revelation as love, a relationship that commands imperatively if essentially nonverbally. Buber explained this same experience of obligation and aspiration as resulting from the I–thou relationship. Two aspects of this situation impinge critically on Buber's doctrine of revelation: command without regulation and God's gift of presence.

The former notion arises from a curious fact about interpersonal intimacy: The meaning born between the partners transcends any-thing they did or said together. In reflection, it must be called ineffable. Yet it was real and, in its own way, commanding; the relationship will not be the same if we do not act on it. What exactly we must now do depends on us, and in filling in the details of our duty we testify to the nature of our relationship. That being so, what was given us in the revelation-meeting can strictly only be called "presence." The other gave us not rules but self and with it the empowerment of the I–thou relationship. So, too, God "speaks" and "commands" by being there with us; and we, heavy with the meaning we have come to know, then create the acts or write the accounts that will carry this truth into our lives. Religious practices and texts arise entirely from the human side of the relationship but do so in living response to encounters with the real God. They remain sacred as long as they authentically reflect or renew our relationship with God.

It remains to be added that an act is involved here. God must give presence or, if you prefer, become present. Without the Other, there is no genuine encounter, and nothing we might do can force it into being: If we cannot produce it on demand even with people, how much the less might we do so with God? When it happens that we occasionally find God before us—mostly as indirect participant in other I–thou meetings but also in direct, "person-to-person" encounter—that is a gift. God, not normally present to us in this way, has appeared and, in so doing, has given us revelation.

More than any other theory I know, this dialogical interpretation of revelation corresponds to my own ongoing relationship with God, my Jewish observance, and my involvement in contemporary culture. My difficulties with the theory arise less from its understanding of God's revelation than from how the two thinkers applied it to create divergent theories of Jewish obligation. Where Rosenzweig so commits us to traditional Jewish law that he slights what God may now be saying to the self, Buber so safeguards our individual intimacy with God that he undermines the corporate nature of the Covenant. I shall try to show in the final section of this work how a personalistic theory of God's revelation can be reconceived to produce a theory of Jewish duty that is both more personal than that of Rosenzweig and more ethnic than that of Buber.

Abraham Heschel's doctrine of God's utter primacy places God's revealing, like God's creation, beyond human experience. Anything we can say about the *process* by which it occurred is but *midrash*; however, the *content* of what was revealed to the prophets is accurate and binding. Their gift lay in being able to have sym-pathos, to feel what God was feeling and to render it in their own words with utter reliability. Their personalities and other particularities come through in their records but their genius is not creativity or imagination but simple faithfulness. God's own truth stands behind the substance of the Written and Oral Torah.

Less traditionally inclined thinkers have argued that Heschel's theory might be reworked to provide a more flexible—that is, Conservative Jewish—attitude toward Jewish law. I do not see how this can be done without doing violence to Heschel's determined theocentricity. As long as revelation is conceived in his terms—giving God hierarchical precedence over any human initiative and hence rejecting effective human partnership in revelation—ethical initiatives and historical developments will have to function within the parameters set by God's revelation. If Heschel's understanding of the essential authority of the Torah tradition cannot be affirmed, then one must find another interpretation of what it means to say that God reveals.

Overcoming the Scandal of a God Who Chooses

(3) **God chooses (the people of Israel).** Two affronts coalesce to make this theme a particular scandal for modern Jews. The first comes from the implication that in a given historical period God, in choosing, suddenly did something new. Choice also implies that God is personal, which is itself a troublesome notion to many people and anathema to others who consider it mythological and anthropomorphic. Second, choosing describes the good God as discriminating, preferring one group to others to receive the utterly precious Written and Oral Torah. While that may give them more responsibilities than other peoples it also gives them unique status with God and in history. Defend it as one will, conferred preferential status violates our ethical and democratic sensibilities.

Mordecai Kaplan considered the concept of God's choosing the Jews to be utterly unacceptable in a modern Judaism and insisted that we forthrightly renounce it. He was not only opposing its supernaturalistic and undemocratic implications but felt that it provided a Jewish pretext for justifying antisemitism by allowing other people to claim that they, not the Jews, were chosen. Recognizing how valuable a folk goal is for ethnic morale, Kaplan urged the

Jewish people to choose a universal, ethical mission for itself: exemplifying ethical nationalism. While the tactic of turning the chosen people into the choosing people had roots that can be traced to its 19th-century spokesman, the British writer Israel Zangwill, Kaplan has been its most recent vigorous partisan.

A generation earlier Hermann Cohen had carried out a less radical, more philosophic revision of chosenness. Cohen's God-idea could not in any sense "choose" a people, but it did command living up to one's rationality. The Jewish people, by its long-term affirmation of ethical monotheism, had given humankind its finest example of what human beings needed to be. Its history gave it a "mission": to teach all peoples its universal faith.

But one did not have to be a Jew to know or live by religion of reason. Hence Cohen, a staunchly loyal Jew, propounded a philosophic reason for continued Jewish distinctiveness. His system rested on the mind's miraculous capacity to move from nothing to an idea that constructed a rational worldview. He asserted that the originators of such fecund concepts always retained some special insight into their meaning even though, once they have enunciated them, any rational person could acquire them. He now applied this to the Jewish people, claiming it possessed unparalleled insight into ethical monotheism and was irreplaceable as its authentic teacher.

Leo Baeck, his revisionist disciple, gave this argument a historical twist. He asserted that the Jewish people had become so identified with ethical monotheism because of its history that if there were no Jewish people the proper understanding of the concept would itself die. Pressing "the mission of Israel" to its logical conclusion, he urged Jews to proselytize for what they uniquely knew to be the universal religion of all humankind.

The far-fetched nature of Cohen's and Baeck's efforts to provide a rationalistic mandate for Jewish continuity highlights the irreconcilability of a stringent universalism and a distinctive, commanding particularity. (I shall discuss Kaplan's reconciliation of rationality and ethnicity in chapter 18.) Coherence requires surrendering either one's reliance on philosophy or one's conviction that there is a certain absoluteness about Jewish particularity. Being more certain of my Jewish faith than of the religious competence of any rationalism, I work at Jewish theology as a nonrationalist, partly because doing so enables me to accommodate a doctrine of commanded particularity, of God's "choosing" the Jews.

Buber and Heschel's Understanding of God the Chooser

Martin Buber believes that God cannot be met in the I–it realm of science but only in the I–thou realm, as persons are met; so he refuses to be scandalized at the possibility of God's sporadic availability. Every I–thou relationship involves a certain measure of discrimination, an outreach of the self to just this specific other, love being the classic, common example. However, this does not yet establish Israel's uncommon particularity, for God loves/chooses everyone and all human beings have their moments of I–thou encounter. Buber thus yokes his particularism to a sturdy universalism and his many empathetic studies of religions other than Judaism attest to his belief in God's genuine relationship with many persons and groups.

For Buber, then, as for the rationalists, Israel's uniqueness arises largely from the human side. Like many other nations, our people encountered God in the course of its history but then, as the Bible stories make plain, a development resulted that has no parallels in the history of religions. As mysteriously as love arising, the Israelite nation in critical mass finally became captivated by their experiences of God. As a result, it pledged itself corporately to the service of God and set about developing a national character faithful to this relationship. Israel chose God, but had there been no responsive giving of presence by God, no real relationship would have resulted. Over the ensuing millennia—in rite, folk life, and historic event— our people has experienced God's continuing gift of presence and thus known that God chose/chooses it. Today too we know from our experience that our Covenant with God remains alive, true, and irreplaceable. I find this understanding, as I shall be explaining in chapter 15, the most helpful way of explaining how the one God of the universe can yet be said to have a particularly precious association with the Jewish people.

Abraham Heschel has given us an even stronger view of God's choosing Israel, as befits his view of God's primacy and the Bible's accuracy. He gives no specific explanation of what it means for God to choose, for his is the God who comes seeking man, as the Bible indicates, not a God whose motives or functioning we could ever hope to understand. Heschel's traditional view of God's choosing again confronts us with the need to determine what balance exists in our faith between God's and humankind's roles, for this issue largely determines what our view of God's choosing will be.

The Great Jewish Silence about Retribution

(4) God rewards and punishes. No Jewish doctrine has more steadily been contradicted by experience than the biblical teaching of God's faithful retributive justice—perhaps the reason for inclusion in the Bible of such "unorthodox" books as Job and Ecclesiastes. The rabbis most vigorously defended God's justice despite everything, and made the resurrection of the dead the Jewish equivalent of a dogma, allowing the failures of God's justice in this world to be remedied in the next. Medieval Jewish philosophers like Maimonides limited divine retribution to groups while Jewish mystics abandoned rational theodicies for *kabbalah* and its access to a realm far transcending ordinary human comprehension.

Despite the many inner theological tensions over this teaching, the expectation of this-and-other-worldly reward and punishment remained central to Jewish spirituality until the 19th century. Thereafter, secularization led to its abandonment by all but the most pious Jews. Even before the Holocaust, no systematic 20th-century Jewish thinker sought to defend rather than interpret away God's effective justice. Since the Holocaust, the traditional theory of this-worldly retribution has survived in theological discussion only as the object of criticism. When, on occasion, a traditionally oriented contemporary rabbi has ascribed the Holocaust or a public disaster to nonobservance, most of world Jewry, including much of Orthodoxy, has deemed it a scandal.

Modern Jewish rationalists abandoned the notion of God's rewarding and punishing as intellectually incoherent. Hermann Cohen thought it mythological to speak of God's acting in nature in response to human acts. Mordecai Kaplan likewise decried retributive justice as supernaturalism and limited God to only those natural forces that support our striving for self-fulfillment. For both thinkers, all of God's effective justice occurs through human agency and they see God precisely in our ethical, creative activity. This view dignifies humankind but also reflects an optimism about us that has made it increasingly less persuasive as our century has proceeded.

Martin Buber, too, cannot say very much about God's execution of justice since it seems odd to speak of reward and punishment in connection with I–thou intimacy. Nonetheless, our acts do have I–thou consequences, our faithfulness intensifying the relationship and our infidelities harming it, our greatest good.

Abraham Heschel's silence on this issue creates a critical problem for him: The prophets describe God as so angry at our wickedness that God threatens to break forth in fury against the people of Israel. Anxious that we not take God's responsive outrage as compromising God's moral stature, Heschel insists that God's passions always remain under ethical control. I do not see this principle manifest in the prophetic writings, nor do I see how this can be applied to God's restraint during the Holocaust. I can only surmise that Heschel's great sensitivity to the distance between us and God, and his compassion for what his family and others suffered during the Holocaust, imposed this pious silence on him.

A Personal Effort to Break the Silence

None of these views speaks to my religious experience and I therefore believe it necessary, despite the extraordinary difficulties involved, to try to say something more positive about God's rewarding and punishing. I begin with two modest, essentially intellectual, observations. First, with God's justice premised on human freedom (and, hence, responsibility), God's justice cannot be perfect but must be rough. In a world with exceptionless retribution, one with every good act rewarded and every evil act punished, freedom would quickly give way to conditioning. That would produce the behavior God seeks but only at the price of dissolving the free exercise of the will into behavioristic automatism. If God wishes people to be meaningfully free and achieve righteousness by the proper use of their unique freedom, God's reward and punishment cannot be mechanical.

Second, behind the rationalist's denial of retribution I sense an acceptance of a view of natural causality as a seamless web. Recent developments, scientific and philosophical, have made this assumption questionable. The triumph of quantum mechanics has introduced an odd mix of freedom and determinism into the prediction of specific events, and the developing mathematics of chaos enables us to visualize a curious mixture of freedom within bounds. The analogy with the old religious sense of a provident God and a free humankind readily suggests itself to the believing Jewish mind. We cannot so readily bar God's acting in nature as did those generations who had ultimate confidence in scientific explanation.

Of course, the best reason for reticence about God's justice stems from the injustice we have seen befall others; integrity demands that we link realism and belief. After the sensible theodicies have helped us refine our faith and we have given as much credence as we can to the distance between God and us, there is still too much about retribution that we do not understand and ought not accept. And all that needs to be said before we speak of the Holocaust. . . .

Were most of us blessed with encompassing trust in God, we might embrace God's activity in our midst though its operation escaped and even pained us. Mystics often teach that, from God's perspective, all our difficulties with retribution have no meaning and uniting one's soul with God can enable us to transcend our former perplexities. I am part of that great bulk of humanity that has not been graced with so overflowing a faith or so soaring a spirit. I must therefore make room in my belief for the limited agnosticism my realism demands. And were I blessed with great certainty about our personal survival in an afterlife, I could at least mitigate the incomprehensibility of our suffering in this world. Much of our modern anguish over the problem of theodicy comes from our lost faith in the world to come; injustice in this world, conceived as the only world we shall know, is terribly bitter. My trust in God for life after death relieves me of the punishing burden of requiring everything to be settled here. But it is not so secure that it eases my hurt at what the good God allows among us.

Though I cannot affirm direct and immediate retribution, that does not require me to deny the presence of *any* justice in human affairs. Seeking its presence, we are tempted to itemize all the occasions on which we were not rewarded. "I didn't deserve that" mostly means we found God or the world unresponsive. It does not often mean all the good that comes to us on which we have no claim, life being the obvious case. If we wish to be fair when we speak about God's justice and ourselves, then we must begin with all that God has given us that we had no right to or had not earned. In my experience, what God gives most people hour by hour most generously exceeds what, as a simple matter of justice, they deserve. When one lives in gratitude, the absence of justice stands out primarily in the astonishing benevolence showered on most people.

Still, I am taking considerable license in calling "justice" a process in which equivalent cases receive an unequal response. And God should not be bound by the limits that allow us to accept the imperfections of human justice systems. I do not deny that, as best I understand it, God often does excruciatingly less than my experience of God leads me to believe God should do—but my anguish over this does not become so determinative that I can say God does *nothing* to check human iniquity and foster human goodness. Rather, I often dimly but really discern God's shaping power making itself felt, now strongly, now weakly, and then inexplicably not at all, in the ordinary flow of reality. Perfections aside, love engenders love and violence arouses hatred, wisdom enriches life and ignorance diminishes it. Even amid the brutal power realities we call history, the trampled human spirit has survived and even triumphed; should a generation that has seen Nazism defeated and the Communist empire collapse from within deny that God has given goodness its own power?

Having forced myself at least to break the silence with these words, I find my mind and imagination inadequate to saying the more that my heart tells me is true.

Humanizing the Ultimate Jewish Hope

(5) **God redeems (Israel).** The *keriat shema* refers only to the past, to God's having saved the Hebrews from Egyptian slavery and pursuit. However, the liturgical context makes the intent of the recitation quite clear: God who has kept Covenant in the past may be relied upon to do so in the present and, most gloriously, in a culminating eschatological redemption—beliefs made explicit in the *shemoneh esreh* prayers, which follow the morning *keriat shema*.

The modern reinterpreters of God's redemption have had little difficulty transforming God's acting into human doing though this has involved them in pulling its eschatological, messianic aspects back into history. Mordecai Kaplan, for example, polemicized against the classic Jewish doctrine of other-worldly salvation—the Days of the Messiah, the resurrection of the dead, Judgment Day, the life of the World to Come—as egregious supernaturalism. Like other Jewish rationalists, he called for humankind to use its moral and political power to create a fully humane and thus messianic social order.

A generation before, Hermann Cohen had given a similar notion a more sophisticated treatment. Cohen pointed to a paradox connected with our pursuit of the rational-ethical ideal. It must never be completed in actuality lest by losing our distinctive activity we lose what makes us human. Yet knowing that the task could never be accomplished would induce a fatalism that would also end our ethical striving. So our self-redeeming ethical-rational activity must be pictured like the mathematician's asymptote, a curve that ever approaches the axis but never gets there. The idea of God, by guaranteeing the ever-nearer/always-distant quality of the ethical ideal, rationally redeems human existence.

One can easily see how this humanized, ethicized doctrine of redemption came to be identified with radical or liberal politics—in Cohen's case, with democratic socialism. More fully secularized Jews could not realistically see what religion contributed to this process of humanizing society and simply devoted themselves to political action, Zionism being its application to our own people. Though both theories have been challenged as overly optimistic, their this-worldly vision of redemption dominates even nonrational contemporary discussions of the topic. Thus Heschel, in his few comments on redemption, does not interpret the doctrine in terms of revelation but only as a human ethical task. Rosenzweig's *The Star of Redemption* similarly scants God's activity in redemption, which he speaks of as what Man does in relation to the World. He does not entirely ignore the third element; in a climactic, typically oracular and obscure paragraph, he says that God culminates the process, thus allowing all the elements to become One. In a similar vein, I cannot provide any content to Arthur Cohen's assertion that God redeems by doing on the ontological level what humans have done on the ethical/spiritual level.

Our Experience of the God Who Saves Us

Martin Buber points to an experience that lies directly behind our trust that God redeems. Indirectly, we gain this trust from God's partnership in our creation of the personal and social patterns that foster and nourish I–thou relationships, what Buber calls "community" and considers our messianic task. But he also reminds us of a not uncommon experience that attests to God's independent role in redemption. When deeply distraught, we can feel utterly lost, beyond anyone's help, especially beyond anything we could still do for ourselves. And yet, it sometimes happens that we emerge from the depths—perhaps more accurately, that something pulled us up from there. It was not any initiative of ours or basic reflex; we were beyond that. As it were, a hand reached out to us and helped us with a power not our own. This unpredictable, inexplicable help that we encounter, says Buber, has taught us that God redeems. And our folk experience of the Exodus and its echoes in Jewish history testify that God liberates peoples as well as persons.

In a sense, this understanding rests on the experience that every I–thou encounter redeems, not merely from the objectification of the I–it but for the humanization of genuine relationship. And because the other must give rather than withhold presence, we sense God continually redeeming us in commonplace "salvations" as well as in the memorable, historic ones. Redemption should be that constant a theme in Jewish spirituality. But Buber would not say anything about eschatology, for that requires speaking about an existence utterly beyond our experience. He simply trusted in the One he loved.

For myself, that God redeems presently and ultimately has a theoretical and an experiential foundation. Knowing God to be good— if sometimes more inexplicably inert than active—and powerful, I trust that God's goodness will one day be fully manifest in creation. I normally distrust beliefs derived logically from other beliefs unless they also have a basis in our living faith. I have been spared any deep experience of the dark despair of which Buber speaks and thus cannot truly attest to the experience of saving power he wrote about. But I have known its analog in the Hand I have regularly discerned touching me and shaping my life in ways I cannot call my own, conscious or unconscious. And I have experienced some great historic moments—the civil rights struggle of the early 1960s, the salvation of the Six Day War, the liberation of Communist Europe in 1990— that I knew to be shaped as much by God as by human agency. God redeems.

I therefore trust that, despite the tarrying, one day—perhaps today—human and divine endeavor will reach its climax and will redeem in the climactic way our tradition calls the coming of the Messiah. I would dearly like to know more about how God will do this and what the culminating divine act will be like, but I remain unenlightened. And I also cannot extrapolate from what little I know about God acting in history to how God will take us beyond it or to what. Yet this ignorance does not keep me from believing it so firmly that I base my life on it.

A Postliberal Theology of Jewish Duty

II

Israel, the People That Creates the Way

אַתָּה אֶחָד וְשִׁמְךָ אֶחָד,
וּמִי כְּעַמְּךָ יִשְׂרָאֵל גּוֹי אֶחָד בָּאָרֶץ.

You are one and Your name is one
And who is like Your people Israel,
A nation unique on earth?

11   What Can We Do about Our Will-to-Do-Evil?

HE ENLIGHTENMENT, powerfully reinforced by social and political forces, gave individuals a radically enhanced stature in human affairs, thereby beginning an increasing moralization of society. Dialectically, as individualism has reached extraordinary empowerment in the United States, we have come to something of a crisis in the troubled modern effort to justify social authority from a person-based axiology. This tension between individual and group intensifies from both sides in contemporary Jewish existence. With social opportunity and security for Jews based on the principle that all persons deserve equality in and of themselves and not because they belong to a class or group, individualism has daily reinforcement. At the same time, there can be no recognizable Jewishness without a significant folk life, a value continually imperiled by the special pressures of being a minority locally or in the world. Thus, while being an Israeli ameliorates this problem substantially, it does not end it. The culture of Israel, both high and pop, is more international and personalistic in character than ethnically distinctive, a characteristic unlikely to change, the speed of communication ever rising.

Any hope of creating a theology of the Jewish people must, then, first deal with the limits of individualism and, at least in my case, without substantially compromising what I acknowledge to be the religious truth of self-determination. I propose to study the social side of individuality by looking at three of its critical aspects. In this chapter I ask how self-reliant we can be, considering the self's propensity to do evil. In the next two chapters I shall first examine the philosophical struggle over the social side of selfhood, and then, whether humanity as a whole rather than any lesser group is our proper social matrix.

Trusting the Self to Be the Measure of All Things

For many generations, Jews taking their places in general society adopted its positive tone and faced history as optimists. They did not overlook the many evils of their societies and the special trials visited upon Jews, but they remained hopeful that things not only could but would get better and they devoted themselves to this end. Much of their ethical steadfastness came from their confidence that human reason, fully employed and properly directed, would enable people to overcome their will-to-do-evil. Modern rabbis regularly demonstrated the Jewish authenticity of this optimism by citing a *midrash* that daringly called the *yetzer hara*, the urge-to-do-evil, "good"; without it, they said, people would not build houses, get married, or have children. This was claimed to be the ancient version of the modern thesis that, with proper education and discipline, people could turn even their sinful urges to worthy purposes. This optimistic assessment of the self's capacities took three major forms in the Jewish community: philosophical, political, and, more recently, psychotherapeutic. Without denying their interrelationships, I propose to discuss them separately.

Since Hellenic times, philosophers have believed that evil originated in passion and ignorance and could therefore be remedied by wisdom. Enlightenment rationalists gave this insight revolutionary power as they showed in case after case that much of what custom or institutions demanded had no basis in fact or ethics. They proposed bringing the light of knowledge into people's lives, thereby removing the ignorance and superstition that had long prevented the creation of a moral civilization. This message had special appeal to European Jewry. In the West it justified extending rights to Jews, and in the East it unmasked the prejudice, venality, and irrationality of societies that refused to emancipate their Jews. Something similar applied inside the Jewish community. The refusal of the traditional rabbinate to accommodate ghettoized custom and law to Jewry's newly equalized status seemed similarly backward, as the Haskalah authors (the secular Hebraists) delighted in pointing out. Before long Jews began looking to the university, not to the *yeshivah*, to improve human existence.

Hermann Cohen gave this point of view status by his neo-Kantian philosophy of personal responsibility. He did not mean by ethics what many a late 20th-century chastened liberal takes it to be: a doctrine of limited melioration. Cohen believed that properly utilizing the powers of reason would enable us to control our will to do evil. To be sure, he meant this dynamically, as the ongoing, unending task of thinking/doing good in each new situation. Our messianism lay in just this humanizing work, not in some mythological future. However, it is not the time frame of Cohen's messianism that is critical to this discussion but the fact that (the idea of) God plays no active role in it (except to generate the system). Whatever will happen depends entirely upon human agency, putting humanity into a salvific role that reason enables all of us to fulfill. So the traditional hope for God's agent, the personal Messiah, now gives way to individuals joining humanity in the common project of bringing the Messianic Age.

Much of the popular appeal of this teaching came from the contrast that Cohen and later rationalists drew between it and the Christian doctrine of original sin. In Cohen's Judaism, people require no miraculous saving act of God (as through the Christ) to redeem them from a congenitally perverse nature. Rather, they need to become more truly themselves, rationally pursuing the true, the good, and the beautiful and thereby attaining all the "salvation" befitting a creature born pure rather than stained by sin. Moreover, Cohen argued, the Christian dependence on divine redemption encouraged believers to put faith where action ought to be and thus made them ethically passive.

I see in this optimistic view of human nature a variation of the theoretical Kantian dictum, "Because you must, you can," which resolved a major conundrum in Kant's system. In the logic of science—that is, of the world in which we live and act—things operate deterministically, by cause and effect. In the logic of ethics, however, only when we act out of the freedom to respond positively or negatively to a given situation can our decision possibly be ethical. How then can I ever act ethically since I must do so freely yet I exist in a world I understand to be deterministic? The Kantian answer comes from the depths of the philosopher's commitment: Because reason requires you to make a free moral determination, you must have the liberty to do so even though you cannot understand rationally how the logic of science can accommodate the logic of ethics and vice versa. To say anything else would be to charge existence with irrationality, the ultimate heresy for philosophic rationalists.

I wish to draw an analogy between this deduction and the Cohenian judgment about our capacity to control our impulse to evil. It is difficult to believe that anyone could ever be so rational as to harness all the energies that seem to direct us to do evil and direct them to ethical tasks. But the essential fulfillment of our humanhood involves doing just that, unequivocally doing the good right now.

Because we must be good as an absolute condition of being a person and not a beast, we can be as good as our reason categorically demands we be. Asserting anything less than "the perfectibility of man" would be irrational.

Approaching Hope Pragmatically and Politically

Mordecai Kaplan's theory of our human capacity to control our will to evil displays none of the rationalistic stringency of Cohen's philosophizing. Kaplan's philosophy even opens the tantalizing possibility that he might envisage limits to what human reason might do about evil since his doctrine of a limited God implies that even the greatest power in the universe cannot now overcome it. But he gives no direct evidence for such a view of limited human power, remaining passionately optimistic about the effects of education and culture. Setting us in our natural context, he ascribes our inclination to evil to our animal origins and envisions the evil in nature as arising in aspects of it that have not yet been given creative order. He exhorts us to use our reason as the best means for winning victories over temptation and confidently anticipates increased knowledge bringing both self and nature under our sway.

Kaplan offers little sustained argument to substantiate this rosy view of the human condition. True to his social concerns, he considers it a given of contemporary culture and thus a necessary premise for any truly modern thought. When in his later years he found the social ethos denying the adequacy of rationalism, he considered it regression and, utilizing Gilbert Murray's famous phrase disdaining the late Hellenic turn from philosophy to religion, termed it "a failure of nerve." Kaplan did, however, give a negative, pragmatic argument for his view. He felt that any less positive affirmation of the power of human reason would so dispirit us that it would paralyze our moral will. He could not believe that anyone seeing the many benefits that arose from people using their power to right wrongs would surrender the only view of human nature he thought would properly empower ethical devotion.

Kaplan's interest in practicality points to the interaction between the intellectual and political manifestations of Jewish optimism. Secularization naturally directed attention to changing social relations. The Marxist analysis of power also had its effect. Whereas traditional Judaism pietistically depended on God to right wrongs, and talk of modern Jewish ethics never got far beyond the university or coffee house, socialism would yoke idealism to practical politics. The shift from philosophy to politics did not change the basic premise of unlimited human capability. To begin with the clearest case, orthodox Marxists knew "scientifically" that evil arose from the inequitable economic structure of society and the class warfare it promoted. The source of the evil could be eliminated by revolution or the ballot, enabling the proletariat to establish a fully egalitarian state. The result would be a new human being as well as a just society. All this lay fully in human hands, though history itself also inexorably moved in this direction. The Marxist analysis of human ills often proved so insightful and its vision of humankind liberated from exploitation excited such hope that Marxism long reigned as the most practical modern messianism, evoking extraordinary sacrifice of person and conscience from many.

Most Jews found Marxist politics too rationalistic to be true and too contemptuous of individual conscience to be right. They preferred to work for universal rights and economic opportunity through more pragmatic political liberalism, ranging from democratic socialism on the left—which attracted a considerable minority of Jews—to the liberal wings of the established political parties—where the majority clustered. Eschewing grandiose claims to transform human nature and society utterly, more moderate activists nonetheless passionately believed their political programs would radically improve the common welfare. And when they momentarily had no solution to offer for a social ill, they had confidence in their method: study by experts, dialogue to reconcile differences, governmental action (including funding), mobilizing public support and, in more recent years, involving those affected in the planning process. The practical nature of these politics should not obscure the messianic emotions with which Jews invested them—feelings that often surface as wistfulness in those who yearn for the days when morally clear-cut issues and thrilling new programs made political activity personally redemptive.

Transposing the Optimism to Psychotherapy

As disillusionment with the messianic adequacy of philosophic rationalism, high culture, and democratic politics grew, the modernist strategy of transforming human nature by human reason shifted from the mind and forum to the psyche (as well as formulating itself in combinations of the three). Freud and his disciples had exposed how thoroughly our emotional inner life, conscious and unconscious, shaped our rationality and pervaded our institutions. The residue of our earliest emotive imaginings brought us self-inflicted suffering and moved us to do evil to others, often in the guise of being generously beneficent. Becoming enlightened emotionally to the realities of our affective life would liberate us from this inner slavery and make possible the effective self-determination of the fulfilled human personality. Moreover, when we stopped projecting our infantile emotionality on our personal relationships and our institutions, we and other mentally healthy people might finally create a benign social order.

The telltale signs of messianism abound among the early protagonists of psychoanalysis and its revisionist offspring, psychotherapy. Even the early papers of Freud manifest it for all their straining to be scientific and their careful qualification of the scope of the claims being made. They communicate the master's excitement with each extension of the theory from intrapsychic to social phenomena and with the ever-expanding applicability of his new hermeneutic. Nothing human seemed alien to psychoanalytic interpretation's revelations until Freud's late papers; by then his moral discipline had forced him to a chastened realism based on the limits of technique and the intractabilities of human nature. In the end, he counseled a stoic acceptance of our aggressive drive, which analysis could never enable us to sublimate fully to its twin impulse, love.

Again, the new difficulties resulted in a change of tactics, not of strategy. The trust in human adequacy merely begot a rush to quicker or simpler or emotionally innovative modes of treatment that promised to release a humanhood untouched by prior technique. From Jung and Adler to the latest self-help bestseller, these methods often prove helpful in certain sectors, then gradually betray their limits and, in turn, make room for new prophets of psychological breakthroughs. Enough experience has now accumulated that, even though successful treatment makes many patients better, one cannot say that the patients and their therapists do markedly little evil compared to the untreated.

We can best summarize this movement of human self-assertiveness by recalling its favorite biblical support, the original meaning of the root ḥ-t-'. Premoderns used this term to designate certain misbehaviors as sin, thereby identifying them as defiance of God's will and laden with divine disapproval. For much of our century, an inordinate sense of guilt often lay behind the ills people brought to their psychotherapists, and ridding people of their morbidity effected their cure. Modern Jewish teachers, inspired by their rationalistic view of reality, delighted in pointing out that h-t-' originally had no such portentous overtones but referred to the prosaic human experience of missing one's way or one's mark. In archery, the verb describes shooting an arrow that does not hit the target. That, said the liberals, properly describes errant conduct. It stems from improper use of our abilities, most probably brought on by faulty social, emotional, or intellectual training. Rather than speak of sin and encumber people with disabling guilt, we should understand misbehavior by its complex causation rather than reduce it to a matter of faulty will. We can remedy it by attention to its origins, by the personal therapy that will transform its emotional roots, and by the humanistic politics that will do the same for its social causes.

This therapeutic view of human behavior has so established itself among Jews that almost no English-speaking rabbi ever calls an admittedly grievous act a "sin" or "evil" except for rhetorical emphasis. Following the counseling mode, they do not wish to appear judgmental or moralistic. They and other Jews commonly respond to serious wrongdoing by seeking its psychic causes or pronouncing the person "sick." Consequently, Jews reared on these models of human improvability simply could not believe that a people as educated and cultured as the Germans could countenance and carry out the Holocaust. The depth of our secularization becomes powerfully evident when we consider how long and how passionately Jews clung to their faith in human perfectibility even after the Holocaust.

The Hopefulness of Jewish Existentialism

Though in many other respects Martin Buber's thought moved beyond modernity's exaggerated emphasis on the individual, his view of evil, while changing the metaphor for its etiology, hardly moves much beyond classic liberalism. Since Buber identifies the good act as one faithful to an I–thou relationship, he ascribes our evildoing to our refusal to engage in encounter or act on its implications. He sees two stages to our misconduct. The first takes place when the whirl of possibility paralyzes us. Intrigued or overcome by all that we might do, we cannot decide to do any one thing. We wait choicelessly and let happen what happens. In this common evildoing of will-less-ness we do the acts that come from never being able to address just this person or situation as a whole self.

In the second stage of evil, what began as a chance disposition of the self becomes its chosen way. The kind of action whose original arbitrariness allowed it to be as easily discarded as done now becomes a full-scale commitment of the "self." It cannot be the true self's decision because Buber believes that self comes into being only in I–thou relationships. Our intensified evildoing can now be identified as utter "self"-concern, living in the service of the pseudo-I of I–it, perhaps even I–I. Buber pointed to this as the source of Hitler's demonic power and terrifying presence; he was, literally, "self"-confident and "self"-determined. Buber boldly took this analysis one step further, saying should this long persist it can harden into a stance that robs the person of the power to "turn from the evil way and live." He does not specify how this could occur but he acknowledges its human reality, citing Pharaoh as the classic instance. In such exceptional cases, evildoing results in the inability to do *teshuvah*, to turn away from one's sinning, a rare note of retribution in a modern thinker.

Buber's admission that human evildoing can become irremediable is telling testimony concerning his hard-won realism, for like the modern Jewish rationalists, he usually glories in the humanity of the rabbinic doctrine of *teshuvah*. As elaborated in the Talmud and ingrained among Jews through the solemn practices of Yom Kippur (though *teshuvah* should be a daily undertaking), it proclaims a certain optimism about human nature. The rabbis teach that, with some modest exceptions, people never lose the capacity to freely stop transgressing, repent of their acts, and turn back to doing God's will. God so "desires" *teshuvah*, the rabbis say, that wholehearted repentance immediately draws forth God's forgiveness. This results in no "cheap grace" for though it restores the relationship, it does not wipe out all the just punishment incurred by the sin. Rather, the rabbis taught that suffering and death as well as repentance and Yom Kippur complete the atonement with God.

Modern Jewish thinkers found this rabbinic teaching most appealing. The rationalists reinterpreted this "turning" as our acquiring greater insight into our motives and goals by means of education, reflection, or psychotherapy. This greater self-understanding would liberate us enough to want to make reparation for the damage we had done and would redirect our wills to be more ethical or loving in our relationships. For Buber, it meant that the estrangement our act had brought into a relationship could always be overcome by remorse, reparation, and seeking of forgiveness, thereby creating a new/old intimacy. Here Buber's characteristic emphasis on human power reasserts itself; though he admits of the occasional loss of the power to repent, he too displays great confidence in our capacity to control our evildoing.

Two things powerfully reinforced this exceptional devotion to the redemptive power of the human mind or self. One came from immediate experience, whether personal, like the Emancipation, or social, such as the end of slavery. In such cases enlightenment made it possible to overcome entrenched prejudice and highly vested interest in order to right ancient wrongs. This emphasis on human self-saving also distinguished Judaism positively from traditional Christianity. Against its celebration of God's miraculous assumption of human form so as to save humankind from original sin—in some churches, by means of priestly intermediaries and sacraments—Judaism proclaimed the essential purity of all human beings, Jew and gentile. This provided all human beings with an inner zone of ultimate neutrality to which they could always return from their evildoing and thence move to restore their relationship with God. Particularly in an era when becoming Christian seemed to many a prerequisite to full personal acceptance, these modern reworkings of *teshuvah* became a major means to Jewish self-respect and commitment. Eager to preserve the spiritual truth that had empowered their freedom, passionate to give Judaism proper preeminence, the liberals did not appreciate the ubiquity and intractability of the human will-to-do-evil. Many of them surely believed that anything less than an enthusiastic affirmation of human self-assertion would open the door to a return of social reaction and religious fundamentalism.

The Rabbis, Premoderns as Postmoderns

After what we have seen of the abuse of freedom and power, the liberal understanding of human evildoing seems naive as compared to the rabbis. They balanced their belief in people's ineradicable potential to turn from evil and do good with the tough-minded understanding that people are very much more the creatures of their will-to-do-evil, their *yetzer hara*, rather than their will-to-do-good, their *yetzer hatov*. They did not believe that human nature was congenitally flawed—though some rabbis, perhaps overwhelmed by what realism revealed, flirted with the notion—but neither did they assert, as Rousseau and later liberals often did, that people came into existence innately good only to be perverted by society. Without compromising their belief in our essential purity, they thought us so beset by our will-to-do-evil that the practice of *teshuvah* had to be the daily counterpart of our life of *mitzvah*. Various rabbis said the *yetzer hara* entered us at birth while the *yetzer hatov* only appeared at age thirteen; that the will-to-do-evil never ceased trying to overpower us; that it had endless wiles, including appealing to our righteousness; that sex was its most immediate channel; that despite our useful strategies for defeating it, none could insure us against its deceit; that all we could hope for was temporary victories over it; that the greatest persons had it in greatest measure; that its goal was our death; and that after tempting us mercilessly in this world it would then testify against us in the next. In sum, the rabbis find human perversity so prevalent that when they use the word *yetzer* without modifier, one may be certain that the evil and not the good urge is meant.

In rabbinic eyes, people are highly conflicted creatures who in principle can do what God expects but more often do just the opposite—and they did not consider themselves exceptions. Their view may perhaps best be contrasted with that of the modern Jewish thinkers in terms of their respective interpretations of a biblical verse they both thought significant, Gen. 4:7. God says to Cain, who is distraught that God has accepted Abel's sacrifice but rejected his, "If you do good, you will be accepted and if you do not do good. . . . Sin couches at the opening and desires you, but you *timshal* it." The root *m-sh-l* means to "to rule" or "master." So to speak, the two eras of interpretation differ over the extent of our rule. The liberals thought we could tame the beast by the full development of our human powers. The rabbis only claimed that we could fend off its attacks by our unremitting effort and discipline coupled with a reliance on Torah's power and God's loving help.

The Nearness of Dualism in Heschel's Neokabbalism

On the issue of human evil, Abraham Heschel's postmodern stance again comes through clearly. Alone among the great teachers of this century, he finds classic Judaism's realism to be more individually and historically perceptive than liberal theories of human competence. His fullest discussion of the topic occurs not as part of either of his two major philosophic statements but in an essay published in tribute to the renowned Protestant ethician and activist,

Reinhold Niebuhr. Its title, "Confusion of Good and Evil," indicates that his own realism went far beyond the rabbis. He praises Niebuhr for having seen that the major problem of human behavior lay not in the struggle between our will-to-do-good and will-to-do-evil—which the rabbis had so clearly enunciated—but in the startling realization that even our purest efforts to do the good are inevitably contaminated by some evil. This doctrine utterly contradicts the basic premise of the rationalistic views of humanhood. Neither Heschel nor Niebuhr denied that our evil also contains a certain measure of good, but sensitive to the ease with which the demonic irrupts, neither suggested, à la Jacob Frank, that we actively seek to sublimate this entrapped holiness.

As nowhere else in his writing, Heschel cites utterances of the Hasidic masters to illustrate his view that the human will is better conceived as having an interpenetrating duality of motives rather than as split between good and evil urges. Utilizing the common existentialist critique of the rationalistic view of human nature, he points to the willfulness of the self as defeating all our efforts to keep it under rational control. But he dissociates himself furthest from modern thought when he argues that we must look beyond the human will for the root of our waywardness. He traces our evildoing to its ontological source: a flaw in the very structure of the universe, reflected by our inability fully to separate good from evil. To provide a Jewish basis for this view, he quotes a substantial passage from the Zohar.

What Heschel does not then do strikes me as critical for understanding his meaning. For after providing us with this unusual text he forebears from elucidating its kabbalistic meaning, much less affirms it. By its lush symbolism the Zohar communicates a near dualistic theosophy. Covertly, but nonetheless identifiably, it teaches that the ten holy *sefirot* have an almost exact parallel in ten profane *sefirot*. God's very own structure has its near counterpart in the similar negative pattern of the *Sitra Aḥra*, "the other side," that is, in the cosmic power of evil. This doctrine contradicts the concept of God's unity and specifically defies the talmudic ruling that it is heresy to affirm Two Powers in heaven. Thus the mystic tolerance of paradox reached an extreme here.

I cannot tell whether Heschel's view that evil infects all goodness is based on this Zoharic doctrine of a divided ultimate reality—a notion that he kept esoteric. Systematically, however, Heschel's reticence seems substantive rather than strategic, a move that enables him to maintain his high regard for ethical acts despite a shadowed view of human nature and its ontological foundation. Affirming, as Adin Steinsaltz does, the reality of the Zoharic *Sitra Aḥra* does not preclude espousing a Heschelian ethical activism. It can be reached, however, only by accepting a radical distinction between God's mystically dualized nature and what the Torah tells us God has specified we must do. From the absolute divine perspective, *mitzvot* and ethics have no significance or meaning, but in the human situation nothing could be more important. Mystics of many religions have not found this inconsistency troubling and Jewish mystics remain highly observant. I do not know whether our contemporary non-Orthodox Jewish mystics will commend a similarly paradoxical dialectic of gnosis and duty. Thus far, the teachings of Arthur Green and Lawrence Kushner, for example, have centered on personally experiencing God, thereby creating a oneness with nature and humankind that mandates us "to mend the world" ethically. Their silence on the kabbalistic doctrine of evil's ontological status or their own views on the root of human evildoing may, like Heschel's, stem from their desire not to compromise God's empowerment of ethical responsibility.

Combining Mystical Realism and Ethical Activism

Isaac Luria's thought offers an instructive example of the difficulty of being enthusiastic about human efforts to do good while ascribing Godlike power to evil. Rather than try "to mend" this "world," Luria followed his cosmogony and sought "to mend the world" of the *sefirot* and thereby eventually change the mundane world. He therefore directed his putative messianic activism to meditative practices (that accompanied the prescribed deeds, particularly prayer) designed to strengthen the holy *sefirot*, rather than to remedying the social practices and structures he saw manifesting injustice. Heschel's higher reward for the immediate if limited redemptive utility of moral action demonstrates modernity's continuing influence on him. But he is far too realistic to return to the old liberalism, asserting instead an ontological base to our "confusion of good and evil." This mediating stance nonetheless leaves him with a perilously problematic paradox: If our every act of goodness necessarily also creates evil, how hopeful can we ever become about any ethical campaign?

Heschel offers two answers. He gives major attention to his

contention that the holy deed possesses self-purifying power. It has a kind of sacramental efficacy that transforms our flawed or evil motives to holy effect. Because we no longer depend on our moral intention but on its sanctifying effectiveness, we can come to our causes with full-hearted dedication. Heschel also reminds us that we can count on God's help. In a theological version of the Kantian principle of enablement, he argues that since God has commanded us to live, God also must have made it possible for our deeds to have a positive result. Thus God's accompanying power refines the tainted issue of our conflicted wills.

I find Heschel's resolution of the paradox of necessary failure despite categorical responsibility both incomprehensible and unrealistic. What does it mean to assert—repeatedly and without explanation—that an act itself can negate the evil we inevitably bring to it? Sacramentalism has had so little place in Judaism that the Temple rites commanded in the Torah can be rendered ineffectual by an errant priest. For someone who argued persuasively against "religious behaviorism" as an adequate theory of Jewish obligation, this affirmation of the virtue of the act-in-itself appears contradictory. Moreover, if good deeds do in fact transmute the evil with which we invest them, why do we so regularly see the finest causes—with religion the chief example—regularly sullied by the evil their leaders and followers do in their name? The appealing candor of Heschel's depiction of the human confusion of good and evil makes his theory of the redemptive power of good acts incomprehensible.

By contrast, one can easily understand his appeal to God's help to remedy our sinfulness since it is the source of our millennial Jewish hope for messianic redemption. But given this emphasis it also changes us from the decisive to the accessory actors in the life of Torah, a change particularly telling with regard to our doing *teshuvah*. Moreover, to have God decontaminating our acts requires continuous miracles of salvation on God's part. Pietists and mystics have no difficulty living in appreciation of God's immediate saving help for them minute by minute, but I find this theory asking too much of God and not enough of us.

The Rift Within, the Snake Without

I agree with Heschel that our experience of the human capacity for evil makes it impossible to return to our old self-reliant strategies of self-transformation. Sooner or later, our will-to-do-evil outwits us.

In this respect the rabbis have shown themselves to be far wiser about human nature than modern philosophers and psychologists. Moreover, the evil has been so pervasive and pernicious that I cannot any longer confidently assert that the origins of evil lie totally in the free operation of our conflicted will and not somehow also in the nature of creation itself. I cannot explain that assertion without lapsing into either mythology or rhetoric. It does, however, have the support of the classic teachers of our faith who, awestruck by the irrepressibility and gruesomeness of evil, continually demonstrated this same theological ambivalence about the source of our perverseness. In Genesis, the snake plays as critical a role in the story of the first sin as does Adam and Eve's weakness of will. The rabbis, too, though mainly speaking of the *yetzer hara* as intrapsychic, also often reify it as a power operative in the world.

I do not know whether my preference for the realism of the rabbis as against that of the mystics stems from a fortunate personal life or a lingering liberal optimism. But two experiences ground my understanding. The first arises from my sense that I have occasionally been able to do an unblemished good. In that respect alone the Bible and the rabbis reflect my experience more accurately than do the mystics. Second, I have an empowering sense of God's helping goodness. This empowerment is not as strong as Heschel's self-correcting tainted *mitzvah*, but it strengthens me in my efforts to do what is right and to overcome my will-to-do-evil. I am confirmed in this by the fact that, in the *teshuvah* I must regularly do, I find my part in the process an effective aspect of a transformation that ultimately depends on God's gracious responsiveness.

The issue in this analysis has not been whether human beings can do anything of spiritual significance or whether Jewish faith makes anything more important than doing the good. The point at stake, rather, has been whether Judaism ought to continue to be a religion in which we have such confidence in the human spirit that we continue to assert that human effort by itself can accomplish all our religious ideals. I am setting forth the postmodern, yet rabbinic, position that a determinedly self-reliant self can never become properly human. We need to have a certain realism about our limits if only so that we can appreciate how individuality implies community, not only with other people but with God. Acknowledging this would allow for a reverse *tzimtzum*, a sufficient contraction of our human self-importance that would leave room in our lives for our community and for God's presence.

This new humility does not require us to deny or scorn our personal spiritual power, and it does not establish the existence of God or the Covenant. But knowing how easily our will-to-do-evil corrupts our will-to-do-good not only checks our ethical pretentiousness but returns us to classic Judaism's concept of human initiative as covenantal. When we seek God as a partner in every significant act we invest our deciding and doing with direction, worth, hope, and, in failure, the possibility of repair.

12   The Social Side of Selfhood

 THEORY OF Jewish responsibility that accentuates self-determination must give special attention to the social nature of human selfhood and I propose doing so by tracing some important philosophical developments that have led to my own understanding. One can trace the Christian roots of the modern idea of autonomy back to Peter Abelard's emphasis on personal intent, to Thomas Aquinas's insistence on the substantial sovereignty of our reason, and Martin Luther's championing of individual faith over corporate tradition.

The passage from the God-centered Middle Ages to the human-centered modern period is customarily connected with René Descartes's decisive new methodological standard: We ought to doubt every idea until we can make its truth clear and distinct to our minds. As methodical doubt became a categorical imperative for the modern mind, sovereignty in the realm of value shifted from the community to the individual. This new starting point empowered single selves to sit confidently in judgment over all proposals and to demand of their protagonists convincing warrants of their authority.

Jean-Jacques Rousseau gave this priority of the self social, specifically political, scope. Accepting individuals as the rightful judges of their obligations manifested itself negatively as indignant criticism of institutions; wherever one applied the new criterion, one realized how little the duties that groups demanded arose from their members' self-determined interests or assent. This led Rousseau to the revolutionary notion that ruling without the continuing consent of the ruled violated their personal dignity. To make politics ethically acceptable would require allowing everyone to share in the power of government. This concept of popular sovereignty engendered democracy, the system our experience has shown to be the most humane system of government we know, though not an unflawed one. For most Jews, participation in democracy has produced over the years an unshakeable conviction of the moral indispensability of personal autonomy and the necessity of its being given adequate scope.

Personal Autonomy as the Heart of Ethics

Immanuel Kant, an enthusiastic supporter of the Enlightenment, subordinated all other considerations in his ethics to the concept of

170

the good (individual) will. He distinguished sharply between will and impulse, deeming the latter little more than animalistic urging and thus no basis for reflective human action. The move from impulse to will allows us to give rational direction to our drive to action—and only when we do that can we be called good. To conform to our rational nature, our ethical will cannot be guided by a merely contingent principle like consequence, for that notion has no compelling logical status but always involves possibility. So, too, one cannot rationally limit the scope of one's ethical will to a restricted group. In keeping with rationality's comprehensive reach, truly ethical commands extend universally to embrace all moral agents. Moreover, they will also manifest the imperative, directive quality of a concluded logical argument. They do not merely counsel or suggest but require. Thus a rationally formed ethical will lives by universal imperatives, that is, law. In sum, a good will follows the moral law that reason discloses.

Enamored of the rational individual's ethical will, Kant became the great champion of personal *autonomy*. His ethics of *nomos*, of law, operates in terms of universal, binding certainties. But in any given situation, each self, *autos*, must rationally determine for itself what constitutes the moral law and, in determining it, thereby legislate the applicable universal ethical duty as its own. Thus, rational ethics depends on rational self-determination, or *auto-nomy*.

The unsophisticated modern ear no longer hears the stringent Kantian overtones of the word "autonomy," for rationality and law have faded from the popular ethical consciousness. Instead, "autonomy" has become radical individualism, doing whatever seems worthwhile to you (optimally, without infringing on others' similar right to freedom). But reason kept the Kantian individual's self in check, for the will rightly subjected itself to reason's imperatives (lest we act out of mere impulse). To the child of 20th-century personal freedom, that answer seems dogmatic and raises the question, "What gives Kantian rationality such power to constrain the self?" The question arises from a consciousness of a gap between the self and its rationality, a sensibility that led to the decline of Kantian ethics and, in due course, to the contemporary confusion about the moral self.

Kant considered it axiomatic that, above all else, rationality makes a person human, and he therefore never bothered discussing it. A century later and only a generation after Cohen had revived Kantian thinking, his follower, Ernst Cassirer, had to admit the baleful effect of a changed philosophical climate. What the neo-

Kantians had taken to be the necessary path of reason channeling the will by moral law had now become only another possible way of posing and answering the perennial questions of ethics.

But if reason no longer supplied the *nomos*, where would the will gain its direction? As *autos* began to dominate not only thought but culture and life-style, the question of duty to others, locally and generally, became ever more pressing. For the ever more authoritative self easily transformed self-determination into self-centeredness, a notion far from the old Judeo-Christian intuition of individual worth. While we cannot avoid something of the heavy individualism associated with the term "autonomy," Kant and his followers so identified it with our experience of the dignity of self-determination that I believe we need to retain it and fill it with postmodern meaning.

Social Surrogates for Reason as the Self's Moral Guide

The two most effective practical challenges to Kantian autonomy, Marxism and nationalism, have charged it with excessive individualism, a matter critical to us as Jews since our folk, the people of Israel, plays so decisive a role in our faith.

Karl Marx believed that our anthropology will be flawed unless we shift the center of authority from the individual to society or humankind. He heaps scorn on the notion of autonomy, charging that the alleged freedom of individuals in bourgeois democracy involves the alienation of our true humanity. Things now play a deleterious role in modern existence, people cruelly exploit one another, economic bondage subjects us to demeaning power realities—all while we rejoice in our Kantian pure inner freedom. In fact, he rudely insists, our individual ideas and the patterns by which we shape them testify far more to the conditions of production under which we exist than to the transcendence of human rationality.

Marx, of course, cared more about politics than philosophy, exactly the point he sought to drive home: Ideas need to be thought in terms of socioeconomic power realities, preferably to change them, not speculatively as in Hegel's thought. Thus, Marx had no interest in gaining rights for German Jewry as such but discusses their situation only to attack the political notion that gaining individual rights constitutes meaningful freedom. Such politics ignores the fundamentally social nature of humanhood. Therefore, only when individuals learn to think of themselves as "species-beings" and organize themselves as a sociopolitical power will human emanicipation be complete.

Marx's concern with society and its structuring of power has been broadly persuasive even to those who have rejected his politics and economic determinism. Nothing has so refuted the claims of philosophers to articulate the necessary paths of universal human reason than the sociological critiques that have unmasked "the conditions of production" of "rational" ideas like objectivity. Practically, too, we now expect our political leaders to concern themselves with the economy and the ordering of social relations, for we know how intimately our private existence depends on our social context. In Kant's defense it must be noted that he indicated the social dimension of ethical responsibility by insisting that all ethical maxims be universalizable.

Marx and Kant differed radically over whether the crux of our humanhood was social or individual. Marx's devotion to the social self allows a party or state to know better than its members what their individuality properly entails, thus making possible a totalitarian "democracy." Against this doctrine Kantian individualism has now demonstrated its fundamental human appeal in the democratic upheavals of the once solidly Communist countries. In an analogous manner, a postmodern Judaism cannot do without strong elements of Kantian autonomy even as it cannot be satisfied with the utter subordination of the social aspects of our humanity to those which are properly individual.

Nationalists likewise find individualism deficient and we can gain some special Jewish insight into this critique by examining the thought of Ahad Haam, "one of the people" (pseudonym of Asher Ginzberg, one which brilliantly epitomized his position). He has particular significance for this discussion because, uniquely among the early ideologues of Zionism, he argued that the Jewish national ideal intrinsically demanded moral excellence of our people. His clearest statement about Jewish ethics came in a disdainful response to Claude Montefiore's suggestion that modern Judaism had to come to terms with the message of the Gospels if it were to remain a great teacher of humanity. Ahad Haam retorted that the two faiths have inconsistent ethics and mounted the customary Jewish polemic against the practicality of a Christian love ethic guiding social relationships. He proclaimed the undoubted superiority of the Jewish commitment to justice for the ordering of human affairs. By this he meant an uncompromising, abstract principle of rational obligation, one that, he contended, has been the distinguishing characteristic of Jewish national life and culture. The Jewish ideal, as he saw it, would be a condition in which justice has become instinctual so that, disdaining all personal and social considerations, people would judge every action with absolute impartiality.

As against the injustice and partiality that often prevail, Ahad Haam's principled justice would be a welcome human advance. But to demand a standard of justice so abstracted from real life that we ought to ignore all human considerations in ethical decision making seems not only harsh but possibly cruel. This theory also censors out of our tradition the dialectical Jewish devotion to *rahamim*, mercy. Since Ahad Haam never produced his promised work on Jewish ethics, we have no way of giving fuller meaning to this statement—his longest on ethics—in terms of its systematic context. Here, however, my concern is how Ahad Haam reconciled his ethical idealism with his sense of each Jew's duty to the Jewish nation.

Ahad Haam regularly derided the privatization of modern Jewish existence and said that the self should be understood primarily as a limb of the national body. This would have the effect of involving each Jew in the ethnic Jewish commitment to justice, more primarily it would require one to acquire so strong a Jewish national feeling that this group standard would direct one's life and constrain one's will.

Logically, this theoretical intermingling of ethical and national obligation should require a loyal Jew whose conscience clashed with our leaders' designation of national duty to abide by their ruling. Yet in the case of intermarriage Ahad Haam becomes ambivalent. He acknowledges that a loyal Jew might, from a personal ethical standpoint, deem such a marriage permissible. He opposes this, with a notable softening of his customary absolutistic tone, not as a matter of principle but of practical consequence. Thus, he appeals to the reader's sentiment: with Jewish life so endangered, should not the nationalistic Jew defend the folk and sacrifice one's personal happiness in this case?

An ethical secular nationalism may not be able to say more on this issue, but in his hesitation before this serious question Ahad Haam reveals how even a strongly social interpretation of human existence must, to win the allegiance of moderns, acknowledge the rights of individual conscience. I do not mean by this comment to deny the truth of his contention that personal Jewish identity necessarily involves a corporate, ethnic dimension. I only wish to call attention to the problem Jews share with all emancipated moderns: Admitting the sociality of the self, how shall we work out the subtle calculus of rightful obligation to one's self and to one's group?

In recent decades, mounting sociological evidence has strongly influenced our sense of the self as substantially a creature of society. And our experience has reinforced this notion. Even in the 1960s, at the height of individual rebellion against institutions, group life manifested its indispensability. An individualistic movement, no less, arose, celebrated its own culture as a counter-culture, and sought to create institutions that allowed for greater individuality, the short-lived communes. Since then, American privatism has so intensified the loneliness accompanying individualization that people create small groups like extended families or *havurot* in order to alleviate it. How, then, can personal autonomy and sociality be reconciled?

The Existentialist Ambivalence about the Self

Retrospectively, this problem of the self's ethical and social nature may be said to haunt the life work of Jean-Paul Sartre. Initially, Sartre was the great philosophic exponent of the utterly free and unrestricted individual. Continuing the critique of Western philosophy that stretches from Nietzsche through Heidegger, Sartre denied that it was self-evident, as Descartes had thought, that the very fact of one's thinking demonstrated that one existed. Opposing such rationalistic dogmatism, he boldly asserted the opposite view, that existence is rationally absurd: it precedes our thinking and therefore necessarily overflows it. No rationalism can hope fully to explain its givens, like temporality or freedom or even reason itself. A self seeking to be authentic—to be truly for-itself—has nothing to rely on but itself. Therefore, to seek any external support to legitimate the use of one's freedom constitutes the primal Sartrean sin.

In the Sartrean redefinition of "autonomy," with the *autos* defined as pure spontaneity (rationality providing no guidance), *nomos* means the self's duty to choose what it wishes, if necessary, by simply leaping into commitment. Sartre does not flinch from this thoroughgoing relativism and writes in the concluding pages of *Being and Nothingness:* "All human values are equivalent . . . all are on principle doomed to failure. Thus it amounts to the same thing whether one gets drunk alone or is a leader of nations." Where Kant constrained Enlightenment individualism by the discipline of reason,

Sartre confirms the collapse of that standard and offers in its place the "law" of authenticity to one's free will.

Sartre does admit one social-moral consideration into his system: The other who stands over against me must be granted the same sort of freedom-consciousness that I possess. In Sartre's own terms, he has no rational basis for this declaration since one could hardly be as conscious of another's free self as one is of one's own. Yet this exception to his usual rigor testifies to his ethical seriousness and presages the problem he continued to face: providing some justification for social responsibility.

Sartre had promised a work on ethics to fulfill the ontological analysis of *Being and Nothingness*, but instead turned to analyze the Marxist interpretation of the sociality of the self. Though acknowledging the many social determinants of our individuality, he saw no way of shifting some legitimate authority from the self to the group. Situating the free self within the interstices of Marxist history did not alter Sartrean autonomy as the unfettered exercise of will. Sartre again promised a successor volume on ethics but it never appeared. Sartre's failure epitomizes the continuing plight of philosophical ethics, which cannot easily discard the Enlightenment vision of individual dignity but can no longer find a common rationalism that requires something like the biblical notion of social obligation. One result has been a call to recognize that discourse about virtue and moral imperatives can only take place within a community whose members share a certain ethical perspective and that universal claims for ethics must be given up.

What Can Rationalism Now Say to the Sovereign Self?

Among social theorists, Jürgen Habermas may be presenting the most compelling contemporary secular effort to situate free individuals in a social context. Habermas has tried to face up to the dire moral consequences of our post-Nietzschean, post-Sartrean ethical agnosticism in a time just when social structures have increasing power. Once again institutional evils impel the thinker to take the self seriously, even though not much can any longer be usefully said in Kantian fashion simply from within one's private individuality. Habermas has instead sought a ground of ethical value in our lived human social situation.

He points to communication as unique to human beings and universal in humankind. Applying a quasi-Kantian transcendental analytic, he then inquires as to its necessary presuppositions. All such interchange requires an effort to be understood and, therefore, to gain the other's assent to engage in communicating. Once this agreement has been gained the fundamental pattern of ethical interaction has been established: the seeking of the other's free concurrence and, conversely, respect for each partner's right not to be coerced but to come to independent determination. Rationality quickly claims its place in this process, for Habermas acknowledges the validity of one form of coercion, what he calls the peculiar force of the better argument. We can then state a new criterion of truth, one that we may not be able to exemplify but that we can always endeavor to reach: that is, an argument that would be accepted by everyone under conditions of perfect communication. In the service of this ideal we must unmask all the present distortions of communication brought on by our alienating social structures and, as we transcend our false consciousness, we can more closely reach truth.

In this theory, autonomy has become the individual's right to resist any societal value or structure that remains unconvincingly explained. Without postulating the Kantian rationalism that demands and structures the use of our practical reason, Habermas has made individual rationality the basis of our hope that we can make normative ethical judgments and, on that basis, authorize moral social arrangements. By older standards this is a somewhat minimalistic ethic, though not to the degree of Sartre's thought. However, compared to the Marxist justification of social responsibility at the cost of denying effective individuality, it powerfully reinforces the Enlightenment enfranchisement of the individual. Habermas is thus making a major contribution to resolving the tension between the autonomous self and social obligation.

Yet the compelling power of this philosophy remains limited by its pragmatic evasion of the metaethical issue of the dignity of the self. For what secular reasons ought we to take the self so seriously and grant it such dignity? A realistic appraisal of most lives, beginning with our own, will rarely yield the conclusion that the quality of people's lives explains why they deserve to be treated with ultimate concern and to be accorded the right of self-legislation. If we insist on the extraordinary dignity of autonomy, it must surely be despite what, in fact, we regularly show ourselves to be.

Moreover, my Jewish sense of content-laden responsibility demands more guidance than merely pointing out the characteristics of a properly ethical imperative. Responsible personhood requires more substantive guidance than that, particularly in an era when many people have more personal freedom than they can handle without anxiety. Where can they gain the consciousness of commanding quality that will mandate the values and thence the maxims by which they ought to live? And what might make this not merely a likely ethical construction of reality but an imperative of such quality that it commands one's utmost, lifelong devotion? I agree with those thinkers who now acknowledge that secular reason cannot as such ever quiet our insatiable Cartesian doubt about rationalistic efforts to ground our ethics and thus properly dignify the self. So beginning with such certainties as have arisen in my life and survived expanding experience and critical reflection, I turn my search for greater clarity from secular to religious thought.

The Related Self: Individual, Yet Social

For me, the diverse strands of this post-Enlightenment spiritual quest come together best in the thought of Martin Buber. Buber knows no utterly discrete Cartesian ego but only a self which, to come into being, must be engaged with an other. The phenomenologists might have told us something like this in identifying how much of our sense of self comes from others' perceptions of us. But Buber says very much more, that self-knowledge is already I–it, that living selfhood exists only in relationship, and that when relationship truly exists, each partner directly knows the other not in part but as a whole self. Indeed the full self emerges only in mutuality with another full self, thereby disclosing the quality which, by its ennobling effect, demands to come into our I–it existence and transform it. The Eternal Thou also participates in each I–thou encounter, serving as the context of our meeting all other thous. Whether in direct or indirect association with us, God relates to us precisely as the unique self we are, thereby endowing our individuality with ultimate value.

Buber gives new meaning to autonomy because it now must become relational. In an I–thou encounter the self must retain its freedom for if I must do what you desire, then "I" in my singleness am not present but only your image of the "me" that meets your needs. For this reason too no Kantian *nomos* can dictate my duty, for universalizable law specifies the common case, not necessarily the particular duty that arose from my-our present encounter. But my *autos* cannot be utterly self-determining for it appears in its fullness only in mutuality. Hence self-determination now must be the lawmaking of the self-with-other; at the least, it involves a dyadic normativity.

This person-based image of authority has weighty social consequences. The qualitative distinction between I–it and I–thou relationships explains why most institutions disturb us so: they regularly treat us more as objects than as persons. We then begin to long for social structures that encourage people to reach out to one another in dialogic concern. Buber terms such a group a "community" and he may take credit for the revolutionary thesis that our highest human duty is to transmute society into community. It is, in fact, his notion of messianism.

Normally this humanization of society takes place quite slowly, by individuals meeting and developing relationships. But Buber also believes that, on occasion, groups as such participate in I–thou encounters. Then, as we may have experienced on a small scale in work, recreation, prayer, or study, we all momentarily become bound up in a unity that does not negate our individuality but fulfills it, not person to person but in mutuality with many others. We highly value communities forged by such experiences and insofar as we renew them in further activity the group becomes even more important to our individual existence.

In historic moments a folk can undergo such an experience, giving it a distinctive national character. This happened to the Hebrews in the events we call Exodus and Sinai, during which they became conscious of being as directly involved with God as with one another. The nation that emerged from these encounters bound itself in a relationship with God they called the Covenant—and renewed it in subsequent experiences over the centuries in the land of Israel. In due course, the Hebrews came to understand themselves as the people Covenanted to God.

Sinai, it must be emphasized, was one group's unusual experience of a universal human phenomenon. Whenever such encounters occur, whether they be momentous or fleeting, they generate a sense of obligation in the group. This prompts the promulgation of specific laws appropriate to the experience and these retain their Buberian legitimacy as long as they continue to give expression to the encounter that gave rise to them. Social forms have a further validity to Buber. People cannot remain in the I–thou state but must spend most of their lives in the I–it mode. Until the next encounter, individuals should seek to transform the I–it by their memories of the quality that permeated the I–thou meeting.

Good law may thus be understood as enabling the continuity of I–thou reality in our I–it existence. Yet inspired law, even though it will continue to maintain its claim of inspiration, always becomes emptied of the spirit. When this happens the law no longer has commanding power. It must again validate itself by the living I–thou situation or be set aside. Relational autonomy, therefore, both validates and invalidates law, providing the basis for the charge that Buber is un-Jewish because he is antinomian in either a halakhic or Kantian sense.

From the Related Self to the Jewish Self

Depending on how actively one interprets this last proviso, this Buberian authorization of value, group, and structure encapsulates much of what I take to be the critical Jewish religious experience of recent years. It knows and honors the self's role in legislation yet grounds it in a relationship with God and community that summons the individual to humanize personal relationships and social structures, in short, that summons the individual to messianic living. Yet for whatever reasons, neither Buber nor Rosenzweig could see this theory resulting in anything other than a practical extreme, universalism in the one case, halakhic passivity in the other.

We see this best in their famous exchange of letters from 1922–1925 on the rightful authority of Jewish law. Though agreeing that all religious authority must finally arise within the self, Rosenzweig urged Buber to accept the *halakhah*, at least in principle, as our presumed Jewish duty in any given situation. Buber rejected the proposal, arguing that if he (or anyone) wanted to remain open to what the Eternal Thou might be "saying" in a given situation, he could not subject himself in advance of a situation to rules made long ago by others. Of course a given *halakhah* might still reflect the I–thou experience that engendered it and thus still rightly command one. However, no one could know that until the validating I–thou meeting occurred in a particular situation. Buber summed up his position in the words, "for me, though man is a law-receiver, God is not a law-giver, and therefore the Law has no universal validity for me, but only a personal one."

A pragmatic consideration also played a role in Buber's determination to give his theory of authority a strongly individualistic reading. He found the *halakhah* as lived and interpreted in his day directed more to its own institutional ends than to fostering a living

Jewish relationship with God. To bring God back to the center of Jewish life, Buber felt he must resolutely resist any prior claims on us.

These many decades later, as the 20th century moves toward conclusion, I find much truth in Buber's obdurate individualism. Again and again, in one place or another, people find it the height of moral responsibility to oppose the many social institutions that purport to benefit us but then abuse or neutralize our freedom. To that extent the Enlightenment's vision of ethical duty cannot be surrendered. Nonetheless, I also do not see this as our paramount spiritual concern. One glance around us reveals that what was once the human liberation of an individualism that reason could be expected to socialize has, with the loss of the old qualitative certainties, degenerated into a threateningly amoral self-centeredness. If only to invest autonomy once again with the high dignity that entitles it to oppose insensitive institutions, we need to oppose irresponsible individualism by specifying the sources of authority that should legitimately limit the exercise of the free self. In our time, resocializing autonomy has become as important a moral imperative as opposing collectives seeking to deny it. Against Buber, we must reemphasize the sociality of the individual self, even as with him we envisage all human selves bound in covenant with God.

This shift of priorities has even greater cogency for contemporary Jewry. We shall have no rich sense of Jewish duty as long as we persist in thinking of ourselves as individual selves-in-general who see Torah as another resource, though an emotionally attractive one, for enhancing our high humanity. Only when we end the distinction between our personhood and our Jewishness and understand ourselves as indivisibly Jewish selves, persons whose selfhood is inextricable from their participation in the Jewish people and its historic relationship with God, will we make possible a vigorous postmodern life of Torah.

13   Fully Human, Fully Jewish

HE KANTIAN VISION of the mature person as a rational self-legislator provided two philosophically justified rationalizations for disdaining Jewish identity. The one endorsed a self-satisfied individualism; the other, an embrace of only those duties applicable to all humankind. It is to the inadequacies of this latter strategy that I now turn.

Modern discourse, by its very logic, places a severe disability on anyone seeking to mandate primary loyalty to a social particular. The self being the foundation stone of all modern authority, corporate demands can rightly be made only in the name of all selves, the universal, and not the particular. By our accepted standards of argument, then, individuality receives its significance by virtue of being an instance of a valued general class or category. This pattern of assigning value indicates that the particular intrinsically has merely contingent status. To compensate for this loss of quality, one then can try to demonstrate the particular's value as an effective means toward the universal ideal. The reduction of Jewish particularity to merely instrumental significance helped undermine dedication to Jewish duty by subjecting its demands to an invidious cost/benefit analysis: How efficiently do they enable us to attain what reason bids us care more about, namely, our universal human goals? The priority of the universal makes the life of Torah that dispensable.

As they modernized, Jews happily ignored this difficulty and enthusiastically made general ethics their Torah; before and without Hitler, the lure of the universal threatened an end to the Jews. In Western Europe it took the bourgeois form of an assimilation that found humanism the fulfillment of everything worthwhile to which Judaism had aspired in its cramped and Semitic fashion. In Eastern Europe, socialist and communist doctrines of political universalism flourished luxuriantly. In their parties and later in the Soviet Union, the devotees of these doctrines anathematized Judaism and Zionism for diverting attention from the proper goals of the workers of the world.

Particularity: From Subordinate to Partner

Personally experiencing the nobility of universal humanhood, emancipated Jews idealistically took on the task of making it the

182

living, historical reality of every human being. Recent history has judged it to be hopelessly utopian to dream of an imminent Messianic Age that reorders all human relationships on a thoroughly universalistic basis. Looking within, as well, this high-mindedness that transcends concern for Jewish continuity contradicts the preciousness of Jewish particularity laid bare by the continuing threats to our people's survival. No caring Jew can easily forget that the very people that proclaimed itself the great example of universal humanism did its methodical best to destroy us while the liberal democracies found ways not to do what they might have done to mitigate the murder; therefore, many Jews were not shocked that as freedom came to Eastern Europe, ugly religious and nationalist antisemitism reappeared.

Fearfulness aside, the many Jews who love their Jewishness will indignantly spurn the disdainful notion that Jewish particularity lacks intrinsic dignity and must justify itself in terms of its service of a greater good. Though we love universalism as democracy, we spurn its becoming an ideological imperialism that seizes all genuine value for itself alone. We manifest a bipolar faith, one dialectically juxtaposing the importance of particular instances to that of ideal universals. Explicating their interplay and entailments thus becomes a critical contemporary theological task.

We need to begin this enterprise by clarifying the worth we assign to Jewish particularity, for it will be a primary determinative of what we consider to be a satisfactory life of Torah. The possibility of the death or fossilization of our people poses the issue most starkly: Do we believe the Jews and Judaism to be ultimately dispensable or not? Would our disappearance from history be only another sociocultural loss like that of the Carthaginians or the Incas, or would it constitute something far more irretrievable, a tragedy with cosmic reverberation, as it were? Practically, how much should we care if our grandchildren are being raised as decent human beings but not as Jews? If Jewishness is only a matter of conditioning, personal emotion, or social habituation, our discomfort at our descendants not being Jewish would be understandable but have little normative weight. If, however, we believe that the Jewish people has a critical role in human history—namely, bringing the Messiah—then staying Jewish and projecting Jewishness through future generations become critical Jewish responsibilities. I speak as one of those Jews whose religio-ethnic experience has disclosed a certain absoluteness in faithful Jewishness, one not derivative of

The top line is missing from page 184. It should read:

anything but God's will and our answering dedication. Though I

shall return to this issue in chapter 17, I will carry on my analysis here in terms of this strong affirmation of Jewish particularity.

We can now frame our theological problem this way: How might we intellectually integrate devotion to the enduring truth of the life of Torah with an equally compelling ardor for the universal equality of humankind? I will present my response to this question in two steps, by first discussing universalism's loss of philosophic credibility, the basis on which it may still claim validity, and its continuing place in a postmodern Judaism. I will then make a brief statement of its limits, returning to this dialectic in greater detail in chapter 16. I will also say something about the role religious faith plays in living with this existential paradox.

Judaism Now Mandates My Universalism

Let us begin with the confident past. Modern philosophers believed their standards for proper thinking only brought to consciousness the logical patterns inherent in every rational mind whatsoever. From that lofty perspective reference to private experiences, like revelation to specific persons on special occasions, had to be termed primitive and retrogressive. Modern rationalism could claim to be ethically superior to the biblical faiths because it had a universal moral horizon, whereas the particularity of the latter placed barriers in the way of a positive identification with all humankind.

Today it has become difficult to ascribe such sweep to rationality. Applying the sociology of knowledge to what once purported to be ideas common to all rational minds shows them to be quite particularistic. Historically, they developed as the conventional languages of a professional guild of male, white, middle-class, European Christian or Christianized university professors. In our more global, more class-, more gender-, more race-conscious pluralism, who can claim to transcend all the contingencies of time, place, and person? Instead of philosophies that present themselves as universally objective and certain, contemporary thinkers must content themselves with identifying the groups whose accepted syntax and logic alone give their arguments conviction, producing the notorious "hermeneutic circles" of contemporary intellectual discourse. In a sweeping reversal of the cultural assumptions of the two post-Enlightenment centuries, secular philosophies can no longer rationally establish universalism and thus the rights that inhere in every human being—surely a major intellectual cause of the ethical decay in Western civilization.

Whereas contemporary philosophy can at best only commend universal human dignity, Hebrew Scriptures command it. Irrevocable personal worth arises from two of its closely related themes, that God created people in God's own "image"—which, for all its ambiguity, links humanhood with the absolute source of value in the universe—and the even more daring assertion that God has an ongoing partnership with humankind. The incomparable status of people among created things stems from this close identification with God and God's purposes.

Perhaps nothing makes this unique status more evident than the Jewish doctrine of *teshuvah*, or turning back to God, which English lamely renders as "repentance." God endows human beings with freedom, a freedom sufficiently real that they can defy God's own stated desires. Paradoxically, this already gives them intrinsic value of extraordinary measure, but Judaism extends it even further. Sinning might be envisioned as permanently estranging people from God and thus stripping them of their essential dignity. Jewish moralists do surround the willfully, determinedly wicked with this aura, but this does not denude them of their covenant partnership with God (and neither does their being subjected to just punishment, the corpses of the executed receiving respectful treatment). Rather, God never deprives the wicked of another unique human capacity, the freedom they retain even in the midst of sinfulness to "turn from their evil ways and live." Every human being can do this and do it on their own, without benefit of special rite or intermediary. So when the vicious Ninevites give up their evildoing and sincerely plead for forgiveness, God accepts them instantly—to Jonah's discomfiture. Human dignity remains that inalienable.

The foundation of the Jewish religious commitment to universalism is the covenant God made with Noah and his children, a theme that authorizes the *halakhah* concerning Jewish relations with gentiles. Already in the Genesis account, the universal human relationship with God has the same structure as that between God and the Jewish people, namely, a covenant. More tellingly, Jewish law further equates the two in its assertion that, before the giving of the Torah, Jews and gentiles had the same duties, and that, after it was given, Jews have no exemption from any prohibition binding gentiles. Of course, the rabbis considered "the nations" idolaters and, hence, utterly reprehensible; but here again, they condemned them not because they had a different religion but because of their behavior, the same standard they applied to the Jews. It comes as no surprise then that medieval Jewish authorities could codify the dictum that pious gentiles, like Jews, had "a share in the life of the world to come."

A similar attitude toward the outsider who comes to live among Jews who are settled on their promised land finds eloquent expression in the law that "you must not oppress the stranger for you know the heart of the stranger having yourselves been strangers in the land of Egypt" (Exod. 23:9). The Torah often links the stranger with two other powerless if Jewish persons: the widow and the orphan. These three symbolize all those likely to be taken advantage of by the shrewd and the mighty. The Torah reminds the people that God has a special interest in their welfare; it is the Torah's only "reason" for demanding decency toward people one could easily outmaneuver. So too one must not curse the deaf, though one knows the words cannot be heard, or put a stumbling-block before the blind, though one knows they will not know who did them harm, for "I am *Adonai*."

For centuries, these teachings did not have the universal scope and democratic aura they have today. Early on, Jews kept aloof from a world devoted to idolatry. Later, when Christianity and Islam brought belief in one God to the Western world, discrimination and hostility toward Jews made Jewish self-concern prudent. For all their straitened circumstances, they never surrendered the connection between one God and one humanity—a spiritual accomplishment of numinous proportions. Then, when persecution gave way to equality, Jewish thinkers had little difficulty recovering the old Jewish insistence on a human solidarity based on each individual's irrefragable dignity.

Particularity, the Necessary Ground of Universalism Today

My Jewish faith teaches me, as Christian belief teaches Christians, that we must fill the word "human" with utterly universal content. This Judeo-Christian understanding once provided the grounding principle of Western democracy. With the one incomparable God of Hebrew Scripture as its source, universal human dignity cannot be compromised or qualified by any merely human authority. But it can give rise to that characteristic modern principle that people

have "rights," that is, simply by virtue of being human a certain
unconditional character attaches to them. Against an overbearing
power, people can stand on their rights and, ideally, stop the
oppressors from doing their coercive will. Any effort to mitigate our
rights will quickly be identified as an infringement of our personhood
and thus unethical. The Judeo-Christian heritage invested the self
with that much moral power and our experience with democratic
living has confirmed the truth of this modernization of an ancient
ideal.

When secular philosophy assumed this vision of humanhood to
be self-evident and universal, it could argue that rationality itself
would give it similar force if not more, considering that it now freed
universalism from denominational coloration. But if contemporary
thought can only recommend or esteem the idea but not demonstrate
the universal dignity of persons, our intuition of the transcendent
quality of personhood has lost its secular footing. The failure of
contemporary rationalisms to invest human beings with undeniable
elemental worth has in no small way contributed to our late 20th-
century wariness of philosophy and our openness to religions, new
and old.

I retain my strong universalism, then, because of my Jewish
faith—that is, because I am a particularist. The same is true of many
Christians and adherents of other religions as well. We cannot
surrender, in the name of humankind, our vigorous commitment to
our own distinctive faith without thereby surrendering the very
mandate that alone can now require us to dignify all humankind. I
do not deny that there are many people without religious commitment who are devoted to and work hard for universal human
concerns. In the western world, they are people who are still living
by an ideal they received from the Judeo-Christian underpinnings of
their culture, or else they pragmatically espouse this ideal as the least
damaging, most peace-enhancing social arrangement. The former
position will either remain grounded in its cultural particularism or,
without a foundation, become reduced to a practical procedure. But
pragmatic conclusions are always open to revision when it appears
that something might work better. The dignity of all humankind
deserves greater certainty than that.

Many Religions: An Argument against All Particularity?

A similar truth emerges when we shift our focus from individuals
to religions. The world is incurably pluralistic religiously, but that

does not mean, as some have suggested, that the simultaneous claims of many of them to exclusive truth disproves the truth claim of any one of them. It only suggests that not all of them can be simultaneously true in the way that they profess to be. To decide among them—or to tease out the limited truth of each or all of them— would require us to have a standard of truth transcending all religion. In the days when professors could un-self-consciously proclaim their ideas to be universally necessary for all rational beings, every enlightened person could take this superior stance. However, when postmodern humility can at best commend universalism as a persuasive construction of reality, proposing it as the judge of religious truth smacks of an arrogance its moral coloration cannot excuse.

I know as part of my inherited and personally renewed Jewish faith that other religions can be true. Rabbinic Judaism teaches that all human beings can know what God wants of them, essentially seven root commandments: not to blaspheme God, worship idols, murder, steal, be sexually degenerate, nor cut limbs from living animals; positively, to set up courts of justice. But as the Tower of Babel story long ago taught, humankind regularly violates its covenant-responsibilities, a willfulness that the rabbis believed, on the basis of historical experience, characterized "the nations." The Torah understands the Covenant with Abraham as God's attempt to compensate for humanity's inveterate perversity—but this new Covenant does not abrogate the one made with Noah. Rather God establishes the special Covenant so that the divine rule may become manifest in history and eventually transform it. The Jews fulfill God's special purpose by living in special intensity under God's law—that is, by the observance of 613 root commandments.

In Jewish law, gentiles do not need to become Jews; they need only be pious Noahides to be "saved." So the Jews have no command to convert anyone and little tradition of proselytization though the rabbis despaired about human collectives ever becoming righteous and speculated that they would not survive the judgment day.

Despite all this doctrine, the rabbis dealt directly only with idolaters. Succeeding generations have had to fill in Judaism's judgment of other religions. With regard to Christianity this meant judging whether its use of icons, its veneration of saints, and particularly its doctrine of the Christ as a coequal person of the triune God were the equivalent of idolatry. Most Jewish thinkers today believe pious Christians and Muslims fulfill the Noahide covenant and thus are "saved." This is about as far as the traditional Jewish theology of other religions has gone.

When believing Jews began experiencing democracy they quickly become passionate apostles of the universal availability of religious truth and its living presence in non-Jewish religions. Their tradition reinforced their delight in the common humanity they found in the societies that granted them effective equality, and the Noahide covenant quickly went from being an old story to a present Jewish ideal.

What secular source might today create such a positive openness to truth in many religions? Surely not the ever-growing data produced by the study of the world's religions. To argue that the very multiplicity of human religions demonstrates that a common truth underlies them all directly contradicts the evidence. The facts disclose only burgeoning diversity. To see a unity in disparate data requires a transempirical standard of judgment. Little could be more important to a discussion of truth in human religions than to examine the nature of such a criterion and to justify it. To take an extreme case, if we wish to avoid all judgment and exclude no one, we arrive at an unrestricted relativism: "All religions are equally worthwhile and none is any better than another." I can understand the virtues of such a position for the academic study of religion, a discipline that seeks only to be descriptive. If, however, our concern is normative and we wish to find a worthy faith by which to live, this unrestricted tolerance dooms us to indecision, a standardlessness made all the more intolerable by our need to guard against the demonic in religion as in politics. And as we seek adequate emphasis for the values we most cherish, e.g., a modernized Judeo-Christian regard for all persons, we must dissociate ourselves from faiths that do not adequately proclaim them.

More directly, when universalism becomes a premise in this discussion, we have a right to ask a critical question. Whence does it arise and what gives it such hierarchical, even moral authority that it can assert the right to negate the truth claims of any individual religion? Since the history and sociology of religion are descriptive, they cannot prescribe what underlies all religions or constitutes their essence without becoming constructive philosophy of religion. Minus a compelling metaphysics or ontology to establish so universal a sense of truth, statements characterizing religion generally can only have heuristic or hermeneutic value, neither of which would endow them with normative authority. In the present wintry discontent of rationalism and the unresolvable competition of fundamentalist theories of religion today, I see no secular basis for a normative theory of universal religion. (Of course, another historical shift in our understanding of reason might so alter its scope that a rationalism might again coincide with what I have been taught by revelation and experience.)

The pragmatic argument for granting all religions some measure of truth, and thus calling for social pluralism, has considerable suasive power for all those of us sensitive to the benefits this has brought to intergroup relations. But for all its rewards, the practicality of tolerance also leads to an abhorrence of limits that requires accepting a lot of allegedly lesser evils and to the possibility that another, less humane pattern might appear to yield a richer balance of benefit and thus be adopted.

The Perils of "Explaining" Particularity

Most people rarely encounter universalism in this abstract form. More commonly, if unconsciously, they meet it in the statements purporting to translate a particular religion's enduring truth into modern terms. Contemporary Western intellectuality being so Hellenic, one establishes relevance by translating a tradition's truth into universally available terms. Thus, as moderns shifted their religious discourse from the truth of divine revelation to that gained from the evidence of personal experience, one of the most appealing hermeneutics speaks in terms of the "truly" or "fully" human.

This notion has had wide currency in modern Judaism, most especially in Hermann Cohen's identification of Judaism with ethical rationalism and Mordecai Kaplan's theory of religious culture as an expression of human growth and development. Perhaps we can gain a clearer perspective on the insidiousness of this discourse-induced universalism if we look at it in another faith, Christianity.

The influential mid-century Protestant theologian Paul Tillich crafted one of the most appealing modern interpretations of the Christ, a personalist or existentialist one. He envisaged Christianity as the faith that proclaimed the "name" of God, God's specific identity, as the same as the "name" of Jesus. Tillich's own universalizing translation of Jesus's name justified this version of the classic Christian equivalence of God and Jesus. He argued that the "name of Jesus" discloses the structure of our "new being," a phrase of overflowing meaning that can be partially decoded as personal renewal and fulfillment. Tillich evocatively analyzed the contemporary human condition in this existentialist mode, illuminating its dark sense of threat and elucidating its religious message of hope.

Despite my admiration for the intellectual and hermeneutic brilliance of this accomplishment, much about it strikes me as methodologically puzzling. To begin with the historical issue, how does he know that the name of Christ means and apparently has always meant "the new being"? I do not recall such language in either the New Testament or in later classic Christian documents about the nature and work of the Christ. Rather it seems reasonably clear to me that Tillich has sought to identify the essence of traditional Christianity with his modern personalistic interpretation of it as full humanization.

I can understand why he wants to do this. The particularity of classic Christianity has become a major "scandal," to use the New Testament word, not only to non-Christians but to many who call themselves Christians. To claim the identity (in the Trinity) of one particular man with the one God and to point to his crucifixion and resurrection as somehow literally saving humankind, affronts the modern soul with its universalistic sense of value. By transforming the meaning of the Christ into a teaching about human existence generally, Tillich has made Christianity less scandalous and more spiritually appealing because he has rendered it more humanistic. Yet, as an outsider, I cannot tell whether his humanizing of the Christ properly carries Christianity forward or as good as empties it of distinctive identity and spiritual substance despite his summoning of key Christian symbols.

I recognize this theological problem as very much my own. All of us today who wish for apologetic and spiritual reasons to emphasize the universal aspects of our faiths face a question we feel we must but cannot answer: How much can an old tradition be universalized and still remain true to its primal religious truth, one it always knew to be significantly particular? In contemporary Judaism, for example, our most significant arguments rage over how much we can departic-ularize the concept or practice of Torah, or the extent to which an Israeli nationalism, no different from any other, can fully translate classic Jewish identity. As I see it, the difficulty goes beyond judging which set of terms most satisfactorily expresses our sense of the universal human truth of our existence. Rather, it arises from the way in which trying to give new prominence to the universalism always present in our tradition unleashes an imperialistic normativity that threatens to wipe out our balancing particularism. Thus, to return to Tillich's case, if Christianity only teaches a certain way of human living, why, other than because of emotional ties to the old symbols or community, does a reasonably self-actualizing human being need Christian particularity and institutionality? If one does not dialectically yoke one's universalizing with an equally powerful profession of particularity, there will be no such need. That has surely been one reason for the modern move to orthodoxies and its spiritual twin, the continuing American affirmation of religion but disaffection with mainline Christian and Jewish religious institutions. To be sure, I have not been fair to Tillich's subtle effort to show how the particular Christian story and teaching correlate with and remake our culture's vague view of humanhood. He sought a dialectic of the universal and the particular, but I find his critics persuasive in charging him with allowing the former to overwhelm the latter.

The Interplay of the Particular and the Universal

This issue takes on special significance because of my earlier argument that without a particularistic religious ground our universalism cannot have the moral power to which our spiritual and human experience entitles it. If our universal language remains unqualified by a strong argument for particularity it will not only delegitimize the particular but that, in turn, will destroy what gives the universal its commanding power. But this priority I am assigning to the particular can breed its own theological difficulties. Indeed, I have given so much attention to the problems universalism begets that I must now make a first statement about the threat of excessive particularism. (I shall return to this dialectic in chapter 16.) An imperialistic assertion of the primacy of the particular has not infrequently given rise in religions to a demonic chauvinism and fanaticism. While no one can give a simple rule for the proper balance of the particular and the universal, I can suggest four guidelines by which to check the hierarchical priority of the particular.

First, assertions about our particularity, not being universals, should be applied only to ourselves, as in the Jewish understanding that only Jews, not all people, need to serve God as Jews, Second, Jews who are not Orthodox believers should take seriously the fundamental principle of non-Orthodoxy, that our human insight into religious truth, while great enough to stake our life on, is always limited and not absolute. Those whose piety differs from ours may therefore well have another true if similarly limited sense of the Ultimate, and thus we must be practicing religious pluralists. Third, all believers properly stand under the moral judgment of religion's secular critics. If we claim that our lives reflect our intimate relationship with the one universal God, we should not act so as to bring discredit on our God who has a living relationship with all humankind. This concern should apply with special intensity should we ever find ourselves with political power, precisely when the temptations to group self-justification grow most irresistible. Fourth, we ought to do our best not to confuse present history with its eschatological fulfillment. Only when God redeems human history from its sinfulness will the truth we affirm fully come into being. Until then we must not confuse our righteousness with God's unique saving power or forget that we stand under God's present judgment. These theses do not relieve me of the problems potentially created by my assigning priority to the particular over the universal, but they ease my practical difficulties when I face situations in which the values clash.

Theologically, one can live so paradoxical a vision of one's obligation by what may figuratively be called the theological suspension of the law of the excluded middle. Greek logic insisted on a sharp choice between contradictories, on the rational necessity of the either/or, in our case, either the universal or the particular. Classic Judaism knows this mode of thought but apparently does not find it inclusive enough to give adequate structure to its intuition of ultimate reality. Its verbalizations tend rather to take the dialectical both/and form, thus comfortably depicting God as limited and unlimited, personal and impersonal, just and merciful, the God of the universe and of the Jewish people.

This un-Hellenic embrace of clashing symbols continues in contemporary Jewish spirituality, perhaps with somewhat greater intensiveness. Though our faith is certain enough for us to stake our lives and that of our community on it—and do so with a messianic timeline—we also acknowledge our finitude and do not assert that we have the whole truth or the only truth about God and humankind. Others we have come to know have what we can recognize as their own spiritual truth. Not only must they, like us, have the freedom to express and refine their faith, we can often learn much from them while all the while believing Judaism to be decisively correct.

Our particularity also demonstrates this two-sidedness. We confess that Jewish tradition has given special power to our dedication to universal human rights. If our people's God were not the good, concerned, unique Divinity we know our God to be, we would not live under the imperative of recognizing every human being's inalienable worth despite humankind's astonishing diversity and moral fallibility. And if our folk had not made our Egyptian slavery and Exodus central to its ethos—an experience profoundly renewed in the Emancipation—we would not be so passionate about extending human rights to every creature. Yet we know many others, in their own ways and out of their own experience, believe as we do. When, as has often happened, they see their deepest spiritual insight in our old Exodus tale we are not surprised, for we know our particular religious vision is also profoundly and inseparably universal.

14   The Sparks of Chosenness

O MUCH has been written about the doctrine of the chosen people—mostly to defend the rabbis from the charge of teaching the superiority of the Jews—that I believe a fresh approach will give us greater insight into the concept and its modernization. I shall therefore devote this chapter to discussing its effect on Jewish life and reserve my theoretical analysis of the concept for the next chapter. Rabbinic Judaism anticipated that the knowledge of being part of God's chosen people ideally would shape Jewish lives in six ways, which, for analytic purposes, I shall categorize as intra- and extracommunal.

Intracommunally, chosenness first founds Jewish existence on the consciousness that the one God of the universe gave the Torah to the Jews alone. Therefore, and second, a Jew should do *mitzvot* as an individual and as part of the Jewish people's corporate service of God. Third, living this way makes Jewish life holy, distinguished from profane existence, and suffused with a sense of contact with God. Fourth, because of this alliance with God, Jews know that their people will survive every historical vicissitude and one day be vindicated when God fully redeems them and all humankind because of them.

The two extracommunal consequences of this belief can be termed separation and service. The Torah's laws aim, among other purposes, to isolate the Jewish people from other groups so that this folk can endure and carry out its special obligations to God; as an instrument of redemption, Jewish separateness therefore acquires sacred status. It also has an unfortunate side-effect. All eccentric peoples suffer for their oddity, but something about distance for the sake of what is ultimate seems to intensify the hatred directed at the Jews. Our history having often been bitter, the classic Jewish view of the relationship of chosenness to suffering demands clarification. God's election does not mandate or require Jewish pain, though that has often been its consequence. Bluntly put: crucifixion is not a Jewish model for serving God. The Torah commands Jews to avoid suffering by all reasonable means. However, should suffering come, the rabbis direct us to see if we can accept it as only another situation in which we acknowledge God as sovereign. We do what we can to sanctify even the excrescences of history—but we neither seek nor glory in them.

The other extracommunal aspect of chosenness can be termed activist. What a Jew does reflects on God, so each Jew should set a high example of personal conduct before humanity. (The standard also applied intracommunally but takes on special intensity in relation to gentiles.) The rabbis term Jewish indecency *hillul Hashem*, "a profanation of God's name"; it tarnishes God's reputation among the nations. In contrast, they call Jewish acts of nobility *kiddush Hashem*, "the santification of God's name." Because this term also became the designation for martyrdom, people often overlook the broader meaning the rabbis give to it, as in their tale about Shimon ben Shetah. He bought an animal he later discovered to be carrying a precious jewel. Having bargained only with the purchase of the animal in mind, he then returned the jewel to the owner, causing the gentile to exclaim. "Blessed be the God of Shimon ben Shetah!" Here and elsewhere the rabbis exhort Jews to act in such exemplary fashion that they will draw people to God.

The *halakhah* makes the relationship between the inner and outer aspects of chosenness hierarchical, assigning the intracommunal responsibilities the higher priority. Most halakhic prescriptions detail personal, familial, and communal Jewish duties, whereas only a tiny number specify Jewish obligations to non-Jews or to non-Jewish society. (The degraded social situation imposed on Jews long rendered such topics utterly hypothetical, as became clear when the Emancipation initiated a radical change of interest.) Though secondary, the extracommunal aspects of chosenness remained indispensable since, despite the Covenant with the people of Israel, God remains covenanted to gentiles as well as to Jews. Moreover, Jewish faithfulness leads to everyone's redemption and therefore inevitably includes a collateral involvement with all humankind.

In our time, the existence of a Jewish state has intensified the possible effects of our people being chosen. Clearly, the classic intracommunal aspect of Jewish responsibility can now best be fulfilled in the State of Israel. Living in our ancestral land, one redolent of Jewish history, legend, and aspiration, and participating in a culturally self-determining Jewish community provides the Jewish people corporately with the optimum situation in which to work out its God-oriented destiny. Perhaps the extracommunal aspects of chosenness can also best be carried out by the State of Israel, for its behavior often attracts the world's attention. On the personal level, however, individual Israelis rarely have as close contact with non-Jews as Diaspora Jews do and mostly do not consider this aspect of chosenness very important.

Equality, Contemporary Jewry's Great Passion

Before discussing the effects of chosenness among Diaspora Jews I think it important to clarify my perspective, particularly since I seek to be aware of how much my view of Judaism has been shaped by being an American (which I take to be the present epitome of Diaspora existence generally). Statistically speaking, I reflect a minority American Jewish experience. Most American Jews grew up in or around the great urban centers of the American northeast, Chicago, or Los Angeles. My formative Jewish memories relate to Columbus, Ohio, in the 1930s, a city of about three hundred thousand with a Jewish community of perhaps eight thousand that had typically inadequate Jewish institutions. I studied for the rabbinate in Cincinnati and had five years of rabbinic service in the American "diaspora" before coming to live in a developing suburb of New York City.

Thus I think of the American Diaspora experience not primarily in terms of ethnically rich, old metropolitan neighborhoods but in terms of the experience of the small pockets of Jews who sought to maintain their identity amid gentiles who slowly became more hospitable. With the continuing geographic dispersion of American Jewry, my broad American perspective has become less idiosyncratic, particularly with more than 90 percent of our community now native born. This background, too, has something to do with my effort to distinguish what I judge to be a love for East European Jewish style from our continuing religious responsibilities as a Jewish community.

If we inquire, then, about how chosenness functions in "my" Diaspora, we must first acknowledge the thoroughgoing secularization of this community. Despite the recent resurgence of religious interest among what is still a minority of Jews, secularity continues to dominate our worldview for two old reasons. First, without the secularization of general society Diaspora Jews could not have achieved equality; as long as states were traditionally Christian or Moslem, Jews could not be equals. As various social sectors become indifferent to religion, Jews gain opportunity. Eager after centuries of discrimination to live in decent normality—a motive critical to Zionism—Diaspora Jews have a great stake in the secularization of general society and, to benefit from it, have willingly sacrificed much of their inherited Jewishness. Second, Jews have found the major instruments of secularization, the big city and the university, congenial to their received values. Clustering at both in highly disproportionate numbers, their socialization by these bodies should not be underestimated.

For purposes of analysis let us distinguish the social from the intellectual changes this process has introduced into Jewish life and its resulting effects on Jewish chosenness.

Modern Jewish life-styles differ most radically from that of the previous period in the decline of Jewish separatism and the full-scale adoption of non-Jewish standards. We dress in "their" clothes; educate in their manner; do research in the form they call scholarship; and consider ourselves cultured if we know their music, their art, their dance. We live by their aesthetics and, with certain limits, we model our life-style after theirs. Consequently we cannot easily employ an old tactic for maintaining ethnic distance: denigration of the other. Terms like *goy* and *shiksa* once left the lips heavy with emotion and powerfully reinforced the superiority of Jewish identity. But we Diaspora Jews have found much in the modern gentile way of life so humanly worthwhile that we have adopted it as our own. For the most part, little distinguishes the lives of most Diaspora Jews from that of the responsible non-Jews among whom they live.

Positively, the extraordinary satisfactions we American Jews have gained from living in a democratic society have made us passionate believers in "humanity." We find most people very much alike and the more we get to know strangers the more we discover how much we have in common. Human beings, for all their personal quirks and historic animosities, turn out to be truly of one sort, thus filling the Adam and Eve story with fresh meaning, one whose impact travel and the media continue to extend. This has given us a strong ethical expectation: People everywhere should not hate or exploit each other but, rather, give full equality to the disenfranchised. We know that Jews only began to get rights when people stopped thinking of us as Oriental barbarians and began considering us human beings with different practices and beliefs. Every time we remember how our families made the passage from degradation and penury to dignity and substance we recognize that we cannot remain content with the old passive commitment to extracommunal Jewish obligation. For us, it must be an active, major component of Jewish obligation. This duty appeals so strongly to us because it touches our self-interest as

THE SPARKS OF CHOSENNESS

well as our morality. We think it hard-headed realism to insure our security by keeping democratic institutions powerful and effective. When no one's rights can be effectively removed and social harmony assures the distribution of benefits to everyone, Jews can sleep more peacefully.

If Everyone Is Equal, How Can We Be Special?

This devotion to the idea of humanity provides the social basis for the almost universal rejection by American Jews of the traditional doctrine of the Chosen People. Despite generations of apologetics, the notion that God chose the Jews "from all other peoples" implies, to people in love with equality, an assertion of Jewish difference and superiority. My Diaspora, living among decent people who are as quasi-Christian as Jews are quasi-Jewish, does not experience the possession of the Torah as making the Jews so special. While the phrase "Judeo-Christian" can be easily abused, it properly reflects the considerable overlap of Jewish and Christian life-styles in a democratic setting, one that cannot be explained away entirely by the secularization of both faiths in recent years.

Surprisingly enough, we approach chosenness from a direction exactly opposite to that of a number of Israeli traditionalists and their inner-oriented Diaspora counterparts. They argue that post-Holocaust Jewry should approach this issue not merely from the divine side—God's choice leading to separation and thus hatred—but from that of Jewish experience. Living with the reality of neighbors who remain eerily obsessed by a desire to destroy the State of Israel despite every Israeli overture of friendship, they urge us to begin our consideration of chosenness by confronting the inexplicable endurance and malignancy of antisemitism. Something cosmic must be at stake in this over-determined hatred of the Jewish people for asking to be allowed to live in peace and security on its long cherished land.

In this reading, the ferocity and persistence of antisemitism become the Jews' unique burden in history, one that separates them from all other peoples. So unparalleled a chosenness can only find validation as God's inexplicable will for us. For reasons that lie beyond human understanding, God's choosing us and setting us apart from other peoples also destines us to this unique suffering. We cry out, pray for peace, await the Messiah, and trust in God's sure if inscrutable rule.

By contrast to their own full-blooded faith, traditionalists characterize our Diaspora rejection of chosenness in the name of universal
humanhood as vapid theorizing, a shallow ideology created to screen
our desire not to be outsiders. I think that charge has some merit
but ignores the fact that our experience of neighborliness has radically
differed from theirs. We do not need to compensate for a heavy
burden of antisemitism by ascribing it to God's singling us out. To
the contrary, though our Anglo-Jewish newspapers rarely miss an
opportunity to play up antisemitic incidents, our lives remain
remarkably free of them. We may encounter a verbal slur or, more
likely, have a sense of quiet exclusion from certain social contexts.
Mostly, antisemitism becomes manifest as the work of spray painters,
tombstone tippers, and sensation seekers, and is the espoused doctrine
of only the American political lunatic fringe, all of whom will quickly
be denounced by those with significant office and power. True,
antisemitism lurks latently in Western culture, and we can never
know when it will make a fresh and virulent appearance. Nonetheless,
my Diaspora's continuing experience of the oneness of humankind
impels it to mitigate its affirmation of Jewish uniqueness.

Can Our Beliefs Support Chosenness?

Other critics have argued that the Holocaust and the unceasing
record of antisemitism since then decisively unmask this liberal
Jewish ideal of one humanity as utterly illusory. Again, I concede
some truth to the charge, at least to the extent that we cannot any
longer maintain modern Jewry's old optimism about humankind's
will or capacity to eliminate its personal brutishness and societal
indecency. But our less idealized view of human nature has not
eradicated our belief in humanity. We would not be so distressed at
the failures of America and Western society if, like so many around us,
we could stop caring about human equality and mutual responsibility.

This reasoning applies most emphatically to what we learned
from the Holocaust. If a unitary humanity is an illusion and there
are only particular peoples with their ethnic interest, why do we
remain outraged that the Germans did what they absurdly thought
best for their nation? We expect every decent person to denounce
their evildoing—and the condoning of it by "good" people—as
intolerably heinous because they violated ethical norms every human
being knows, most particularly by ruling us out of humankind. Once
the Nazis' spurious theory of racial superiority stripped the Jews and

gypsies and some others of their human status, they could move toward their extermination with a clear conscience. The bitter history of this century should make it perfectly clear that excluding any group of people from our common humanity is a Nazi doctrine, and no Jewish mouth or mind should ever contain so profane a notion. Belief in one humanity may not be a basis for realistic political action, but it has gained sufficient moral power to have become a factor in human affairs and a major determinant of my Diaspora's view of chosenness.

There is an intellectual side to this religious development. Most modernized Jews find it cognitively dissonant to explain Jewish particularity as God's arbitrary choice of the people of Israel. To them it asserts more than they can easily say about what God does and much less than they believe about the human role in religion. God acting as an agent in the natural order clashes so with the scientific view of reality, and God's manifesting preference seems so patently unethical, that no modern Jewish thinker has espoused a strong doctrine of God's choosing. In fact, none appears to have much ambivalence about abandoning chosenness and devising a surrogate for it. Despite the marked postmodern skepticism toward science and its worldview, there has been little non-Orthodox movement to resuscitate the classical doctrine.

The relative passivity of the human role in the traditional view of chosenness has also proven difficult. Modern Jewish thinkers, eager to assert human dignity, made great capital of the Hebrews' free acceptance of the Covenant at Sinai. Yet in rabbinic literature as in the Bible, the majestic God dominates the alliance, setting the rules by which the Jews can enter it and remain acceptable partners. By contrast to religions that lay great stress on God's sovereignty, the Judaism of the rabbis allows human beings, particularly the pious and the learned, exceptional liberty toward God. However, compared to the modern conception of personal dignity involving self-determination, the freedoms granted seem constricted and minimal, leaving people more its accepting subjects than its active cocreators.

Our modern sense of our spiritual capacity and the resulting worth that inheres in us requires us to claim a more active role in our relationship with God, Zionism being the classic example. We cannot any longer see the religious legitimacy of limiting our action to waiting for the Messiah to bring us back to the land of Israel. We believe in taking more personal responsibility for our destiny than our traditionalist forebears did, so we pursue politics as well as *mitzvot.* The return to the land, which another generation of sages called heresy, and toward which some still have great ambivalence, appears to most of the rest of world Jewry a proper exercise of Jewish initiative in the service of God. Our theological reinterpretation of chosenness must reflect this revised view of the relationship.

Tracking the Benefits and the Difficulties of Chosenness

Before undertaking that, I want to extend this analysis of the social foundations of this area of belief by sketching in my impression of how our residual belief in "chosenness" still manifests itself in our lives. I shall do so by indicating how I see it in some of the best and worst aspects of American Jewish life.

Since most of my analysis of Diaspora Jewry has focused on its secularized majority, let me redress the balance somewhat by some comment about those Jews who have rejected modernity, primarily the Hasidim and "the *yeshivah* world." In treating the continuing effects of a traditional view of chosenness, I can trace them in the lives of the more numerous Orthodox who have secularized to the extent that they see *halakhah* permitting it. At their best, both groups, knowing they serve the one and only God, conduct their affairs with piety, filling them with *kedushah*, holiness. Impressively, this spirituality characterizes not merely exceptional scholars or noted leaders but ordinary Jews who ennoble their everyday routines out of their consciousness of being part of God's chosen people. Though they may occasionally share the dejection that contemporary existence begets, they can meet it with the inner certainty that by living by the Torah their lives incarnate a cosmic significance. They therefore understand their separateness from other peoples and why Jews sometimes suffer specially for it. Though they do not welcome such affliction, they often can transcend it, since no mystery can obscure the fact that God still reigns. American Jewry can proudly point to their lives as one of its most attractive models of contemporary Jewish existence.

This same sense of chosenness creates what my Diaspora considers the worst of this Jewish way. Some traditionally devout Jews concentrate so on the duties detailed in the classic texts and the customs practiced in their communities that they ignore or reject the outer aspects of chosenness. They are concerned about a Jew's relation to the world only insofar as it obstructs or facilitates performance of their intracommunal Jewish duty. General human problems like natural disaster, mass starvation, over-population, and the depletion of natural resources they leave to the gentiles. If accused of narrow unconcern for others, they quickly remind one of the texts obligating certain Jewish duties to gentiles "for the sake of peace." They interpret this not as a summons to social activism as do most modern Jews but, rather, as a precept limited to the minimum Jews must do to avoid disruptive antisemitism. Thus, some have argued that the *halakhah* does not require Jews to pay taxes and we must do so only if we believe we might be found out and thus cause a problem for all Jews. This rigorous inner-directedness also creates an oppressive defensiveness that admits no humanly significant discovery not already contained in the Written or Oral Torah. It also rules out in advance any possibility of historical or ethical fallibility in a classic Jewish text. To some extent, this self-centeredness can be understood as a reaction to our recent unprecedented suffering. Yet in this context, appropriate self-concern can easily become Jewish self-aggrandizement, as in the contention that the Holocaust entitles Jews to special consideration but requires no Jewish reciprocity. For such Jews, chosenness implies societal get but no societal give.

Theologically, this truncated version of chosenness identifies God so intimately with the people of Israel that what is good for the Jews becomes the exclusive good. One need not be highly secularized to find this stance Jewishly objectionable. It offends against the classic Jewish doctrines that God's choice of Israel confers greater responsibility, not special privilege, and that the God of Israel remains most truly God of all humankind.

The secularized bulk of American Jewry shows similarly commendable and objectionable interpretations of being chosen. Their modernized Jewishness expresses itself most notably in their service to humanity, that is, in terms of the extracommunal aspect of chosenness. No worthy humane American endeavor, governmental, communal, or private, that has welcomed Jewish participation has lacked for significant Jewish support, leadership, skill, and imagination. In science, literature, and the arts—as creators, financial sponsors, or faithful consumers—American Jews participate in humanistic enterprises in overwhelming statistical disproportion. They have been a direct cause of much of American culture's world stature. For these Jews, chosenness primarily means universal ethical mission. Their general social accomplishment has brought them a pervading sense of personal dignity and Jewish fulfillment. They appreciate being part of an elite folk, one historically devoted to high human achievement and properly proud of its exceptional recent contributions to the enhancement of humanity's welfare. They consider Jewish ethical responsibility a matter of ethnic *noblesse oblige*, a unique folk standard that distinguishes us from all other peoples. They have surely shifted the balance of duty in the traditional pattern of living our chosenness, but the enlarged scope of this duty clearly derives from it.

As a result of this compelling outer-directedness, these Jews often fail to have a counterbalancing devotion to the inner obligations of chosenness. Taking *mitzvah* rather exclusively in its sense of good deed, they have little sense of it as commandment and almost none of it as particular Jewish discipline. While they may esteem a vague Jewishness they call "tradition," they may maximally see it as providing guidance, but not anything that might be called a mandate. The insidiousness of this slight Jewishness may be gauged from the odd case of the large proportion of Jews who proudly term themselves "Orthodox" because they prefer to *davven* in an Orthodox *shul* (when they go), though otherwise being only arbitrarily observant. At least these Jews still maintain a modicum of Jewish usage while most other Jews use their ethical concerns to justify their Jewish apathy and unconcern. And with their hearts turned to humankind, their rate of intermarriage continues to rise. Perhaps their worst trait is their Jewish self-hate. They dedicate themselves to high-minded humanitarianism because unconsciously but decisively they cannot accept being Jewish. In their extroverted version of chosenness, they can grandly work to ameliorate the sufferings of any needy people—except of course their own.

Theologically, these Jews err in identifying themselves so with the covenant God made with the children of Noah that they forget they learned about it through the Covenant of Sinai. If they do not sincerely share its particular faith, one they learned as part of their ethnic socialization, they will not long feel or transmit this compelling need to work for the good of all human beings.

Flashes of Chosenness amid Our Secularized Existence

Somewhere in between these extremes of sanctity and sin lies the ongoing folk continuation of Israel's ancient Covenant, which surfaces at largely unnoticed moments. Consider, for example, the uncommon pride most American Jews have in high humanistic attainment. They deem it something of a personal confirmation when

Jews like Saul Bellow or Cynthia Ozick make another substantial contribution to American culture. While normally quite impressed with money and popularity, they have a rather different, so to speak, less "Jewish," regard for authors like Belva Plavin or Irving Wallace who have far more readers but far less staying power. We connect Jewishness with Nobel Prize winners because, in some residual way, we know our people to be special and expect that to manifest itself in high human attainment. This indicates to me our residual sense that being Jewish has something transcendent about it, for we would not have such expectations if we considered Jewishness only a matter of ordinary ethnic identity.

A second locus may be identified in the realm of civic behavior. Though they love equality and wish to be thought of as being like everyone else, most American Jews emphatically feel that our community ought to stand apart from other groups in rates of alcoholism, philandering, divorce, rape, or murder. When a prominent Jew, even one only peripherally connected with the Jewish community, commits egregious knavery all Jews feel besmirched. Supreme Court Justice Abe Fortas forced from office because of doubtful morality; Jewish leader Bernard Bergman convicted of gouging the aged and ill in his nursing homes; billionaire Leona Helmsley debasing employees, chiseling suppliers, and cheating the government; Ivan Boesky and all the other Jewish names connected with the Wall Street insider trading scandals of the late 1980s—all of these disgraced their entire people. Even Jews who had never heard the Hebrew phrase *hillul Hashem* were Jewishly judgmental when they heard what had transpired. We are rightfully sensitive to giving our enemies ammunition for new attacks. Yet beyond our ethnic defensiveness lies our commitment to the notion that Jews ought to exemplify high human values.

A special word needs to be said in this regard about the State of Israel. If what one individual Jew does affects every other Jew, how much more is that true of the State of Israel's behavior. Thus were the State of Israel to conduct itself with the limited idealism of most other nations—particularly like that of its neighbors Syria and Iraq— I believe most of world Jewry, despite their secularization, would feel such normality to be a Jewish loss. This does not mean most of us expect the State of Israel to be saintly or perfect; that is a standard only political debaters raise to deride others, and most Jews are too realistic to employ it. The real issue is how to combine the realities of power with the furtherance of Jewish ideals in a time when the abuse of power has become a most pervasive and hateful sin. Positively put, world Jewry long took exalted pride in the State of Israel because it used its power for high human achievement despite extraordinary challenges. Pressured by enemies on every side, poor in natural resources, socially unintegrated because of an openness to Jewish immigrants, manipulated and tempted by the world's great powers, the Israelis have been uncommonly humane. And they have fought often and hard without becoming militaristic, have lived with terrorism without giving way to indiscriminate hatred for their enemies, and, above all, have not surrendered their democracy to a military junta to meet their crises. Theirs has largely been a noble human accomplishment, exactly the sort of unusual achievement Jews expect of Jews. And this unbroken sense of Jewish chosenness prompts every caring Jew to have a personal concern about how the State of Israel eventually resolves the vexing question of the status of the West Bank Palestinians.

Reflection and observation proceeding hand in hand, my description of the social realities of chosenness today already has reflected something of my theological views on this topic, and I now turn to the task of making a direct statement of them.

15   Covenant, Not Chosenness

POLEMICAL MOTIVE largely prompted me to select the word "covenant" to characterize the substantive focus of the theological movement that emerged in the 1950s. We rebels thought it unseemly for the ruling rationalisms to rely on general culture to tell us what remained true in Judaism and prevent the validation of a rich theory of Jewish particularity. We also believed they had effectively reduced God to a figment of the mind or the psyche. We affirmed the intrinsic truth of Jewish particularity and knew it had to do with our people's response to God's "commanding," which prompted us to more fully Judaize the non-Orthodox theology of Jewish duty. Though the term was not yet in common use, "covenant" seemed to me to point to our commitment to an actional piety of *mitzvah*. (I later learned that one stage of early American Puritanism had used this word in a somewhat similar way.) I can best approach the meaning and application of the term by following the intellectual trail that firmly embedded it in my theology. I begin with a consideration of three rationalistic efforts to offset rationalism's own general delegitimation of Jewish particularity: the identification of folk and idea, the appeal to science, and the sociologization of Judaism.

Two Early Efforts to Fashion a Rationalistic Particularism

In the mid-19th century, Nahman Krochmal attempted to link Jewish particularity with rationalism by means of an argument with Hegelian overtones. Krochmal utilized Hegel's teaching that Absolute Spirit was the reality moving through nature and history to establish the Jewish people's eternality. Though Spirit itself survived all change, it had to take concrete, finite form to make itself effective in time. Therefore, as long as the Jewish people identified itself with Spirit—effectively with monotheism—it bound its own destiny to it and would never die.

Early in this century, Leo Baeck made a somewhat similar case for the eternal particularity of Jews as long as they remained devoted to universal truth. As a disciple of Cohen, Baeck's rationalism prohibited him from making quasi-metaphysical claims about history and spirit as did Krochmal. Yet Baeck defied his customary neo-

Kantian approach to reality by his argument identifying the Jewish people with the key universal idea. Since ethical monotheism is a rational conception, any people could have discovered it. But, claimed Baeck, only the people of Israel did so with such impact that they made it the basis of their folk existence. Over the centuries this folk and this idea became so identified with one another that were the people of Israel to die, Baeck asserts, so would the authentic concept of ethical monotheism. It is an astonishing notion. That a rational idea cannot be known without the people most devoted to it seems thoroughly self-contradictory. Without a Hegelian philosophy to link eternal ideas with historic groups, this proposal has little but its Jewish devotion to commend it.

Far more appealing to rationalists have been arguments for Jewish distinctiveness based on scientific models. Before the rise of sociology, biology provided a handy explanation, the nascent notion of race. Thinkers like Kaufmann Kohler, Franz Rosenzweig, and the young Martin Buber attributed the special character of Jewish life to our racially distinct "Jewish blood." Increased knowledge and hard-headed observation soon made that theory untenable; since Hitler, even its figurative use has been an abomination.

The study of human behavior provided another possibility as thinkers applied the concept of personality to nations, giving rise to the discipline of "folk psychology." Its most influential Jewish proponent was Ahad Haam. Acknowledging other peoples' ethnic talents, he identified Israel's genius as the creation of a high culture characterized by an exalted ethics. His Zionism, therefore, emphasized culture rather than politics and envisioned a revived Jewish state serving as the spiritual, that is, cultural, center of world Jewry.

Despite the appeal to the nonreligious of construing Jewish folk culture or nationalism as the vehicle for Jewish continuity, Ahad Haam's secularized theory of chosenness has fared poorly in the State of Israel and the Diaspora. Since sociologists created and elaborated the notion of "culture," folk psychology and the idea of peoples having specific ethnic talents have become intellectually unsupportable. Moreover, the more open-mindedly one studies the history of Jewish culture, the less one can argue that it evidences a gift for high culture and a distinctive ethics.

A Third Solution: Redefining Judaism Sociologically

Mordecai Kaplan rejected the concept of our chosenness as supernaturalistic and undemocratic. He dismissed ideational solutions to the problem created by rationalism because one cannot convert universal ideas into any one people's special property. And, though considering himself Ahad Haam's disciple, he rejected the Zionist master's theories about the Jewish psyche as unscientific. Instead he turned to sociology to speak rationalistically but positively of group individuality.

Human beings always live as part of social groups that powerfully shape human individuality. They provide us with language, values, manners, and a worldview encompassing the near at hand and the ultimate—in short, with a particular culture (or, as Kaplan termed it in the 1930s, a "civilization"). While all cultures have elements in common, they become distinctive as a result of the natural interplay of the ethnic group with its physical environment.

The operative word here is "natural"; things simply work this way and this knowledge exerts a certain normative force. Seeking to live universally contradicts the ingrained particularity of human existence and is therefore irrational. Of course, all thoughtful people will respond to certain universal motifs in nature but they will also necessarily express them in terms of their particular culture. Judaism's distinctiveness came not from its ideas, for insofar as they were true they were universal. Rather, it came from Jewish culture, the specific ways that Jews over the ages have appropriated, articulated, and transmitted their people's version of these generally available insights. Those of us born into the Jewish people should naturally live by its dynamic, ever-evolving civilization; anything else would be unnatural.

Kaplan also advocated a vigorous Zionism to give our culture the rejuvenating power of a national home. Yet, making peoplehood and culture the focus of his Judaism, he also commended Diaspora Jewish existence, which he envisioned as living in two civilizations. Fortunately, democratic nations consider the mutual fructification of cultural styles beneficial and Jewish culture has something particularly valuable to contribute to America, namely its fusion of ethnicity and religion, something the American folk culture has not yet developed. This bicivilizational approach has had considerable appeal over the decades, initially as our postimmigrant generations sought to preserve their folk styles, then because its cultural emphasis enabled acculturating agnostics to be at home Jewishly, and more recently as Americans generally came to value cultural pluralism.

However, the theory makes possible a troubling eventuality that Kaplan faced unflinchingly. If every mature civilization climaxes in a religion, then we can expect that the American people will one day fulfill the promise of their sociality and create an American faith. With the American civilization then humanly sufficient, what reason will there be for Jews to continue living in the Jewish civilization? Kaplan candidly says there will be none. Of course, some people may still enjoy doing Jewish things but should they not, there will be no theoretically compelling reason for them not to abandon Judaism. Kaplan's sociological Jewishness thus foresees and accepts the possible end of the Jewish people and its culture.

What Depth of Value Adheres to Jewish Particularity?

Once again an instrumental legitimation of particularity raises the troublesome question: When one particularity might do as well as another, why should we devote ourselves to the minority way with its attendant special burdens? Kaplan's theory compels us to ask what degree of ultimacy we ascribe to the Jewish people. The issue is not an either/or choice between having supreme value or none at all but the more subtle one of whether Jewishness is only very valuable to us or whether it has a certain absoluteness about it. To be sure, advocates of the former position would grieve at the demise of the Jewish civilization but that would result from a personal emotional loss and a sadness at the decrease in the world's social differentiation. These temporary griefs would be compensated for by the benefits that would soon come from having one's natural social needs satisfactorily met by another civilization.

This apparently hypothetical conclusion has, in a way, become something of a reality in the continuing drift of American Jews into intermarriage. One's appreciation of the Jewish civilization hardly seems a reason to stand in the way of consummating one's love for a person who gets the same rewards from the American folk. Perhaps many of the resulting families may well carry out their stated desire to raise their children as Jews. However, the rising rate of intermarriage demonstrates how substantial a proportion of our community feels that cultural Jewish identity offers little not already well celebrated in American decency.

I do not see that any contemporary rationalism can effectively cope with the deeply troubling problem of our decreasing bent for Jewish particularity—but I admit that many Jews, in America and elsewhere, do not share my distress. Some sleep peacefully with the recognition that they and their children mark their family's transition out of Judaism into a local version of humanity. Others so enjoy their social and spiritual freedom that they can accept equality's dissolution of Jewish identity as long as their descendants remain good people. And most Jews, I think, simply do not want to face the clash between their two great loves, Jewish and general identity; they certainly would be most uneasy about our erecting new barriers between ourselves and our neighbors.

I am convinced, however, that many Jews have also been moved to rethink their putative democratic unconcern about long-range Jewish continuity by the recurrent, massive threats to Jewish existence in our time. At some primal level, they have discovered that Jewish survival means more to them and the world than mere ethnic loyalty can explain. Most would find it difficult to say baldly what they deeply believe—that the Jews are, in principle, not dispensable. I seek a theological statement adequate to this intuition of absoluteness about the Jewish people, and I do not see that it can be derived from theologies that limit themselves to what can be extrapolated from the human grounds of faith—the standard liberal procedure. I believe we must supplement human choosing with God's own action if we are to explain to ourselves our fundamental commitment to the continuity of the people of Israel. Yet I believe the traditional view that God "chose us from among all peoples and gave us the Torah" clashes too much with our sense of history and reality for us to reaffirm it.

The Shift to the Mutuality of Partnership

This explains to me why, for all the veneration American Jews have lavished on Abraham Heschel, his treatment of the Jewish people's special character has had little resonance. Heschel asserted his God-centered view—the sharp contrast with Mordecai Kaplan's humanism was almost certainly intentional—as a simple consequence of the reality of revelation. God's never repeated act at Sinai turned the escaping Hebrew slaves into God's chosen people and set them apart from all other peoples to serve God in special devotion. Heschel balanced this neotraditionalism by arguing that Judaism contains far more human interpretation than divine revelation and that the law functioned as a personal, spiritual way to God's presence. Nonetheless, once he made the incomparably transcendent God the authority behind the Oral and the Written Torah, obedience became the leading motif of Jewish piety. He meant by this doctrine to deny the modern exaltation of self-determination and in so doing stated a position more extreme than I believe true. Though my postmodern religiosity acknowledges God as the ground of my personhood and the standard of my behavior, I also find something sacred about exercising my personal autonomy in relation to God. This goes far beyond what the biblical authors and the rabbis thought appropriate to the relationship between God and humankind. Yet it seems to me that their term, "Covenant," lends itself to a personalist reinterpretation that allows me to express my belief in an enhanced reciprocity between God and people.

The idea first occurred to me as a result of my impression that Martin Buber and Franz Rosenzweig had succeeded in balancing an activist human religiosity with an unabashed avowal of God's independence, authority, and relatedness. In their view persons replace rationality as the standard of proper thinking and relationships supplant system in supplying structure to existence. Buber and Rosenzweig know a God who is both other than us and as real as we are. Each made the relationship between that God and us the heart of his thinking and understood this intimacy to provide a radically new, nonverbal version of God's revelation and choice. Though they both speak of the Covenant relationship from time to time, neither made this motif central to his interpretation of Judaism. Yet had they not taught me the theological virtue of the metaphor of relationship, I would not have been empowered to find a way between Buber's antinomianism and Rosenzweig's dogmatic legalism and disdain of ethnicity.

Rosenzweig's view of chosenness closely resembles that of Heschel because Rosenzweig also utterly identified Jewish peoplehood with the receipt and observance of Torah. Having God's law, we have no need of the common sinews of nationality: land, secular language, and culture. We even have no real interest in history, the arena in which people who do not yet have God seek to find God, for by Torah we know ourselves already allied to God. For Rosenzweig, therefore, we are God's chosen people in the classic sense that we have been given the Torah.

With revelation and chosenness so closely linked, we may say that Rosenzweig's non-Orthodox view turned choice as God's gift of words into God's presence in love. This resolves some of the standard modern difficulties with chosenness, for we know love to be selective and preferential yet we do not normally deride it as unethical. It also explains why we, like all lovers, consider our relationship different from those of all other lovers, though similarities abound. And, like all who have found a true love, we seek to be faithful and cannot conceive of abandoning our love to seek another.

Heschel could not accept such personalizing of chosenness for it does not yield the kind of God-authorized Jewish discipline his theory of prophetic sympathy establishes. Rosenzweig remains sufficiently a modern to refuse to grant authority to the law simply as a matter of inheritance. Instead, he gave each Jew the task of relegitimating the received rules by transforming them through observance into personal commands. Otherwise, Rosenzweig placed all Jews in principle under the imperative claim of the law and only existential "inability" might temporarily excuse them from it.

Rosenzweig's view of chosenness has had little better reception than that of Heschel, for he too keeps us passive before the law's inequities, minimizes the significance of effective Jewish ethnicity, and denies the importance of recent Jewish history. As a result, though right-wing existentialism has been widely admired for its reaffirmation of Jewish law, its theory creates a new problem: How can we reconcile the personal autonomy that our sense of self requires with the corporate nature of the Jewishness that is basic to our being?

The Necessity and Limits of Individualism

In Buber's version of revelation/chosenness as love/I–thou the personal element is radicalized, thus creating the existentialist left. By transforming God's act into a divine–human relationship and the one-time event of Sinai into a long-term, historical development, Buber turned the contract of Torah into the bidding that arises from intimacy; in other words, he replaces *halakhah* with the marital I–thou. This led him to a specific kind of antinomianism that we can best understand if we first clear up some common misunderstandings of his thought. He believed God commands us in the sense that entering a relationship with someone always imposes duties on the partners. He did not deny the legitimate authority of institutions and practices that effectively mediate God's presence. And he had a strong social component to his thought, believing that in exceptional moments peoples confront God and thus transform mere ethnicity into authentic nationhood.

According to Buber, the Bible spoke of a real experience the Jewish people had at Sinai and subsequently, for centuries, under the charismatic leadership of the prophets. A relationship unique to human history resulted: A nation bound itself to serve God through history by transforming its corporate existence. Experiencing God as an active partner in this process, it called itself "chosen."

This strong social theory led Buber to become an early leader in cultural Zionism and general religious socialism. Nonetheless, when it came to religious duty he undercut this theory of the group by insisting rigorously that only the person-based I–thou meeting can rightly command us. Thus, prior communal enactments exercise a legitimate claim on us only as they can continue to involve us in a legitimating I–thou encounter. Practically, he felt that in our time the minutiae of Jewish law and custom inhibited rather than enhanced the possibility of personal encounter with God. Refusing to carry out any practice unauthorized by such a personal experience, he lived as a nonobservant Jew.

Much in Rosenzweig's and Buber's theories of chosenness/ revelation speaks to my own sense of religious truth. By knowing command yet honoring persons and establishing Jewish uniqueness without invidiousness, their views commend themselves to my postmodern theological sensibility. Yet neither provides me with a satisfactory theology of Jewish obligation. Buber, despite his nonrationalism and philosophy of relationship, remained a faithful child of the Enlightenment in demanding that the self exercise final authority over previously defined duties, albeit as part of an immediate I–thou encounter. Rosenzweig, intuitive as ever about authentic Jewish existence, knew we had to have more tradition and discipline than that. Nonetheless, he could only Judaize our devoted individualism by dogmatically asserting the binding power of the Law, a thesis he qualified by his notion of nonverbal revelation, by calling for the personalization of statutes, and by acknowledging the right of temporary dissent.

Toward a Jewish Selfhood

We shall not arrive at a theory of robust Jewish duty as long as we do not transform the Enlightenment's self into a Jewish self, the kind of person I contend our religious experience has shown many of us we are. As I reached this understanding of our problem, the notion of Covenant as relationship appeared to me to open a way toward its solution. It provided me with a metaphor keyed to the involvement of the whole self yet pointing to the priority of the

Jewish people in our relationship with God—the Covenant being made with the folk as a whole, not with Jews as isolates.

This understanding of the sociality of the self explains how one of our major societal ills, privatism and its associated loneliness and depression, intellectually derives from taking persons atomistically rather than as intrinsically social. The same is true in the Jewish community. The theological root of Jewish nonobservance is the doctrine that we are persons-in-general who happen-also-to-be-Jews. But if Jewish particularity does not require external legitimation and has a self-validating quality, theologies built on the primacy of universal selfhood can never give adequate dignity to being one-of-Israel. Moreover, with the modern notion of universalism itself now revealed as particular to a given sociocultural situation, our intuition of the universal dignity of human selfhood itself requires a particular base, one that Covenant/covenant provides.

Where the self-in-general finds its ground in the Noahide covenant with God, the Jewish self has its roots in the Jewish people's historic relationship with God. This Covenant-Jew is no schizoid person-in-general who incidentally though gratefully participates in Jewish ethnicity but is a Jew/person at once, in utter existential depth. Throughout biblical times, the Israelites maintained a sufficient number of these people oriented to God and folk that they became a critical ethnic mass and the choosing/chosenness of the Covenant came into being. Today that critical core group has dwindled perilously and simple ethnicity must carry a burden of continuity that it cannot long sustain. Theology seeks to supply the intellectual component that a self-determining generation requires in order to change its Jewish ways. Jews living as part of a community bound today, as for millennia, in a true relationship with God will find their individual responsibilities arising from being commanded as part of our personal-yet-folk intimacy with God. God's quality exalts the relationship, making its entailments compelling. At the same time we, the humans who must live out the Covenant as given selves in a specific time and place, determine how our tradition must be continued, modified, or newly expressed to reflect our continuing faithfulness.

I shall return to these themes in the succeeding chapters. Here I wish to extend my analysis of the hermeneutic fruitfulness of Covenant as relationship by applying it to two diverse themes: Jewish religious unity and the nature of rabbinic discourse.

This Concept Helps Us Understand Jewish Life Today

From the Covenantal perspective, one can see two primary spiritual challenges facing contemporary Judaism, the one taken up most notably by the Jews of the State of Israel, the other by Diaspora Jewry, though both communities share each other's concern. In the former case, an extraordinary historic opportunity, seized by Jewish initiative and courage, enabled our people to reassert its ethnicity with a fullness of land and sovereignty we had not known for two millennia. The Covenant classically involved our people living as a nation and attempting to deal with realpolitik within the tensions of survival/sanctification. Zionism at its best has pursued this Covenant-ideal, and in the many ways the State of Israel has fulfilled this unique theo-political vision it has exalted the spiritual life of Jewry worldwide.

At its best, Diaspora Jewry has pursued the other great spiritual opportunity of this era: to discover what it might mean to be an enfranchised self as a believing Jew. Our Emancipation prompted us to radically amplify our tradition's high regard for individual dignity and the place of human interpretation in delineating Covenantal obligation. Two centuries of experience have led us to attach such religious worth to democratic pluralism that we have sought to reshape personal and communal Jewish life in its terms. As a result, modern Jews have been uncommonly effective workers for our society's improvement and have brought a historically unparalleled tolerance into Jewish communal affairs.

By Covenantal standards, neither of these agendas should be permitted to become the exclusive concern of our people. With some exaggeration, we can say that the bipolarity of Covenant has now made itself manifest geographically. Jews of the State of Israel, who seek ever better ways of expressing Covenanted nationhood today, know they need to give significant attention to the modern reinterpretation of God's grant of individual dignity. This theo-political agenda seems so central to Covenant-continuity that it regularly becomes the focus for Diaspora Jewry's pride or dismay at Israeli actions. The converse holds for world Jewry. The individualism that motivates its admirable voluntarism and pluralism also causes its thoughtful leaders to worry about its limited sense of ethnicity and community. With the Covenant constituting an ethnic commitment to historical survival into a messianic future, caring Jews everywhere cannot fail to feel the dangers that accompany its triumphs.

Thinking this way also quickly exposes the crux of our contemporary controversies over what unites and divides the Jewish religious community everywhere. If God chose Israel and distinguished it by the gift of the Oral as well as Written Torah, then not observing the *halakhah* or interpreting it in ways not sanctioned by its most devout students and scholars makes one a sinner and perhaps a heretic. From this perspective, democratic pluralism and individual dignity do not justify transgressing God's commandments, and the observant and the profligate are not one happy family of faith.

Despite this theoretical chasm and the consequent tensions that have roiled our community, a considerable measure of communal goodwill has persisted among us. Much of this can be ascribed to Jewish realism, to our revulsion at doing the antisemites' work for them after all we have suffered. No small part of it also arises, I suggest, from our intuition of our common meta-halakhic foundation. Covenantally, caring non-halakhic Jews can be understood as fervently seeking to serve God as participants in the Jewish people's historic relationship with God and guided by its tradition, though convinced that Covenant-faithfulness today mandates their deviance from the past. They persist in seeking communal unity because they believe that what binds them to all Jews far exceeds what separates them. So too the notion of relationship makes many of our old labels— Orthodox, Conservative, Reform, Reconstructionist, secularist— largely irrelevant. Instead, one can best gain insight into people's Jewishness by judging with what personal seriousness they take it. A Judaism that functions essentially as a leisure-time activity or occasional adjunct to one's core concerns seems an unworthy expression of Covenantal identity regardless of the ideological label its bearer claims. By contrast, Covenantal selfhood begins with the effort to base one's life on one's Jewish faith and then seek to give it expression in all one's ways. Wherever such devout non-Orthodox Jewishness makes itself evident it will, I am convinced, evoke a certain measure of respect from many of those who, in principle, consider it deviant.

The Covenantal Basis of the Rabbis' Uncommon Logic

I had expected thinking Covenantally to give me greater insight into contemporary Jewish life. I was, however, surprised and delighted to discover its virtue in explaining the Jewish past, specifically the rabbinic "logic" that had long been considered eccentric by Hellenic standards. In the Greek model of argument, the syllogism, truth is a direct deduction from the major premise. Moreover, it insists on the law of the excluded middle, that something must be specified as either "a" or "non-a" with all other possibilities being excluded. When one reasons from a single, dominant premise and proceeds unambiguously, what follows must be unitary and without contradiction. But as participants in the Covenant, the rabbis' discourse begins, as it were, with two quite different "premises," God and Israel. In such a system, radically clashing opinions may be quite logical, for a thinker may validly make deductions from either "assumption" as long as one retains a place in one's thought for its corollary.

The notorious rabbinic hospitality to contradiction arises from the substantial differences of the two Covenant partners from one another. Where Israel is particular, historical, limited, and error-prone, God, so to speak, is transcendentally universal, enduring, more limitless than limited, more perfect than anything else. The rightful demands or needs of one or the other Covenant partners can radically diverge, yet we know them to be intimately involved in lasting intimacy: "*Adonai,* [whom we know to be] our [Covenant] God, *Adonai* is [the only/our only] One."

In fact, this relationship gives rise to a logic in which legitimate arguments may be made from any of three perspectives. A rabbi may speak from the standpoint of either partner in the Covenant: What does the One God require of us now? Or, what does the Jewish people now need? Or he may proceed holistically, seeking the balance between the concerns of God and Israel. For centuries now, scholars have carried on both *aggadah* and *halakhah* by this Covenantal dialectic, as even a cursory exposition of some familiar tensions in rabbinic teaching makes clear.

The *aggadah* overflows with acknowledgments of God's omnipresence, e.g., God is the place of the world but the world is not God's place. Yet the rabbis also often speak of the Divine Presence, the *Shekhinah,* withdrawing from the land of Israel due to sin or going into exile with Israel. Where Greek rationality rejects the simultaneous assertion of God being everywhere and absent or in a specific place, the Covenantal Dialectic accepts their combination in its logic. God, thought of only as God's very self, is of course omnipresent; how could there be a place without God? Yet God as the Covenanted One associates with Israel both by withdrawing when they sin and becoming present when they suffer.

Similarly, knowing God to be the Creator, Sovereign, and Ruler of the universe, the rabbis consider it heinous to suggest that there might be a Second Power with God. Yet rabbis can also unhesitatingly diminish God's greatness by saying, "When the Israelites do not do God's will, they, as it were, weaken God's power"; or by having God say, "When ye are My witnesses, I am God, but when ye are not My witnesses I am, as it were, not God." In these latter dicta bold voices speak out for Israel's importance under the Covenant, and since their faith is bipolar, their words can be Torah though they approach blasphemy.

Again, the rabbis teach that God's love rather than Israel's merit brought God to choose them to receive the Torah and be God's own special people. Or they say that God legally acquired them by redeeming them from Egypt or, when they hesitated to accept the Torah at Sinai, coerced them into doing so by lifting the mountain over their heads. So classic Jewish theology ruminates on the divine prerogatives. But it also does so from the perspective of Israel, perhaps the most famous being the legend of God unsuccessfully peddling the Torah to the nations until Israel joyfully shouted, "We shall do it and hearken to it." So too the Sinai coercion story has a rejoinder from the human side, that in the days of Mordecai and Esther the people willingly accepted what had once been forced on them.

The Covenantal Dialectic also clarifies the clash between the two authoritative views as to when the Messiah will come. One insists God will send the Messiah only when God wills to do so, or, which amounts to the same thing, when Israel is utterly bereft of good deeds. The other view insists that the Messiah will arrive when Israel's acts merit it, such as when they all repent, or hearken to God's voice even for one day, or keep a Sabbath, or two.

Rabbinic *aggadah* joyously accommodates sweeping opinions from either side of the Covenant because it extends an equal welcome to categorical dicta from the other side. Then, even if no great number of teachers seeks to make the dialectical tension of the views explicit, the inclusiveness of the literature itself will transmit the fullness of Covenantal thinking.

The same pattern can be observed in the dialectical tension one often finds in the development of the *halakhah* on a given topic. A *posek* (decisor) can be described as being a *maḥmir*, stringent, in this case (or in general), or perhaps as being a *mekil*, lenient. Yet the logic of the *halakhah* recognizes that, all things being equal, though one respected decisor rules that Jews should act one way and another esteemed *rav* concludes that we should do the opposite, both positions are authoritative. This has nothing to do with reverence for pluralism but derives from the logic of Covenant. The *maḥmirim*, identifying the *halakhah* with God's own authority and holiness, let the law make its fullest demands upon us. The *mekilim*, recognizing that the law was not meant for angels but for human beings with all their limitations, allow human considerations to come to the fore in their decision making. Both approaches to the law have a rightful place in the life derived from God's partnership with the people of Israel. The halakhic process itself, by encompassing both tendencies, has a dynamism reflecting the Covenantal Dialectic.

In sum, the concept of the Covenant commends itself not only as the best metaphor we have for speaking of Israel's continuing uniqueness but for understanding its contemporary religious struggle over identity and for explicating the uncommon intellectual structure utilized by our greatest teachers to expound Judaism's meaning and delineate its duties.

16   The Dialectic of Living in Covenant

HAVE BEEN CRITICAL of the modern notions of the solitary self and self-validating universalism in the hope of permitting the consciousness of our particularity to make itself felt and make its proper claim on our selfhood. At the same time I have tried to insist that this strong religious particularism must allow for self-determining persons and a central regard for humankind entire. Let me now indicate something of the proper balance I envision between these potentially clashing Covenant commitments. How shall we live with the conflicts that arise between the Jewish self and the Jewish polity? And then, how shall our people be true to itself without losing its proper involvement with humanity?

I begin by restating the first premise of this position: The self gains its inestimable worth neither by the self-evident nature of its quality nor our willing it, but by being convenanted to God. It cannot then demand a Kantian or Sartrean radical autonomy or self-legislation without regard to God, the Source of our freedom and the Standard of all value. We employ our will rightfully when God serves as its limiting condition, better, as our partner in decision making.

Today, with selfhood fundamental to our philosophic theories and political practice, we cannot as easily indicate why human collectives ought validly exercise significant sway over us. Let us set aside the extreme possibilities: totalitarianism and the absolute primacy of the group, and a radical individualism that proceeds without primary involvement with others. Practically, most of us will accept group authority for the sake of simple social order or group functioning, but we retain the right of conscience to dissent or withdraw from a beloved community should an exceptional issue arise. We face our greatest perplexity when our dialectical commitments pull us in two directions.

The Group's Rightful Authority over Autonomous Selves

Acknowledging a certain primacy of selfhood, I begin my analysis of this problem with a repudiation of the self as a monad. God makes

221

us individuals but also an inseparable part of humanity. Our finitude also makes each of us necessarily dependent upon others and inevitably bonds us more closely to some people than others. We therefore stand under a religio-moral charge to live in communities and to exercise our personal autonomy with social concern. In turn, our communities may justifiably require us to curtail our freedom so that they can function and persevere. Moreover, because certain of them such as country, family, and religion substantially make us who we are, they can also legitimately make exceptional demands on us. They can rightly insist that we curb the free exercise of our consciences when their promptings conflict with the group's central affirmations.

Our postmodern humility about selfhood also requires us to grant our groups greater esteem than the modern ethos did. People having shown themselves to be far less rational, selfless, and morally competent than we once thought, we can freshly appreciate how community standards and traditions can benefit the mature self. They often embody a sagacity far more profound, comprehensive, and time-tested than anything we might create. In conflict with a community that still shapes us, we cannot assume, as we once imperiously did, that modernity has given us far greater insight into our duty and destiny than it has. Rather, we now often find that we must bow to what, after initial rejection and open reconsideration, we concede to be its superior wisdom.

I do not mean by strongly arguing for the sociality of the self and thus of its self-legislation to also make a case for Dostoevski's Grand Inquisitor. But I am regularly exasperated by an American Jewry that, wallowing in freedom, prates piously of the sanctity of personal choice and uses it mainly to sanction casual nonobservance and flabby ethics. I seek only to restore a proper tension between our autonomy and social responsibility, one the contemporary idolization of the self has grossly distorted. I too equate all human dignity with self-determination, but only within the context of a Covenant with God that gives us our personal significance and makes all God's covenant-partners an essential element of our selfhood.

That being understood, when an institution suggests that I should regularly rely on its judgment rather than on my own, I will reassert the sanctity of personal autonomy and oppose its effort to diminish my personhood. I concede that in any such controversy my community may legitimately ask for my social *bona fides* and ask what sacrifices I, as more than a selfish self, have in fact made for its/our welfare. As long as I can present reasonably satisfactory credentials, I will then unabashedly ask for its *bona fides*. What sacrifices has it made of its power, its ambition, and its self-serving nature for me and others of its adherents, we who are not merely its beneficiaries but independent centers of worth and wisdom, and not infrequently the source of its authority? Most institutions still function without essential regard for the rich personhood of those they serve. Their leaders seek compliance by quickly reverting to paternalism, punishment, or tyranny. In the dialectical arrangement of living in covenant, just as autonomous individuals must live in responsible sociality, so our institutions must structure and activate themselves in elemental respect for the God-given dignity of their participants. We properly yearn for the messianic day when the common course will fully represent the common will. Until then, we must ask for its practical equivalent: that our organizations manifest a major, activist commitment to achieving true community and make regular progress toward that goal.

I cannot specify a rule by which we can settle serious confrontations between these valid authorities or even identify the signs that indicate we have reached reasonable limits of individual sacrifice or institutional patience. But we have an old-new model for such open, unsettled, but mutually dignifying relationships, namely, "covenant," now less a contract spelled out from on high than a loving effort to live in reciprocal respect. As the pain of trying to create egalitarian marriages indicates, we cannot know early on what forms and processes most people will find appropriate to such relationships. We can, however, accept covenantal relationships as a central ethical challenge of our time and pragmatically learn how we might sanctify ourselves by living it. For some such reason, I take it, God has given us freedom and opened history to our determination.

The Special Responsibilities of Religious Groups

I believe the foregoing analysis applies to secular as to religious social structures, but it takes somewhat altered form when applied to the corporate life of a biblical religion, most specifically, of course, Judaism.

In the Bible and Talmud the interests of the Covenant people heavily outweigh concern for its individual members. True, individual Jews have extraordinary religious scope in Judaism. Simply by knowing and willing, any Jew may do what God requires of Jews.

Even the legal authorities who determine the details of our obligations do so not by institutional selection but by an authority invested in them by an informal community recognition of their personal religious attainment. Yet classically, this heady Jewish recognition of individuality functions only within our folk contract with God.

Non-Orthodox thinkers have broadly extended the role of individual autonomy in Judaism, all the while insisting that our Jewish legitimacy also requires ongoing interaction with the Jewish community. I link the social, the theological, and the personal levels of our Jewishness by utilizing the existentialist metaphor of relationship. In my view, Jewish autonomy becomes the use of our freedom in terms of our personal participation in the people of Israel's Covenant with God as the latest expression of its historic tradition.

Two intensifications of general human sociality arise from this conception of the Jewish self. As in all religions, living in Covenant involves a human being's most utterly fundamental relationship, namely, that with God. Hence our religious communities and duties cannot be peripheral to our lives but must be at their center; anything less than profound devotion and commitment profanes our professions of Jewish faith. Moreover, because the Covenant was made primarily with the Jewish *ethnos* and only secondarily with the Jewish *autos*, the Jewish people, its local communities, families, and progeny, remain the immediate channels through which we Jews sacralize existence. Since modern life immerses us in an individualistic ethos, all contemporary Judaisms must stress the sociality of Jewish spirituality so that we may live in proper Covenantal duality.

For their part, we must admit, our religious leaders bear impossible burdens. Does anyone truly know how to transform impersonal institutions into humanely interactive communities and not lose the stability that enables a religion to survive? Not every individualizing change we have advocated or they have initiated has proved entirely beneficial. Others, which they have resisted, have shown only ambiguous value when implemented elsewhere. Besides, in recent years tradition has often held up well against modernity. Surely the accumulated wisdom of centuries should not easily be surrendered for what may announce itself as our fulfillment but what the passage of time will show to have been one period's passion. Moreover, our leaders must guide us in terms of what they believe God wants God's people to be doing now. Though they know they cannot speak as

God's special intimates, they also may not evade the special obligation created by their preeminence, for it inevitably invests their
decisions or their inaction with something of God's own authority.

Jewish leaders find these theoretical problems exacerbated by
the persistent threats to our existence. With our people requiring
vigilant defense against its foes, how can it easily tolerate vigorous
critics and conscientious dissenters? At the same time, our community knows and practices so little, believing even less, that its
indifference alone threatens meaningful Jewish continuity. Then
shall what has been preserved of our tradition be further vitiated for
the sake of individual conscience?

Though our religious leaders can find strong warrant for resisting
further experiments in personalizing our faith, they should not
expect that we will passively accept significant disregard of human
autonomy. We not only expect religious institutions to model the
humane values God demands of us as individuals, we expect them
to do so in exemplary fashion. Though we cannot demand perfection
of our religious leaders and institutions, we can and must expect them
to demonstrate more corporate righteousness than the unconsecrated,
for we can find individual holiness by ourselves. They legitimate
their communal roles under the Covenant only as they make it
possible for us to fulfill the necessary social dimension of our
responsibility to God.

Most Americans today apparently do not find that their religious
institutions meet these spiritual expectations. Against everything
sociologists keep saying about secularization, pollsters regularly find
that the overwhelming majority of Americans continue to profess
belief in God and a broad range of other traditional beliefs. Yet they
do not greatly involve themselves in organized religion and its
practices—and that is more true of Jews than any other religious
sample. Of course, this picture of a massive Lincolnesque defection
from religious institutions stems in part from the limitations of
polling people about religion. But I think it tells us much about our
righteous intolerance of religious bodies that do not clearly exemplify
their vaunted values.

Here too I can adumbrate no rule for resolving discord between
the conscientious self and Jewish religious leadership seeking to be
true to God. Though our tradition has honored obedience more than
innovation, inspirited Jews have continually enriched our heritage
in amazingly diverse fashion. Today, with individual creativity a
primary cultural good, we may expect that those who achieve

intimacy with God will make quite unpredictable demands upon our institutions. But if these innovative spirits also know themselves to stand in Israel's Covenant with God they must also acknowledge a summons to live by the discipline of the Covenant community. We will initially assess the Jewish authenticity of their demands upon our institutions by asking how they have met their obligations to our people. What do they know of the tradition they have brought into judgment? What sacrifices of self have they made for Judaism's continuity? What place does the people of Israel have in their personal vision of the proper Jewish service of God? Does their individual version of Judaism give promise of continuing Israel in faithful corporate service to God until the Messiah comes?

Only when they have satisfied these social claims can individual Jews claim that their prophetic protests against our institutions arise from a Jewish ground. Then they may rightly ask: How have our organizations used their power in relation to individuals and in pursuit of their corporate aims? How much dissent and pluralism have they tolerated or encouraged? How far have they sought to lead us and our society toward a more humane existence rather than merely mirror or modify its present virtues and vices?

Our special contemporary difficulties with this clash between self and community derive from our need to refashion the relationship that once shaped our institutional life. Heretofore it involved only two centers of authority: God and the folk pledged to God. Now our commitment to the religious significance of the autonomous self requires us to factor into this alliance a new and demanding third partner, the self-determining individual. This must not be taken to mean that God's primacy in the Covenant ought in any way be diminished. The existence of the people of Israel corporately and of Jews as individuals devolves from God and they therefore ought to be dedicated, beyond all else, to God. I am only saying that our religious experience requires that our religious institutions recognize that the individual Jew is neither bereft of God's presence nor insensitive to God's present command. So each Jewish self must now be factored into our understanding of the community's obligations under the Covenant. This means to me that we require more help from our institutions than we have commonly received as we seek to work out the meaning of our personal existence in Covenant. That will likely mean tolerating greater dissent in ideas and divergence in practice than they have previously found congenial, but that alone can make it possible for us to become more the persons as well as the people of God.

God's Uniqueness Demands a Universal Horizon

Broadening our horizon from the intra- to the extracommunal arena of Covenant responsibility essentially recapitulates the clash of self and community in the tension between devotion to our people and to humanity. Again I wish to redress the imbalance I may have created in stressing Jewish uniqueness by offering an appreciation of the Jewish roots of universalism.

The modern Jewish dedication to humanity has often been scanted as an apologetic ideology created by 19th-century modernizers. Clearly, it became an explicit, major motif in the non-Orthodoxies that appealed to many Jews because, among other reasons, their universal teaching justified giving high Jewish priority to the non-Jewish problems and ideals in which they now happily found themselves involved. However, this development had a considerable basis in some of the underpinnings of classic Jewish belief, namely, its doctrines of first and last things.

The Torah does not begin with the first Jew or the first *mitzvah*. For eleven chapters it tells how everything began and how world history gained its sorry character, thus eliciting the call to Abraham and its consummation at Sinai. Messianism, too, has universal significance, as in the dramatic prophetic vision of all nations living in peace and everyone dwelling in security. Of course, the Bible and the Talmud both have more dominant particularistic eschatologies, which strikes me as reasonable for a people highly conscious of its eccentric, minority status among the nations. But what normal ethnic development explains the accompanying Hebrew national self-transcendence? And why did it persist over the centuries? I can explain it only as a logical consequence of Israel's experience with its unique God, the entailments of which took considerable time to work out.

Consider the implications of God's stature, uniqueness, and goodness. Creation establishes God's sole right to rule and any effort to establish another ultimate authority must be resisted to the point of martyrdom. Every other center of power in human history therefore derives its legitimacy from God. No clan, tribe, nation, class, party,

228 A POSTLIBERAL THEOLOGY OF JEWISH DUTY

or race can call for unconditional allegiance without becoming idolatrous.

God's uniqueness integrally complements God's sovereignty. Asserting oneness alone might leave God unified but cosmically insignificant. Proclaiming God the only real God gives God's commands unchallengeable, irreplaceable, imperative quality. The ubiquitous old, now troublesome, political metaphor, "King," once aptly symbolized all this: Only God sets the order of creation and God alone has ultimate authority in all that follows. Moreover, being good, God cares about human beings and the quality of their action. God wills that singly and collectively they sanctify their lives by their deeds, manifest God's goodness in their character, and direct their freedom by God's behests. Therefore, the supreme, unique God of the universe makes a covenant with humankind, all humankind.

Were the notion of God covenanting not paradoxical enough, the picture of the resulting relationship makes the behavior predicated of creation's sole Sovereign even odder. God creates beings who are free enough to say "No" to the One who made them. Then, apparently because of this distinctive power, God summons these creatures into an alliance of mutual responsibility. For whatever reason, people refuse to fulfill their part of the ennobling pact. Yet the scorned God does not abandon, overpower, or—except in one unsatisfactory experiment—destroy them. Rather, the Ultimate now manifests a tenacious purposiveness. Creatively, God tries numerous ways— revelation, prophecy, punishment, a Covenant with a special people— to save the unique creatures from their obduracy and to realize the divine rule on earth. Messianism is the logical culmination of this view of God, and though the dialectic of Jewish faith makes it possible to assert Israel's sole salvation, God's universal concern must in due course also be voiced.

Surveying the extent to which Judaism's implicit universalism became explicit over the centuries suggests that only when exclusion eased have Jews been moved to articulate their comprehensive ideal. The literatures of the Jews of Hellenistic Alexandria and, later, the Moslem-Jewish symbiosis give ample evidence of this. So, in turn, the more complete social equalization of the Jews in the Emancipation motivated its expression with a fullness theretofore unknown. Assimilationists, Marxists, and others made universalism their exclusive faith and scorned Jewish particularity as superfluous, a charge most Jews rejected, dialectically reaffirming the lasting importance of Jewish particularity. More recently, the Holocaust and its resonance in subsequent threats to Jewish continuity have reminded us of the preciousness of this specific folk. So we live in the uneasy tension created by simultaneous devotion to our people and to humankind.

The Sovereign God and the Proper Authority of Nations

Much of our theology of clashing group loyalties derives from our understanding of nationhood, whose *locus classicus* is Genesis, chapters 10 and 11.

Had humankind remained simply Noahide, we could speak of the historic reality of universalistic existence, but the Torah realistically acknowledges that we meet humankind entire only in the form of "tongues, languages, lands, and nations." It appears to transmit two different traditions about the division of a universal, Noahide humanity into diverse nations. In Genesis 10, ethnicity evolves as a natural consequence of the postdiluvian population explosion. Genesis 11, however, depicts the division of languages and the scattering to many lands as punishment for seeking to build a tower into heaven, God's abode, and to wrest a (divine?) name. In consequence, God creates divisions among people to diminish their united power to do evil. Elsewhere biblical authors say God assigned a particular folk character to each nation, implying that their number and culture are fixed for all time.

The sages had little difficulty integrating these views. The differences among people emerge "naturally" as a result of their customary sinfulness, attested by their decreasing longevity in the generations after the flood. God divided them into their various groups to turn their blasphemous self-assertion against one another and only the superior rule of the Messiah will bring them to live with one another as God's faithful servants. What the rabbis observed of the paganism that surrounded them simply confirmed the biblical judgment: Nationhood is a natural expression of the human will-to-do-evil, for collectivity intensifies individual lust. When the rabbis speak of "the nations" one may be reasonably certain that their point will be derogatory. Despite this, they did not renege on the belief that God had made a covenant with all humankind. This allowed them to rule that a righteous individual gentile could attain the life of the world to come, a judgment they never made of a collective other than Israel. Seeing "the nations" behave abominably, they, like the prophets, confidently expected God would one day punish them drastically.

Until recently, Jewish thinkers have been too overjoyed at being granted citizenship to say much about the dark side of nationhood. They have responded to existence in freedom with messianic fervor, believing that the enlightened acts of their states showed them reaching moral stature. In the latter part of the 19th century, Isaac Mayer Wise described American democracy in eschatological terms while Hermann Cohen argued, about World War I, that the German nation enshrined humanity's highest ideals. Today political realism has become such a burden that one can easily become wistful at their naiveté. Nations still show themselves to be a pretty ugly bunch, exponentially exemplifying our human will-to-do-evil. History remains God's problem—and ours. Theologically, rabbinic realism carries as much conviction on the social as on the individual level. While all human beings stand in covenant with God and some individuals live up to it, the nations and peoples generally do not. Collectivity distorts and displaces our personal sense of Noahide covenantship. I mean this not as a Rousseauistic description of society as the despoiler of our congenital individual goodness. Without our collectives, we still would not be back in Eden— something anarchists do not understand. I am only saying, with the rabbis, that as we organize our nations we empower and give scope to our will-to-do-evil.

But God has not made a covenant with humankind for nothing. Without violating the freedom that makes us possible covenant partners, God still proposes to bring us to covenant holiness and therefore does not abolish the alliance with the Noahides. Instead, God makes a new, more involving Covenant, the one announced to Abraham and consummated at Sinai.

The Unique Character of the Nation Covenanted to God

The Torah accounts specify God's repeated promises to turn Abraham's descendants into a great nation and thus they assert a unique origin for the Hebrews: a divine summons to special obedience to replace arrogance and its punishment. So too the Hebrews do not begin with a land of their own, only the promise of one as God's Covenant partner. Even as they approach it, Moses warns them that they can occupy it only as long as their behavior reflects loyalty to God. For Covenant reciprocity entails Israel's life-and-society-transforming acceptance of God's rule and rules. By the new multiplicity of deeds commanded by God, Israel shows itself to be God's partner without parallel.

In this nation, the Transcendent uniquely grounds the collective enterprise and character. Realistically, and with an absence of the defensiveness we expect of institutional documents, the biblical authors do not claim that the will-to-do-evil no longer functions among the Hebrews. They sin, sometimes egregiously, but they also know it to be a special responsibility of their odd nationhood to keep the nation in thrall to the true sovereign, God. In the stories of the kings who embody Israelite responsibility we find the model of our people's intuition of its idiosyncratic, sacred nationhood. Being human, the kings demonstrate the will-to-do-evil; being rulers, they do so on a grand scale. But their political preeminence does not exempt them from God's reproof and judgment by those extraordinary figures, Israel's prophets. That the Israelites remembered and transmitted as sacred teaching the history and messages of the prophets attests to the perception of Covenant-distinctiveness that came to animate this unusual nation.

The incongruity of Israel's political behavior in the light of its Covenant ideals prompts the theological wonder that God did not choose another social form for them rather than subject them to the awesome risks of collective power. Two suppositions—one substantive, one functional—respond to this query.

God makes Abraham's family a nation in history in order to show that collective power can be sanctified through subordination to God's rule. This does not, however, require Israel to fulfill its Covenantal responsibilities through political autonomy or any other given social structure. The specific form in which the people should organize itself devolves from the historical circumstances in which it finds itself. Thus, Israel could be content with a loose federation and occasional charismatic leaders until the Sea Peoples threatened its existence, bringing about a shift to monarchy. In their extended Middle Ages, the Jews had no hope of political independence and carried on their corporate career through autonomous community existence. In our time, a numinous combination of tragedy, international guilt, and Jewish will made it possible for us to renew Jewish statehood, this time in democratic, secular form. And world Jewry has acknowledged its vital role in keeping our people alive and providing us with new opportunities to pursue our millennial quest.

Being organized as an ethnic group also has functional value in the Covenant. Israel must live in intense fealty to God amidst nations who will to ignore or spurn God's behests for them. The Jews have therefore had to bear an uncommon burden of contumely and suffering, a human condition the Covenant does not proclaim a virtue and Jewish prayer often asks God to end. God's redemptive power manifesting itself only sporadically, the nations remaining obdurately perverse, the Messiah tarrying, Israel lives in jeopardy and continues its service in history with difficulty. Where other groups may seek a future out of biological drive, social inertia, or ethnic self-assertion, Israel fights to live so that God's reality will become known to all humankind.

The multiple ties that ethnicity engenders help the imperiled people endure. Bound to one another and their Covenant memories by land, language, customs, heroes, jokes, foods, gossip, and other aspects of folk life, the Jewish people can defend itself from history's blows clothed in a many-layered ethnic armor. Infusing its folkways with Covenant sensibility, it can powerfully transmit, reinforce, and renew Israel's lasting purpose. This socialization carries such power, Israel can for some period continue being Israel despite times of relative indifference, illiteracy, and faithlessness.

In sum, Jewish ethnic individuality has a universal telos that affects and directs it, but since that purpose must be accomplished in history, it can only be achieved in premessianic times by this particular group in quite local ways. The dialectic of telos and means can be sinfully distorted at either pole. Modern Jews giddily believed that benign politics would imminently realize universalism and sought to sublimate their particularity to it. And the nations have often so abused us that self-concern has blinded us to our involvement with humanity. But we cannot avoid the dialectic of duty imposed on us by our people's Covenant with God, which teaches us of God's covenant with all human beings.

The Theological Context of Jewish Politics

I have spoken in the generalities appropriate to reflective discourse but it would be a denial of Jewish responsibility to avoid applying them to the critical locus of our contemporary clash of values, the State of Israel.

The Holocaust searingly made plain that the Jewish people must never again surrender to others our responsibility to do all that we can to assure our people's survival. We can no longer blithely expect the nations of the world to take up our cause because of their moral progress. During the Middle Ages we could often count on the popes to save us from local despots and fanatics (and then be appropriately compensated). Our sorry experience with Christianity during the Holocaust and our ambivalent relations with it since make it a questionable support in a time of great Jewish trial. Perhaps nations occasionally act out of moral considerations and religion can still affect political decisions. Nonetheless, it does not hurt that we are remarkably loyal and productive citizens worldwide and effectively self-reliant in the State of Israel. For all that we can and must do, the future of our various communities remains in the hands of others, and only as democracy functions truly can there be some hope of Jewish security—another indication of the intertwining of ethnic self-assertion and involvement with humanity at large.

Having returned to independent ethnic status as a sovereign nation, we do not wish ever again to be denied corporate dignity. Though our forebears found ways to sanctify ghetto existence, they considered it the epitome of exile, a metaphysical as well as a political debasement. Having tasted the rights of self-determination and self-expression, we wish, like all the other peoples of the earth, to make our contribution to humankind by being allowed to be ourselves in our own way.

The State of Israel came into being on some such surge of particularism and since its existence has so continually been threatened, one might reasonably feel that it fulfills its role as a Jewish state merely by keeping our people alive. That continues to be all many Israelis and some Diaspora Jews feel ought to be asked of it. Many other Israelis and much of world Jewry, though agreeing on the necessity of Jewish survival, also press our corollary Covenant commitment to high humane standards. For many years they took special Jewish pride in the State of Israel's exceptional moral accomplishments, which are made all the more impressive as a conscious ingredient of Israeli national purpose despite requiring special sacrifice from the citizenry. In recent years, as the West Bank remained under military administration, as Jewish irredentism increased, as the incursion into Beirut helped destabilize Lebanon, as the Intifada expressed a Palestinian will for independence, the discord between Jewish self-interest and universal values split Israelis into opposing camps of near equal size. Diaspora Jews, reflecting their less ethnic, more humanistic situation, began exhibiting a new sense of distance from the State of Israel. Remarkably, in this excruciatingly difficult situation, few Jews could argue that particularity or universality alone could satisfy the demands of Jewish responsibility. The double entailment of the Covenant remained that clear but also, therefore, unresolvable by any one-sided proposal for action. The dialectical understanding of our duty does not remove us from the indeterminacy of history and its testing, but helps us to understand why we are torn—and that too may incline us toward one practical decision or another. At least it helps us to be more responsible about our decisions. To say more than that, I believe, is to pass from theology into politics.

A Postliberal Theology
of Jewish Duty

III

The Torah Born of Covenant

וְתֵן בְּלִבֵּנוּ לְהָבִין וּלְהַשְׂכִּיל,
לִשְׁמֹעַ לִלְמֹד וּלְלַמֵּד,
לִשְׁמֹר וְלַעֲשׂוֹת וּלְקַיֵּם אֶת
כָּל דִּבְרֵי תַלְמוּד תּוֹרָתֶךָ,
בְּאַהֲבָה.
וְהָאֵר עֵינֵינוּ בְּתוֹרָתֶךָ,
וְדַבֵּק לִבֵּנוּ בְּמִצְוֹתֶיךָ

Put it into our hearts
to understand and to discern,
to heed, to study and to teach,
to observe, to do and to fulfill
all the words of instruction in Your Torah
with love.
Enlighten our eyes in Your Torah
and make our hearts cleave to Your commandments.

17 When God Dominates

OW DO WE KNOW what properly constitutes a life of Covenantal *mitzvah?* The two most widely accepted responses, Orthodoxy and ethnic loyalty, fail us by over-emphasizing the role of either God or the people of Israel in determining Jewish duty. In analyzing here the first of these, the contemporary claims of orthodoxies, my mind goes back to a personal experience still fresh in my memory through it took place in March 1950. The Reform rabbis' association, the Central Conference of American Rabbis, perturbed by the changing religious mood of the postwar world, held an unprecedented assembly for its members, an Institute on Theology. I attended one of its several discussion sections, that on revelation, and recall that despite two days of rewarding discussion we could not compose a consensus statement for the plenum. Our report merely indicated the eight problems that engaged the group, many of them related to God's role in revelation.

This failure to reach a consensus so startled the chairman of the Institute, Ferdinand Isserman, that he broke into the proceedings with a personal response. He was astonished that we had made no reference to the Documentary Hypothesis and its conclusions about the creation of the Torah. As far as he was concerned it had settled the matter of revelation. Like most other religious "liberals"—a term I shall use here to refer to all non-Orthodox Jews—he considered the Bible a thoroughly human document, though an endlessly relevant one because of its incomparable account of humankind's spiritual quest.

Liberal religious thinkers often added that it was inspired by God, but this seemed more deference to traditional usage than a living sense of God's partnership in the process. They had little doubt about the truth of their radically modern view, for it was supported by university research and organic to the zeitgeist, the social optimism that expected cultural enlightenment to empower steady human progress. The rabbis attending the Institute would no doubt have hooted down a suggestion that in a few decades fundamentalism—or its less terminologically troublesome Jewish equivalent, Orthodoxy—would claim best to express the zeitgeist and win the willing allegiance of many university graduates.

The Social Causes behind the Turn to Fundamentalisms

The totally unanticipated resurgence of orthodoxies in the four decades since then has surely had little to do with new findings concerning the biblical text. Rather, it has come as a reaction to the failure of the cultural messianism espoused by liberal religion. The modern ethos lost its cultural hegemony largely because of the demythologization of its allies, university rationalism and science. Once we thought them our finest sources of truth and our surest means to ennoblement. Today the sophisticated know they deal only in possible constructions of reality and the masses sense they commend ethical relativism more than necessary values and compelling duties. For, having brilliantly unmasked all the ethical cant around us, they abandon us to the free promptings of the self. Liberal religion has fallen on such hard times because many believe it has abetted this modernist gutting of standards. By turning God's revelation into mere human growth and self-determination, it helped destroy our faith in stable human values and made us prey to moral anarchy. Conscience alone, which for so long seemed to mandate a turn from orthodoxies, should now rather prompt our return to the old religious paradigms of reality with their strong, clear teaching of what a person, a family, a community, and a nation ought to be.

The uncertain status today of liberalism's former academic cornerstone, the Higher Criticism of the Torah, amplifies the ethical bankruptcy of liberalism. My seminary teachers said they were teaching us "biblical science," a method so reliable that one professor regularly assigned a numerical probability to his emendations of our printed Bibles so as to restore the original biblical text. They all not only espoused the Documentary *Hypothesis* but confidently, perhaps even arrogantly, taught it as "the facts."

Today the theory is an academic shambles, used largely out of habit and for want of a better explanation of the messily discordant data. No one can specify an empirically verifiable description of the distinctive language of the Torah's alleged documents, or resolve the doubts as to their century or sequence, or clarify their relation to the redaction process or to the local traditions present in the text, or satisfactorily explain how the oral became the written, or describe the role of literary coherence in all of this, much less how the unique religious vision of the Torah, its most significant characteristic, utterly transforms the cultural images it employs. The older scholarly work in Bible seems, for all its academic hermeneutic, essentially another *midrash*, one that tells us more about the author's trendy professional suppositions than about the text's own apparent concerns. Surely one ought not urge the perplexed of our day to stake their lives on such flimsy grounds. Rather than trim our religion to what one generation or another's celebrated professors teach, should we not rather live by what our religious tradition tells us a good God has graciously made available to us?

Some such case, I believe, grounds the conservative religious zeitgeist of our day. Hence my response to it focuses primarily on the issue of the consequences of our theory of God's revelation and only secondarily on how we can best understand the biblical text.

To facilitate the central discussion, I shall shortly grant this conservative statement of the case. But I should like to be quite explicit that, in fact, I consider it false when stated so unconditionally and, even when properly nuanced, so altered in meaning as to lose its decisive effect. Permit me, then, a few counter-comments before I turn to the central argument.

I know of no major liberal religion that advocates drugs, child abuse, family violence, robbery, hard-core pornography, graft, cheating the government, or other staples of the nightly news. Liberals often get tarred with the brush of every social pathology because they think it morally responsible to confront and talk about the human realities in our midst, from mental retardation to wife abuse. The orthodoxies generally prefer another strategy. First they deny that their communities have such problems or simply exclude such sinners and defectives from the community of the faithful; later they admit that such problems do occur among them but suggest greater faith and devotion as the best therapy; and, finally, when humanistic treatments have long been established elsewhere and prove themselves efficacious, the orthodoxies coopt them with the guidance of a suddenly more accommodating Scripture and tradition.

Orthodoxies do present a legitimate challenge to liberalism, claiming that its emphasis on individual freedom leads to an impoverished sense of duty and a virtual abandonment of limits, a charge that I shall answer in chapter 20. Here I approach the issue of moral consequences comparatively, that is, by juxtaposing the problems orthodoxies can engender to liberal religion's approach to the same issues. That should clarify why the nonorthodox know their faith to be truer.

The Orthodoxies' Limited Tolerance

Had orthodox religions not behaved so badly when they had effective power, liberal religion would most likely not have come into being. The rationalists of the Enlightenment scornfully charged that religion—by separating people into the saved and the damned, by its persecutions, inquisitions, crusades, and wars—had created more evil than good. Religions that claim to bring peace into the world stand doubly damned by such inquity. More important, this divisiveness and controversy arise from fundamental, not peripheral, claims of the orthodoxies. Insofar as a faith claims to know in some detail what God wants of all humankind, then loving one's neighbors as oneself can mean hating the one who is not like you and lovingly forcing him to be like you. Thus, the *halakhah* restricts the neighbor I am commanded to love as myself to the one who is like me in religious observance. It classically grounds this negativity in texts like Ps. 139:21–22. "O Lord, You know I hate those who hate You, and loathe Your adversaries. I feel a perfect hatred toward them; I count them my enemies."

By internal standards one cannot logically impeach the theology of such orthodoxies. Their founding faith avers that God, who alone has every right to do so, has made perfectly plain how human beings ought to live. To spurn God's holy law not only contravenes the highest good but personally affronts God. When the pious do nothing about this perversity they become deeply implicated in it, for by appeasing transgression they teach humankind to accept evil and thereby do the devil's work. Moreover, they also retard the coming of God's rule and draw forth God's punishment on the righteous as well as the sinful. So for God's sake and their own, those who love God should fight and uproot sin.

This limited tolerance or intolerance arises precisely from what the orthodoxies claim to be their great strength: against moral flabbiness and uncontrolled freedom, their faith and discipline are certain. And because that knowledge is unqualified and absolute, no argument can logically challenge or refute it. One cannot range human understanding against what God has ordained since God, who set these standards, is the ultimate ground of all human existence and dignity. One hears this same understanding in the talmudic retort, "The words of the master and the words of the disciple, to which should one listen?"

Indeed, a special horror must greet any serious challenge to God's behests. With absolute good at stake, what normally would be a sin can now become a virtue; one kills flagrant sinners to save their souls. Given full social power, or access to it, orthodoxies have been known to utilize it against those demonic souls who deny God. Thus, in the Spanish Inquisition, Jews who had converted to Catholicism but, under torture, confessed that they had reverted to Jewish ways, still received capital punishment but of a somewhat more humane kind.

I am not arguing that orthodoxies necessarily or inevitably lead to these harsh consequences, nor am I saying that religious orthodoxies have learned nothing since the Middle Ages. All the traditional faiths I know have beliefs that could counteract such absolutism—God's love for every creature and God's desire for their genuine repentance being the most notable among them. And there have always been leaders in our religions who have been revered for their compassionate embrace of everyone, even vile sinners. Orthodoxies *can* be tolerant. That is not the issue between us. Nor is it one of determining which approach to faith is wholly correct and which wholly wrong. Liberal and orthodox faiths share too much of their views of God and humankind for such simplistic judgments. I think it irresponsible to charge that the orthodox ignore human self-determination or that the liberals forget that God, not the human mind, ultimately grounds our values and being. Both affirm the transcendent preeminence of God and ascribe some independent dignity to humankind. We radically diverge, however, over the issue of the proper balance or relative significance we ascribe to God's sovereignty and to human will.

Liberals reject orthodoxy not because, given the power, orthodoxies *will be* intolerant but because their basic faith can generate extremism, zealotry, and fanaticism—something they have often done in the past and still do today. These, simple human experience has taught us, desecrate God's name while claiming to exalt it and therefore are among the foulest of human sins.

The Positive Consequences of Finite Religious Knowledge

By contrast, non-Orthodoxy arises from a stance that intrinsically affirms religious pluralism. It does so because its adherents' experience of closeness to God resonates with a consciousness of the active human side of the relationship and thus the limited though commanding nature of our human comprehension of God. Hence liberalism affirms each individual's and each generation's right to find a better approach to God. Few of us are wiser at this than our inherited religious traditions. But, in principle, with none of us able to affirm that ours is the only, the absolute way to God, we are led to affirm the rights of others to go to God in their own way, even if it differs from ours. Such pluralism as the orthodoxies know is limited to groups and movements that are loyal to their revelation though odd interpreters of it. But to those who differ radically, even in their own communities, no such positive pluralism applies; the orthodoxies draw the circle of tolerance relatively close to them while liberalism seeks to make it ever more inclusive. The *halakhah*, for example, tolerantly rules that one need not be a Jew to know God and gain the life of the world to come. But it also asserts, in Maimonides's famous ruling, that in a Jewish state gentiles must accept this universal religion as a matter of Jewish revelation or be put to death—and that from the greatest of medieval Jewish rationalists.

Sensitive to this problem, many spokesmen (and they are always men) of contemporary orthodoxies have indicated their spiritual unease with extremism and used their influence to oppose it. In the Jewish community no one has more eloquently and consistently undertaken this task (and endured the pains it brings) than Emanuel Rackman, though he has been joined in it by such other North American immigrants to the State of Israel as Eliezer Berkovits, David Hartman, and Shlomo Riskin. While admiring such leadership greatly, I cannot help but see their struggle with their own community as growing from a recognition of the genuine merit of the liberals' religio-moral passion for pluralism. Human nature being what it is, we cannot be asked to rely long on compassionate leaders regularly arising to offset the exclusivist thrust of orthodox religious belief. Consider, for example, how the years continue to go by, and all the theory that the halakhic process can do something about just complaints of feminists still had led to little significant authoritative action. I must also add that if proper leadership can satisfactorily be relied on to offset a religion's shortcomings, then that should also apply to nonorthodox as to orthodox leadership.

Besides, prudence suggests to liberals that the occasional groups of the religious right who manifest a more positive attitude toward pluralism do so more from a lack of effective power than from a principled commitment to pluralism. Were there not so many orthodoxies fighting for preeminence in the United States, for example, were one of them able radically to influence our country's leaders, their view of how much sin they should be asked to tolerate would most likely narrow. This assessment of the orthodoxies' political potential lies behind the deep distress most American Jews, including spokesmen of American Orthodoxy, feel at the power wielded by Israel's Orthodox political parties. Knowing that many of the Israeli Orthodox have never lived in a truly pluralistic society and that others believe the Torah militates against modern expressions of Jewish responsibility, most American Jews devoutly hope the Orthodox never become a majority in the State of Israel.

What Legislative Power Properly Rests in the People?

Orthodoxies have a principled problem with democracy. This is most evident in the functioning of their communities, and it carries over to what they tend to find most desirable in a government. God being One, indeed incomparably so, any institution properly representing God will speak with hierarchical authority to its members. The will of the community may still have an important role in orthodoxies. At Sinai, for all that God spoke directly to the Jewish people and summoned them into Covenant, their willing assent was solicited and memorably gained. (One *midrash* explains the purpose of the first "commandment" of the Decalogue, God's self-identification as the people's redeemer, as the data they needed in order to know with whom they were being asked to join in partnership.) Nonetheless, by ethos and formalities, orthodoxies strictly limit the functioning of the individual conscience to that alone which God's own law and institutions permit.

Consider, for example, the logic of the halakhic regulations concerning menstruation. To begin with, no other body of biblical ritual purity laws continued in operation after the destruction of the Temple (the focus of all the practices related to ritual purity). In postbiblical times the menstrual laws gained a somewhat surprising addition. Though the Torah prescribes a separation of husband and wife only during the period of the menstrual flow, the later law added a further seven days to the period of ritual impurity. Although the sages do not agree about the basis of this ruling, most came to ascribe it to a custom Jewish women voluntarily adopted. (To the extent that custom can occasionally make law in Judaism, something like democracy has a place in it.) Nonetheless, wherever Jews have modernized, Jewish women have overwhelmingly abandoned the practice of the menstrual laws; they would thus seem to have retracted their previous decision. Except they apparently cannot do so. The sages of each era, all male, retain the exclusive authority to determine not only the law but which customs can become law and which must be opposed.

Perhaps that issue agitates only a small number of the pious among us. What, then, shall we say of the issues raised by feminism generally? Setting aside for the moment the merits of one specific issue or another, Jewish feminists appear to care most fundamentally about the critical issue in democracy: participation in the power to make binding decisions. Little touches the modern spirit more than self-determination, having a realistic role in fixing the rules by which one is expected to live. In the established orthodoxies I know, God has commanded or God's appointed authorities have long decreed that religious authority is reserved to males. Liberals will surely agree with the orthodoxies that the content of a religion should not be determined simply by ballot. Nonetheless, the nonorthodox esteem autonomy in principle because they believe the human self always mediates what we know of God. Hence each individual's quest for God concerns them as much as does what the past or the present community discerns as God's reach toward humankind. This alliance of self and communal spiritual experience becomes the foundation of a religious life that enshrines democracy because it fundamentally esteems individuality.

By extension, the same contrast in attitude toward democracy may be seen with regard to government generally. In the Bible, God can be pictured as considering the Hebrews' call for a king to be a rejection of God's own rule over the people, obviously the most desired state of affairs. Historically, then, governmental structures that provide the stability of enforcing or at least encouraging what the orthodoxies know God requires of all people have been most congenial to orthodoxies. By contrast, democracies, with their shifting determinations of how people ought to act, with everyone equally entitled to a say in what ought to be done, can be far more problematic to them. Consider, for example, how much easier it would be to resolve our continuing American religious tensions over abortion with less democracy. Were our governmental leaders more independent of the people and congenial to a given orthodoxy, or were one or another of the orthodox faiths decisively in power, the issue would move decisively toward a conclusion. Surely one reason why no constitutional amendment on abortion has thus far been approved by Congress has been that our orthodoxies themselves cannot agree on a specific delineation of God's own truth about abortion.

This brings us to an important qualification of the orthodoxies' claim that they would bring order into our anarchic society. This could happen if one orthodoxy dominated our nation or the several orthodoxies could agree on a policy. But orthodoxies often disagree as to what constitutes God's own will. When this happens, they can generate intense social conflict—and do so today as in the past. Traditional Jewish law, for instance, does not consider an abortion performed by a Jew murder but, on the contrary, mandates an abortion when the mother's life, or according to some, even her basic mental health is at stake. At the same time, it rules, for reasons that are obscure at best, that gentile abortions are murder.

I quickly add that liberals need not necessarily be pro-abortion, though their high regard for the individual leads them here as elsewhere to make the decision of the person immediately involved, in this case, the mother, their primary concern. And this religious appreciation of the individual will makes them, in principle, enthusiastic about democratic governance despite its occasional vagaries.

What Role Shall We Grant to the Rights of Conscience?

In some orthodoxies thinkers have sought to make room in their midst for "the rights of conscience," though only uncommon exegesis might find the equivalent of this modern notion in Hebrew Scripture, the New Testament, or the Koran. I see such orthodox efforts at accommodation as another silent acknowledgment of the religious truth that more centrally engages liberal spirituality. Obviously, orthodoxies that have greater regard for individual spirituality find it easier to work out a reconciliation with democracy, but the difficulty of harmonizing God's own truth with individual self-determination should not be underestimated. Thus, I see no institutional acceptance of the rights of conscience in traditional Islam and only a limited measure of it among traditionalistic Christians. In the latter case, though Roman Catholics and Southern Baptists in their diverse ways have sought to honor individuality, those among them who conscientiously seek new ways these days often find themselves forcefully reminded that in an orthodoxy obedience has precedence over autonomy.

I know of only one Orthodox Jewish thinker, Michael Wyschogrod, who has sought to legitimate democracy in a Jewish polity. He acknowledges that classic Jewish tradition, despite some hints of a similar notion, has no fully self-conscious concept of conscience. With our primal Jewish certainty that our people possesses God's highly contentful revelation we must reject the autonomous conscience in its common, humanistic form. That, as Heidegger penetratingly argued, radically destroys obedience to anything other than ourselves. To replace this faulty concept of conscience, Wyschogrod carefully elaborates one he believes would be acceptable to Judaism. He describes the individual's sense of right as a faculty given humans by God so that they might discern and respond to God's will. This formulation avoids two philosophic evils. By linking individual autonomy with God—theonomy—he has maintained individuality but limited arbitrariness. And with God the ground of human and thus individual value, linking conscience to God prevents a clash between what the self truly commands and what might seem to be religion's alien impositions—heteronomy.

Wyschogrod then seeks to situate conscience in contemporary Orthodoxy by arguing that the willingness to remain Orthodox must be made against the crowd and thus may be said to arise in a significant exercise of autonomy. To be sure, should the promptings of the *halakhah* and one's will conflict, one must sacrifice one's self-determination, a personal version of the binding of Isaac. Since this process of overcoming of self can occasionally be sensed, one has a phenomenological indication of autonomy's reality within Orthodoxy.

He admits that the concept of autonomy correctly points us to a critical locus of human dignity. Without some such self-actualization, we would be less the creatures that God formed us to be. Hence Orthodox Judaism needs to make room for the concept of conscience, a theoretical amplification his unique intellectual enterprise seeks to accomplish. But I believe a practical consideration, though unstated, can be deduced from a consequence he derives from his argument. If conscience legitimately commands, he boldly inquires, do we deny its validity when someone utilizes it against God-given standards? Catholic teaching once specified that error has no rights. Wyschogrod daringly asserts the opposite, that as long as one has come to a wholehearted decision after reverential study of God's revelation (Hebrew Scripture), we must grant individual conscience rights even when we know it to be in error. To say otherwise would allow a heteronomous revelation to override our

God-given right to think and judge for ourselves, thus negating the very essence of conscience.

I believe Wyschogrod's unique Orthodox appreciation of conscience has a high moral purpose: to provide an Orthodox theological justification for allowing Christians to be Christians. He does this not by a relativism that would sacrifice the absoluteness of God's revelation but by carefully providing room for individual conscience within it. Consequently, those who cannot read its message as others do may still claim the right to go their deviant way. Some years back, John Courtney Murray, the noted Roman Catholic theoretician of democracy, mounted a similar argument that the Second Vatican Council made official church teaching.

To the best of my knowledge, Wyschogrod's sophisticated argument has had no echo even in the centrist Orthodox Jewish community. This may change, of course, but I find it more an indication of the resistance of orthodoxies to the concept of conscience and its entailments than of the weakness of his argument.

How Broad Our Vision? How Deep Our Tradition?

The general discomfort of orthodoxies with sinners and evildoers creates another of its problematic manifestations: the limited moral horizon we call ethnocentrism. Their characteristic high self-esteem comes from knowing that their community, having uniquely received God's truth, now alone lives in full loyalty to it while others do not know it—or ignore, or pervert, or even reject it. As a result, the orthodoxies tend to tilt heavily in their own direction the balance between the love of all God's creatures and of those in their community. When the common human preference for the known and the familiar over the strange and alien coopts this sense of cosmic group worth, others can easily appear to be uncanny, unnatural, and perhaps even inhuman. At the extreme, pietists seclude themselves from a defiling world so that they may live as exclusively as possible with their sacred kin. Yet even in less self-ghettoized settings the orthodox appreciation of the universal can highly constrict and charity, most broadly construed, not only begins at home but tends to stay there.

Modern Jews are often startled to learn about the *halakhah*'s interpretation of neighborly love, the commandment Rabbi Akiba called the most inclusive generalization in the Torah. Over the centuries our authoritative sages said it applied only to fellow Jews (and, essentially, to righteous ones). The law requires Jews not only to have regard for a fellow Jew's honor and body but for his money. This led some authorities to rule that Jews should give preference in their business dealings to other Jews, our community's version of the Christian Yellow Pages.

No religious community that hopes to maintain itself, indeed that believes, for all its humanity, that it contains a true insight into the Divine, can do without some separatism and self-differentiation. In recent years many Jews have reasserted their Jewish particularity and some have even built a cultural ghetto to do so. But modernized Jews, though they have participated in this same cultural development, believe that the *halakhah* engenders a restrictive ethos that underestimates the sacred quality of the common humanity they encounter wherever democracy functions truly.

All these unhappy consequences of orthodox theories of revelation come to a climax in the orthodoxies' necessary subordination of persons to text, interpretation, structure, and precedent. God stands behind just these words and no others, behind just these interpretations of the words and no others, behind just this institution by which proper interpretations are mediated, and behind just this inherited wisdom that largely fixed what is and what is not God's will. Let individuals testify that to serve God most responsibly they believe they must significantly depart from these dicta and their spiritual leaders will tell them that their "conscience" must defer to what their religious heritage knows to be God's will. God knows best, they will be told, and so, as a consequence, do the leaders of one's faith.

To the nonorthodox, an alternative explanation seems very much more probable. Instead of functioning as the privileged channel of God's instruction, religious institutions behave very much more like other human structures. All we have learned about the history of groups, of their transition from charismatic beginnings to institutionalization to bureaucratization, for good and for ill, seems to explain much better than does God's revelation or providence why they act as they do. Few orthodoxies today will deny their institutional humanity, but, as God's own legatees, they regularly claim to be exempt from the same sort of correction we think appropriate for other human structures. Liberals also hope that God's will manifests itself in their own activities. But putting the balance on the human partner in our faiths, they deem it a duty, in principle, to be open to those new human experiences which, while deviating from the past, now appear to express its contemporary meaning.

The *halakhah*, like the regulations of other orthodoxies, contains many rulings where text and precedent are reinterpreted by the law's own means to permit what moderns see as greater personal fulfillment. Thus, the *lex talionis* remains God's immutable law, but the rabbis so interpreted it that it calls for monetary compensation instead of physical retribution. To make possible a second marriage, one witness instead of two may be acceptable to the rabbinic court, and that one may be a woman as well as a man. And, perhaps most tenderly of all, though Jewish husbands should divorce wives who do not bear children after ten years of marriage, we have no record of that law being enforced, only waived. Only a caricature would depict religious orthodoxies as without heart.

For all that, the principle of tradition over person substantially maintains itself. The classic Jewish cases have long been the *agunah* and the *mamzer*. In the former instance, a woman cannot remarry because she cannot legally prove that her husband has died or divorced her. The latter case covers the Jew born from adulterous or incestuous intercourse. That Jew may never marry a *kosher* Jew. Liberals cannot understand how such rulings can be considered God's will for us today. They also do not understand how those traditional Jews who agree that these laws should be made inoperable continue to be appeased by authorities who say that the *halakhah* has the flexibility to remedy these inequities, when for decades now its authoritative figures have not significantly modified them.

A further example, not any the less interesting because the public furor over it was initiated by a hoax, pivots on the Mishnah's ruling concerning a structure that collapsed on the Sabbath and buried someone in the ruins. Though breaking Sabbath law makes one technically subject to capital punishment, in this emergency we immediately set aside all the usual prohibitions of labor on the Sabbath and work as hard as we can to dig the person out. Saving a life supersedes every law in Judaism—except the prohibitions of murder, idol worship, and sexual offense. To this extent, the *halakhah* gives the personal priority over the legal. But the Mishnah further specifies that, should we discover that the buried person is a gentile, the Sabbath laws immediately go back into effect and we stop digging. No liberal Jew I know can face such a law without a protest and at least one Orthodox Jewish legal authority has by some similar sentiment been led to reinterpret the Mishnah rule. However, precedent having the weight it does in all orthodoxies, we cannot say what proportion of observant Jews would follow this liberalized ruling. Believing non-Orthodox Jews have little doubt that persons as such—whether in or out of our communities—have a major claim on received religious law and precedent. To us, this rule from the Misnah involves an outdated human understanding, not God's own will.

Our Clashing Views over the Torah's Authorship

Thus far I have sought to show how the deleterious social consequences that fundamentalists associate with religious liberalism must be balanced against the evils that can arise—and have arisen—from orthodoxies. For liberals, these humane, ethical considerations are generally decisive. But since this dispute began, at least on the surface, in relation to Scripture, I wish to return now to the debate over our sacred texts.

In principle, orthodoxies avow God's authorship of the explicit verbal form in which, all things being equal, we have Scripture. Thus, should we, reading it, be surprised that God stated what seems contrary to presently established fact, or that God enjoined or condoned what seems an inhumane act, then our understanding of it must be faulty. As Rabbi Mana said, it is we, not the verse, who are empty. Thus Abraham, Isaac, and Jacob cannot be charged with what, from the stories in the text, we would otherwise consider lying or deceit. So, too, the command to the invading Israelites to kill every Canaanite man, woman, and child of the seven local nations must have religious validity despite its ethical abhorrence. And the apparent duplication of stories in the text, the close parallels the Bible sometimes has to other Near Eastern texts, the statements of the Torah that seem post-Mosaic, the shifting chronology of the narrative, the odd orthography—all these must be there to serve a divine purpose. In perhaps the most popular contemporary traditional Jewish commentary to the five *megillot*, that of the Artscroll series, the author deems it heresy to suggest that the Song of Songs celebrates human sexuality rather than, as tradition teaches, allegorically describing God's love for the people of Israel. To the liberal eye, these and other such exegetical strategies seem a defense against what contemporary common sense suggests: that the text is very much more human than divine, though surely a mixture of both.

The non-Orthodox hold to their divergent, more humanistic

theory of revelation because it gives us a more fully integrated view of the data before us and accords much better with all else we know and have experienced. Once one concedes a considerable role to the human partner in revelation, most of the ordinary difficulties we have in reading the Bible fall away. Few today will be shocked that human beings, even ones with rare human sensitivity to God's will, would express themselves in terms of the worldview and values of their day. However, it is awe inspiring, literally so, that these same authors often completely transcend their time and culture and speak of ultimate truth and sanctifying duty in words through which we still can hear God addressing us.

Orthodoxies often insist that if one does not accept their Scripture as entirely God's word, then, by making it largely human, one renders it insignificant. Liberals find that dichotomy utterly distorts their religious experience. For them, precisely because rejecting Scripture as God's own truth liberates them from the burden of explaining away the innumerable problems in the text, it frees them to appreciate fully the spiritual genius that produced it.

Should Our Religion Be Segregated from All Else We Know?

The critical choice between liberalism and the orthodoxies centers upon their different approach to religious truth. For the liberals, faith in God needs to be understood as but one aspect, if the crucial one, of the seamless whole of human existence. The orthodoxies, on the other hand, all assert that their particular Scripture is unique in human experience, a revelation never fully given before and now never to be superseded. Its proper meaning, then, cannot be ascertained by our customary methods of reasoning. Occasionally, orthodox religious philosophers try to demonstrate the coherence of common reason and the unique revelation of their faiths. But there are so many radical discontinuities between sacred texts and scientific data, to give one critical instance, that they presently prefer compartmentalizing truth. Religious truth is assigned to one mental chamber while clashing modern knowledge is segregated in another. Some few true believers seek to resolve the tension by rejecting modern knowledge altogether.

Liberals can appreciate the respect for God's uniqueness that lies behind this schizoid existence, but they find it distorted by its lack of a balancing appreciation of every human being's ability to know God. They would agree that God's incomparable indwelling presence must be accorded proper respect and dignity rather than become debased by being reduced to people's ordinary, workaday sense of things. At the same time, the non-Orthodox reject a compartmental-ized spirituality because they believe that the human soul, created in God's image, ought to strive to be one even as God is one. And that means coordinating the discordant elements of one's personality into an ever-expanding whole, integrating one's spiritual experience with that of one's faith community and, reaching beyond that, with the experience of all God's children.

Hence liberal spirituality ideally knows no barrier between what we learn from every other human discipline and from religion's teaching. Explicating that unified sense of human existence has turned out to be a more difficult task than early liberal religious thinkers estimated. Not the least reason for this has been the unexpected shifts our modern worldview has taken as people have studied humankind and pondered its recent sorry behavior. Nonethe-less, liberals know that their distinctive way of serving God centers on this pursuit of the integrated soul.

This dedication arises from a compelling sense of what the human spirit can achieve when empowered to use its gifts of intelligence and creativity freely in God's service. In youthful exuber-ance, the non-Orthodox grandly proclaimed the doctrine of human perfectibility and practiced social action as messianism. Today that soaring self-esteem appears naive and destructive, but not so much as to refute two precious liberal truths. One, in significant if limited ways human beings can substantially transform the world and make it more just and loving. And two, God's mandates still may be heard, directing each generation in new as well as in old ways.

Simple realism requires us to acknowledge immediately that even the supposedly mature self can easily collapse into willfulness or idiosyncrasy. On this score the challenge of the orthodoxies to the nonorthodoxies has considerable merit, and postmodern liberals need to respond to it. Thus, as I shall explicate in more detail later, I believe the Jewish self ought never think of its existence as merely individual—hence the modifier "Jewish"—but always as existing in Covenant. It will then exercise its autonomy in partnership with God, with the Jewish community of the present, with the community of the past through its tradition, and with the Messianic Age through working for the Jewish people's future. Living the Covenant in this postmodern fashion will surely not enjoin the specificity that often makes the orthodoxies attractive today. But it also cannot, for all its emphasis on human self-determination, be called anarchic, libertine, or uncommanded. In its devoutness it finds the imperatives arising from our people's Covenant with God more directly through the self than through any text or tradition.

In the backlash against modernity that has swept across Western culture, the orthodoxies have shown how deeply they still appeal to the human spirit. But despite their continuing power, most people who have tasted the personal dignity that modernity has conferred upon them have rejected orthodoxy. I see this judgment arising from a quiet conviction that the secular movement to individualism, pluralism, and democracy has a lasting spiritual validity that cannot be denied. Or, more rhetorically, it expresses a sense that God has spoken to us through the personal freedom modernity has conferred upon us so that, for all that we may have abused it, only in its affirmation and responsible use can we truly serve God.

I have conducted this analysis in the broad context of our Western religious experience so as to correct what seems to me a widespread misconception in the Jewish community. People often feel that our inner struggle over the contemporary meaning of Torah hinges essentially on our Jewish loyalty or willingness to sacrifice some measure of selfhood for our Judaism. Though that may be partially true, it overlooks the greater human spiritual/social development of which we have been a part. Our essential problem is not specifically Jewish but historical. Little that we argue among ourselves cannot be paralleled in other religious communities challenged by modernization, secularization, disillusionment with those trends, and now the possibilities of postmodern nonorthodoxies. We, like them, must decide on the mix of modernity and tradition we believe to be faithful to what God demands of us. That, more than any other issue, will determine what we mean by Torah and how we envision its substance.

18   When Community Takes Priority

WHERE SHALL non-Orthodox Jews, who deny that God's revelation comes to us in verbal form, find a compelling sense of Jewish duty?

For nearly two centuries this question has been at the heart of Jewish non-Orthodoxies. Despite our intellectual and practical experience with it, we have reached no consensus in either theory or practice. If anything, the issue has become more perplexing as the years have shown the early responses to it inadequate. Caring Jews find themselves increasingly conscious of a clash between two of their most authoritative intuitions, the value of self-determination and that of Jewish being. How shall we create an integrated self when, on some primal level of awareness, we find our selves directed to be simultaneously individualistic and oriented to the present yet also communally and historically shaped?

Only the doctrinaire will seek to resolve the issue in either/or fashion. Though most of us insist that without effective autonomy we have no self-dignity, Vladimir Jabotinsky won many adherents to a Zionism that proposed creating a nation that would act as one in unquestioning execution of its leader's will. Most of us also take it for granted that there will be no meaningful Jewish continuity without the Jewish heritage and community being able to make some demands on us. The critical difficulty, then, is one of balance: What are the proper roles of the self and the group in determining what a Jew *ought* to do?

Taking Our Jewishness Seriously

I stress "ought" because I believe it critical to this discussion to highlight the urgency associated with Jewish doing. Consider, for instance, the weak sense of "ought" one can gain by aesthetic validation, by commending Jewish acts as emotionally rewarding and personally enriching, the "art form" we utilize to enhance our existence. This approach has a certain strategic value when we seek to draw into our midst people estranged from our community. But

254

by validating Jewish acts in terms of the personal satisfaction they afford, we make Judaism only another activity that must continually prove its worth to us or be discarded. The competition is severe, for we are inundated with other possibilities of improving our lives and realizing our ideals. Any Judaism that did not largely cater to our needs but made significant demands on us could not then long hope to compete and survive.

If Jewish continuity means anything to us, we need enough Jewish seriousness to provide a certain measure of steady Jewish doing. As a matter of simple practicality, if we, like all minorities, do not differentiate ourselves from our culture's homogenizing tolerance, we will as good as disappear. Choice, dedication, and a certain measure of sacrifice must hold back the debilitating social entropy today as they did in centuries past. Only now that we have given up the belief that God made us unique we must take upon ourselves a greater responsibility for the perpetuation of our Jewish way of life.

That simple pragmatism does not take us very far along the road of Jewish obligation. When we want to judge realistically how significant something is to us, we ask what, in fact, we will do for it. What do we demand of ourselves for its sake? What sacrifices will we make for it? That standard applies with particular power to what now purports to be the life of Torah, and it provides the bite of the common Orthodox critique of non-Orthodoxy. Though the liberals claimed modernization would halt assimilation, the result has only been to slow its depredations somewhat. Non-Orthodox Jews commonly do little, know little, and care little. Whenever a substantial conflict occurs between society's and Judaism's demands on their time, energy, or attention, Judaism regularly loses out. The reason is clear: Essentially, they expect Judaism to serve their needs, not to require dedication, self-denial, or sacrifice. The life of Torah has become that devalued.

Because my Judaism teaches me the ground and goal of my existence and serves me only as I serve God, I think this attack has considerable validity. Reducing Judaism to an adjunct to our lives rather than what structures our existence entire, betrays my experience of Judaism as the ground of my values, breaks with our people's traditional self-understanding, and clashes with the post-Holocaust awareness that has brought many of us to a more intense Jewish self-consciousness. The sacrifice criterion of value can be carried to unreasonable extremes, as in the suggestion that the best Jews are those who take on the greatest number of halakhic stringencies, *ḥumrot*. Neither extreme will do; scrupulosity does not demonstrate Jewish good faith and the self as the measure of all things trivializes our Covenant with God.

I am moved by recent Jewish history to intensify this discussion. Might martyrdom ever be required of contemporary non-Orthodox Jews? I pray wholeheartedly none of us ever faces such a situation, even in the skewed ways that our world might present it. Nonetheless, I ask: Does our present sense of non-Orthodox Jewish duty ever require us, under very special circumstances—so, already, the *halakhah*—to die for our Judaism? If not, if Judaism is not ever worth dying for, then it is hardly significant enough to live by. Acknowledging this strong sense of ultimacy and urgency about Jewish duty, I cannot be satisifed with a weak Jewish "ought." I seek a theology of serious non-Orthodox Jewish obligation that respects the self's autonomy.

Giving the Authoritative Self Covenantal Obligation

This analysis already indicates the intellectual core of our problem: Modernity has taught us the spiritual value of locating authority in the individual, not in tradition or community, where Judaism largely lodges. I do not intend by this bald endorsement of individualism to mitigate my argument (chapter 12) about the sociality of the single self. Most of us owe our passion for autonomy to our socialization, first through the human relations of our families and later from participating in democratic institutions. I only wish to point out the radical disparity that modernity introduced between the authority of the self and authority derived from any power external to it.

Jewish thinkers over the years have had some special difficulties to face in addressing this problem. Two reasons born out of compelling Jewish experience have made it imperative for them to defend a strong doctrine of individualism. First, Jewish rights in the modern world legally derive from it. We have been welcomed as equals into our societies as persons, not as a community or nationality. Any Jewish argument that groups as such may legitimately place their corporate interests ahead of all individual rights would empower other groups to do the same, opening the way to discrimination and the ghetto. Second, individual conscience authorized the modernization of Judaism despite the protests of the traditional rabbinate; it created a *de facto* democratization of Jewish decision making.

Paradoxically enough, Zionism also grounded itself in the individual will. Though it sought to make nationhood the essence of personal Jewishness, its development counted on the right of individual Jews to break with past patterns and join with others to assert their common national vision.

These socio-religious reasons for commitment to self-determination remain so cogent that despite its baleful effect on Jewish observance, most modern Jews live by it. A postmodern theology of serious Jewish duty must then take the form of reconciling an effective autonomy with existence in Covenant.

Only one substantial theory to this effect has stood the test of time, that of Mordecai Kaplan. He argued that our folk has substantial authority over us because Jews, like all human beings, naturally work out their individuality in terms of a particular ethnic culture. At one time there was another widely accepted theory of Jewish duty, that of Hermann Cohen. He bid us constrain our autonomy by our reason, structuring our lives by "religion of reason." Though Jews continue to uphold his insistence on the centrality of the ethical, they no longer agree that people are as rational as he supposed or that an adequate Jewishness can be attained through practicing universal ethics.

Kaplan's Effort to Empower the Jewish Community

Mordecai Kaplan encountered this problem in an earlier form than it takes for those of us who have in recent years, in Rosenzweig's terms, been making our way back to the center of Jewish existence from its periphery. Kaplan's appreciation of particularity came from being part of a wave of immigrants who found the older, German-Jewish patterns of accommodation to American churchified and alien. In reaction, they attempted to keep their rich ethnic Jewishness a vital part of the new life they sought, and Kaplan gave this affirmation of Jewish particularity a theoretical formulation.

One measure of his accomplishment may be gauged from what he knew he had to accept from his liberal predecessors, rationalism and universal ethics—and thus too the problem of the socialization of autonomy. He resolved this difficulty by shifting the universe of discourse from idealistic philosophy to that of the science of human behavior. Sociology—and occasionally psychology—furnished the hermeneutic with which he read Jewish experience and extrapolated the direction of its reconstruction. This ingenious move linked his two interests. By basing himself on a science, he maintained modern rationality, but by basing himself on sociology he could emphasize the power of ethnic groups to shape individual existence. The universal, which seemed so great a threat to Jewish survival, now made his case for Jewish particularity.

Kaplan affirmed personal autonomy, granting the single self an internal authority significantly independent of its socialization and insisting that the moral law constituted an independent criterion of acceptable folk creativity. His commitment to the rights of conscience is made more impressive because, to maintain it, he had to argue a thesis that contradicted the scientific worldview: that the moral law inhered in nature. He also passionately espoused democracy and pluralism, insisting that they must be the principles by which the modern Jewish community operated. Perhaps in all this he was stating the truth of his own life, that of a maverick who exemplified the moral power of the single self over against Jewish tradition, yet who knew himself to be intimately one of the Jewish folk.

He held this individualism in tension with the power and importance of the community. Social science demonstrated that individuals naturally function in social groups and, with few exceptions, even our individuality manifests itself only as a counter-current in our culture. Thus, while we do have the dignity of our autonomy, we normally give it expression through our people's civilization. That is simply the *natural* thing to do—the highest accolade in this kind of system—or, to shift to contemporary metaphors, it is the "healthy" or "mature" way to live. Where that is not commonly taking place, as is true in modern Jewry, Kaplan's diagnosis was that our culture was failing to meet the social needs of Jews, essentially because we regarded ourselves as a religion rather than as a folk civilization. He therefore argued that identifiably Jewish acts should have a twofold value: They should meet individual human needs while also providing survival value for the Jewish people. Thus, in his dialectical view, individuals cannot be detached from their community, yet the group must validate itself in significant part by satisfying their rightful desire for self-determination.

Kaplan also presented a pragmatic argument for social participation. As a confirmed democrat, he expected community norms to be made by the group as a whole, making it likely that we who were involved in making the decision would abide by it even when we disagreed with it. More than an astute social-psychological observation, this thought also points to Kaplan's concern for the individual will in a community-centered system.

Can Kaplan's Community "Command" Us?

With what sense of urgency would democratically adopted particularistic norms confront the individual Jew? This is not an easy question to answer, but it is critical to the search for an adequate theory of Jewish duty. A look at various scenarios should move us toward an answer.

Suppose the community calls on us to act in a way fully consistent with our highest moral standards. Then, with the individual and community in close agreement, the potential issue conflict between them disappears. Should the community by its action have aroused this Jew's somnolent conscience, the individual would have been guided by it, should be grateful to it, and should do what it suggests. Yet we must note that whether in initial or subsequent agreement, the autonomous individual conscience has, in this instance, invested the community norm with its authority.

Something similar occurs when the community calls us to observances we usually find pleasant or enjoyable, as happens with many rituals or customs. Then I am likely to follow its behests partially because they come from my community but very much more because my experience provides a reason for my doing so. We find a good instance of this meeting of concerns in Reform Judaism, a movement often faulted by caring Jews for fostering self-determination to the detriment of communal Jewish discipline. Despite their principled espousal of individualism, most Reform congregations have been able to strengthen the Jewish education they provide by stiffening two congregational standards. In the one case, the confirmation ceremony that took place originally when students were in the eighth grade, thus thirteen, has twice been raised so that the standard has now become the tenth grade, occasionally the eleventh. In the other case, almost no congregation will allow the full social celebration of a *bar* or *bat mitzvah* if the child has not been in training for two, more often three, years. In both situations, the agreement of most Jewish parents that they wanted a reasonably adequate education for their children made the community norm possible and effective. Numerous other examples of harmony between autonomy and community could be adduced from the Jewish community or elsewhere. In these examples of communal-individual congruence we can feel the truth of Kaplan's insistence that a people continually reshapes and reinterprets its folk norms in accord with its ethos so as to meet its members' needs.

The more interesting cases occur when I am indifferent to or put off by a norm that the community considers significant. In such instances we are all somewhat willing to extend ourselves and do sometimes simply for the sake of the group. We will rouse ourselves to go to certain meetings or participate in certain activities. We will also feel compelled to do certain other things we might not personally care about simply because we know other people expect it of us, like serving a socially acceptable repast at a *simhah*.

The problem is that turning *mitzvot* into *folkways* sharply reduces the urgency behind them. Consider the fate of some duties Kaplan's system makes central to Jewish folk existence. He deems the land of Israel the center of our ethnic civilization and its culture the preeminent substance of Jewish folk life. Yet despite the claims this theory makes on individual Jews, Reconstructionism, like most pro-Zionist groups, has not moved many American Jews to make *aliyah* or even gain sufficient proficiency in Hebrew that it becomes a significant medium of our Jewish cultural life. Here, where apparently central community concerns clash with what we believe to be a proper though more personally oriented Jewishness, we refuse to give the group, even one we cherish, very much sway over our lives.

This is often true even when community decisions have been arrived at democratically. To begin with, experience has taught us considerable cynicism about many such determinations, for we do not have much effective democracy in Jewish life, surely not in our American or world Jewish organizational structure, which passes for our polity. Moreover, few seriously suggest that much of the ordinary stuff of Jewish life can be subject to community reconsideration. The solar-lunar calendar with its annually wandering dates for the holidays and its mid-week occurrence for many of them; a Hebrew language that reads from right to left and has vowels above and below as well as in the middle of the consonant line; the system of blessings for all sorts of events; these and much else that still constitute everyday Jewishness might be refashioned in some of their detail but hardly as institutions. Insofar as we remain part of a continuing Jewish heritage we shall not be partners in determining the continuing validity of much of our Judaism. It simply comes down to us from prior ages. Though some of it must go, though we add our own contribution to it and interpret the rest in our own way, what remains

may well be not what we personally or even communally would
have devised or find most attractive. But it is the tradition our people
created and bequeathed to us, and not fundamentally the result of
our democratic decision even in reaffirmation and reworking. As a
result, as long as Jewish communal norms have only social sanction
behind them, they will exercise only a limited claim on us.

When Ethics Outranks Critical Folk Needs

Kaplan understood something of the limits of his pragmatic
argument for Jewish obligation, but he thought that identifying
certain practices as critical to Jewish continuity would make them
an accepted part of Jewish citizenship. Specifying some acts as having
high social significance may momentarily invest a group norm with
high urgency. If we feel that our people or community faces an
emergency, especially a direct threat to its existence, many of us will
be roused to action, even to sacrifice. But that is the exceptional case
and like the halakhic doctrine of *pikuah nefesh*, the threat of death,
it cannot be the principle on which we hope to carry on everyday
Jewish existence through history.

In the latter third of this century much of world Jewry successfully energized itself by the normalization of emergencies, by con-
verting threats to Jewish survival to spurs to Jewish living. With the
Holocaust in the background and the perils of the State of Israel an
immediate reality, our people disciplined itself for survival's sake.
Customarily fractious Jews long sat on their consciences and re-
strained themselves from public protest against what they saw as
disturbing Israeli acts. And when the Communist empire collapsed
and Russian Jewry was free to go to Israel, world Jewry, regardless of
other considerations, extended itself to make possible a speedy,
effective emigration. In these experiences, Kaplan's vision of the
authority of the group over the individual found concrete exemplification.

So too did his teaching that universal ethics overrides the duty
of group loyalty. Three times in this same period, grassroots Jewry
rejected for ethical reasons what its leadership said was "good for
the Jews" and insisted on a shift in direction. In the earliest instance,
well before Gorbachev's liberalization, American Jewish leaders
refused to accede to Israeli pleas that we stop being so hospitable to
Soviet Jewish emigrés coming to the United States, in order to
encourage them to go to the State of Israel. Despite the high priority

given to the needs of the State and the obvious importance of immigration to its survival and well-being, our community could not in good conscience comply. Our divergent values were decisive. We believed so in the rights of individuals to decide where they wanted to go that our leaders resisted the demands of the Israeli statesmen whom they normally considered to be the leaders of our people.

The second clash of values surfaced in the American Jewish reaction to the Israeli policy on the Palestinians and, by extension, to its incursion into Lebanon to destroy the P.L.O. In the mid-'70s, the community, determined to demonstrate solidarity, massively interdicted and destroyed Bereira, the first organization with numerous Jewish scholars and Zionists to challenge openly the State of Israel's approach to the Palestinians. From that point on, the community discipline of solid American Jewish support for Israeli actions continually eroded. By the time of the Lebanon foray,. the penetration into Beirut, and the Israeli support that made possible the massacres at Sabra and Shatila, many American Jews could no longer repress their moral outrage at these results of political-military realism. The Intifada finally canonized this change in attitude and many American Jewish leaders and organizations began taking public stands that not many years before they had branded treason to the Jewish people. This development reached something of a climax when the Israeli government gave financial support to Jews enabling them to occupy a multiple dwelling in the Christian Quarter of Old Jerusalem. This made even AIPAC, a registered Israeli lobbying organization, and the Anti-Defamation League, a long-time apologist for Israeli actions, publicly criticize the Israeli government.

The third example of the limits of asserting the community's good over individual values was the near-revolution brought on in American Jewry by the threat, after Shamir's reelection, to reintroduce the "Who is a Jew?" legislation in Israel. Suddenly, the long sacrosanct "unity of the Jewish people" reversed its meaning. Where it had meant repressing moral dissent for the State of Israel's sake, the proposed change in the Law of Return made such "unity" unconscionable. Most American Jews understood group unity in a quite American sense, that is, as implying a oneness based on a vigorous pluralism—and, of course, itself based on the rights of individuals to be different within a social order. The extraordinary passion this issue aroused may be gauged by two facts. It had little relation to reality since few non-Orthodox converts to Judaism make *aliyah* each year. It also caused an upheaval in the institution most impervious to Jewish difference of opinion but the one whose views on such matters counted most: the American Jewish fundraising apparatus. Over the years federations have carefully positioned themselves above all discord in the community so as not to jeopardize their mission. Yet the revulsion at the power grab by one element of Orthodoxy ran so deep among so many that, to survive, federations nationwide had to break with their long-established, well-founded practice of never getting involved in controversy and take a public stand for pluralistic Jewish unity.

I have not thought by this analysis to invalidate Kaplan's teaching, only to point up the limits of his social argument for community authority as long as it continues to give autonomy effective veto power. Experience over the years indicates to me that our ethnic group, simply as such, has little practical sway over us.

The Need for a Theological Theory

Intellectually, too, Kaplan's argument is unpersuasive. He based his theory of group authority on social science's findings about human nature and human needs. This procedure immediately raises the methodological question as to whether any science, by setting the necessary framework for our thinking, is competent to set the character of a religious group. That issue aside, two logical problems still press in upon us. First, the sociological data on which Kaplan relied extrapolated from the study of groups living in premodern fashion, that is, relatively untouched by modern technology, science, and political organization. How do we know that what once held true of social life in those circumstances continues to be true today? More specifically, why should one assert that the character of a culture developed by a substantially secularized, urbanized, and institutionally educated society exhibits the same characteristics and the same integration as that of a people untouched by these formative influences?

Second, assuming the logical permissibility of the extrapolation from the "primitive" to the modern, what logical basis can be adduced in this instance to justify Kaplan's jump from what *has been* the case to what now *ought to be* done? Kaplan sought to validate the group's claims on us by saying that they always functioned this way and did so in response to human needs. This does not, however, lend them much normative power since now that we know how they operate we can ask whether we want them to function this way. To argue that we cannot change what sociology has shown to be the regular structure of social arrangements lends a determinism to sociological findings—here actually a theory of society—that goes far beyond the usual claims of the discipline. Moreover, insofar as this theory has cogency, it is the same for all groups and does not apply only to the Jewish people. As Kaplan admitted, one day the mature American culture will meet all the needs of Jews and there will then be no reason for them not to make Americanism rather than Judaism their ethnic context. Anyone who believes that Judaism ought to have far more claim on us than that will find Kaplan's theory of Jewish duty inadequate. In addition, I do not see any other secular intellectual resource that can endow a tradition or a community's injunctions with anything like the power that secularity assumes to be vested in personal autonomy.

Despite the difficulties it engenders, the autonomy of the self must somehow be a foundation of any contemporary theory of Jewish duty seeking to reempower tradition and community. It appeals to the one source of authority to which, because of experience and intuition, the contemporary intellect attaches credence: the self. Our problem then becomes showing how, in consonance with our sense that our Jewishness rightly lays ultimate demands upon us, Jewish responsibility somehow inheres in the self. As we have seen, that cannot effectively be done as long as we follow the customary pattern of beginning with a universal selfhood and then seek to build a significant Jewishness upon it. Rather, to be true to our insight, we must overcome the schizoid Jewishness of the-human-being who happens-to-be-a-Jew. My Jewishness is not secondary to anything but primary to my being, a notion I understand Rosenzweig to have discerned but which it has taken some seventy years to clarify and articulate. Instead of construing Judaism in terms of law, idea, nationality, or ethnicity, a postrationalist—that is, a postmodern—Judaism needs to be defined in terms of utter human being, that is, as the faith/life of a particular selfhood, the self that knows itself to be a Jewish self. Only in that way, I believe, can we specify how autonomy, normally so destructive of the particular, might be the basis of a readily identifiable Jewish life. I shall return to this theme in chapter 20, but one further step must first be taken.

It derives from my prior polemic against the secular empowerment of the self, one so great that we trust its authority against all inherited wisdom or established institutions. I see no rational basis for such confidence. The more we learn about the self, the more we are open to the full range of experiences that are part of its ongoing reality, the more we have reason to question its reliability. Indeed, because we have asked the self to carry the salvific burden of creating all meaning and guaranteeing all hope, it has inevitably disappointed us. The self is more our problem than the source of our answers.

I believe it necessary to carry out this polemical argument not because I wish to deny that the self has any significance but only to indicate that on its human own it cannot command the dignity and worth we have found it to possess. When, however, we understand all human selves to be covenanted to God we can understand their inalienable dignity and the ground of the responsibility that properly makes them human. And Jewish selves relate to God not simply as one of humankind but as part of the people of Israel's historic, ongoing Covenant relationship with God.

I must, therefore, first discuss how God interacts with us. That cannot be through verbal revelation of what we ought to do as Jewish selves lest the truth of our autonomy be lost. But if there can be a form of revelation that does not overpower selfhood while endowing it with something of God's own authority, then the *benei noah* and the *benei yisrael* can each come to a new sense of the concord of autonomy and community.

19   Knowing What God Wants of Us

S AN ADULT, I have often been conscious of the Transcendent coming directly into my life. Sometimes its presence has been fairly clear and definite; mostly it has been rather general and unspecific; always, as I have reflected on it, it has been unspectacular and ordinary. Often my awareness has come as a result of study, observance, prayer, or interaction with people; but, mostly, my direct, personal exposure to Divinity has helped me grasp the spiritual depth of these somewhat indirect experiences rather than the other way around.

Whatever the case, I early overcame my middle American skepticism about it and knew I was involved with an independent Other and not merely in a new intrapsychic activity. Of course, I cannot "prove" that or even say very much about It/Her/Him. Valuing community and leery of self-deception, these limitations trouble me, for thoughtful public deliberation can make us more responsible. However, I have become convinced that the essential difficulty lies not with what I allege without warrant but with the reductive discourse that secularized sophisticates require. This restricted cultural vision has also led to a massive inability to assert the authority of ideals, the reality of persons, or, for that matter, the nature of any complex reality like love or goodness. Knowing them not to be illusory, I have become skeptical of skepticism and remain confident that this One I confront is real. Moreover, I find this Ultimate to be of such superlative quality as to lift me far above myself in aspiration and, often, in consequent action. I am surprised, grateful, honored, commissioned by this intimacy with the Other that I and our people call, let me say it, God.

This reality lies behind my effort to think about revelation, about our knowing what God wants of us. I find considerable continuity between my experience of God and what in a wondrously more exalted way must have happened to the prophets, psalmists, codifiers, chroniclers, and their transmitters; their old words regularly evoke a deep, disclosive resonance in me. I feel a kinship too with all those ordinary Jews over the generations who have known personally that God maintains and renews the Covenant and sends them on their dutiful way; carrying out the practices they created

266

and performed, I not infrequently find myself feeling at one with them as I do with God.

Critiques of the Relational Metaphor

I know of no contemporary language-pattern that would allow me to communicate this faith with reasonable fullness. Being unable to create my own, I metaphorically utilize, as the least constraining medium available, the constructs of Martin Buber's thought. Buber interprets revelation as the by-product of the I–thou relationship, the result of our mutuality with the other—as we now reflect on it— bestowing on us new self-worth, meaning, and mission. I will not add here to what I have already written about this understanding but explore my sense of revelation by presenting my rejoinders to Buber's critics. Philosophic rationalists have objected most to the notion of revelation as relationship, while other thinkers have scanted his view out of ethical or Jewish considerations. Though these critiques often overlap, I will treat them separately in turn.

The most comprehensive charge by rationalists focuses on the evasiveness of calling for a source of knowledge that is exempt from our usual canons of debate and evaluation. Revelation now becomes so private, though interpersonal, an experience that it does not allow for the articulation and description of what transpires and what is communicated. Its validity, in part or whole, cannot be assessed or analyzed as would theses from other areas of inquiry. For many, to demand this privileged status for revelation seems but another defensive maneuver of religionists desperate to salvage something of their logically inadequate faith from the triumph of science's superior worldview.

Conceding that the claim of a privileged source of knowledge and authority can be abused, I have sought to set out my theological views in this detail and to subject them to the scrutiny of others. To the extent that this can be done, I think it important and responsible to do so. But what if the premises of contemporary rationalistic systems—the requisite empirical falsifiability of true propositions, for example—invalidate the reality and truth confirmed in one's self-critical life and in the long history of an estimable human community?

The basic trouble with trying to satisfy rationalist critics of religion is that their definition of what is true or real already excludes most significant religious assertions. I charge that their definitions or axioms are as much "privileged" as are those of religious experience; they are not essentially debatable since they set the ground rules for how to go about having a debate. Consider, for example, the arguments philosophers have over the proper nature of rationalism. Some of the key terms of one system are insufficiently rational for employment in another system, e.g., the pragmatists' "utility," the phenomenologists' "forms," the existentialists' "self." Philosophers differ so over what they mean by "rational" that there cannot be a "rational" determination as to which school of thought is most truly rational; it all depends on how you define the term. If such prerational determinations have so much influence over philosophical method and content, why should it be inappropriate for religious thought to ground itself in analogous insights?

In Plato's time rationalists could freely speak of love and refer to myths; only in recent centuries has the effective range of the rational been radically narrowed to include only objectively verifiable propositions. Should philosophic rationality again become hospitable to the broad flow of human concerns, religionists would not be driven to speak of separate realms of discourse. Moreover, if rational discussion permits refutation by psychological analysis, in this instance charging religious thinkers with "defensiveness," it can equally be leveled at the philosophers. Eager to protect their objectivity or their guild, they insist that only when one reasons by their standards may one be said to be properly thinking at all.

Critics also point out that speaking of revelation as relationship involves a contradiction. On the one hand, one claims that the experience involves such fullness of self–Other that it cannot be put into words; it is ineffable. On the other hand, theologians write a good deal about it. If the I–thou resists articulation, how can we make our assertions about God? Shouldn't theologians more logically follow the rule with which Wittgenstein climaxed his early thought: About that of which one cannot speak, one should be silent?

Judaism and other religions have often urged silence as the most appropriate human mode of speaking of the Divine, for silence cannot profane God's holy otherness. This hiddenness made revelation all the more precious to believers. What they could not do from their side—gain access to God's own truth—God had done for them, disclosing what they needed to know in language they could understand. Nonetheless, it is the nature of human beings to search for ways to communicate the limitless meaning they encounter at the heart of things. People worldwide have devised staggeringly diverse ways of conveying knowledge of the gods/God. These rarely include rigorous analysis but, more commonly, story, aphorism, parable, song, dance, and rite. Religionists regularly find it necessary to invent what by contemporary rationalistic standards are odd forms of symbolic discourse, in order to honestly convey their experience. Jews today still find these indirect, evocative, semiotic activities effective, though diminished in effect from the days when revelation was considered literal truth.

Abstract reflection on revelation also has pragmatic religious legitimacy. One undertakes it despite its impossibility, hoping to accomplish several purposes: to clarify things somewhat for oneself; to give helpful pointers to others; to see what might be learned from public discussion; to extend one's sensibilities by attending to others' insights. Such exchanges usually climax by people asserting that they do not know what other people mean or what experience they are referring to—the same thing that often happens among philosophers arriving at root disagreements. Facing our divergent premises, we can sometimes gain critical perspective on our own formative insights and, in reappropriating them, gain understanding of why we believe as we do. The same is true of the effect of our thinking on others. What we have managed to articulate may bring others to fresh awareness of what they have been experiencing, adding a new richness to their religious lives. Any living religious symbol might also do this, and the practice of religion—including reflection about it—draws its living power from this possibility.

Might Objects Disclose God to Us?

Objections also arise from the claim that a relational revelation might occur in encounter with anything. Critics understand that people in premodern cultures might find God in crags and brooks, or that prophets like Amos might be sensitized to God's message by a basket of figs, or Jeremiah by a seething pot. They do not understand how people in our time can believe that revelation as mutuality can take place between us and inanimate objects, such as trees.

I find a distinction of Buber's helpful in this regard. We find it easiest to understand the I–thou relationship on the basis of our experience with other people (the model I have generally used in this book for heuristic purposes). Buber, however, uses the notion more comprehensively, as signaled by his preference for the term "address" to indicate our turn toward the other. He too recognizes the special quality of interchange between persons, for they can indicate mutuality through words. He also suggests that relationship occurs on two other levels, each without language—in the one case, with preverbal entities; in the other, with what he calls transverbal "forms." Many things in nature, alive or dead, "speak" to people and, in the human spirit, music, art, ideas, and the like "address" us with a richness that beggars words. I know an artist who discerns things in color and shape that I do not see, and a landscaper who regularly becomes deeply intimate with land and plants. Despite my efforts to learn from them and others, I have come to recognize the limitations of my receptivity in these areas. I think my problem lies not with inexperience but with decades of conditioning to our cultural convention that questions about "how" things happen always be answered in I–it terms.

I am, however, much more in my element on the transverbal level. Ideas and music, for example, communicate to me in ways that go far beyond pleasure. I have known a mathematician who felt this way about a "beautiful" proof, and my colleagues who dance know something similar from movement. In reflecting on such transverbal encounters, I find it difficult to distinguish between what has been a moving emotional experience and what was genuine "address." As a consequence, I am more guarded about what I learn from meeting God on this level than I am about encounters on the interpersonal level. On the other hand I do not consider it truthful to my experience or that of others to deny that relationship of this kind takes place and may have major impact upon us.

In one respect I wish to qualify the foregoing generalizations about my experience of direct encounter with God. As my relationship with God has ripened over the years to a certain familiarity with God's presence—and thus with God's absence as well—I have found this intimacy to be the least problematic of all my *a posteriori* "evidence" for the truth of my life and faith. It has become the standard for my judgment of my encounters with things, people, and forms.

Is There Direct, Unprocessed Apprehension?

I must no longer delay speaking to the problems raised by my assertion that it is possible to have experiences unmediated by concepts and language. Two lines of attack can be mounted here, both rather technical. The first concentrates on the sequence of processes involved in "having" an experience. How can we assert that, so to speak, something "outside" us makes its way "inside" us unchanged? To the extent we call the experience "ours" and have little difficulty distinguishing it from those that occur to others, some personal acquisition of the "outside" must take place. Once we take into account our act of appropriating it, we can no longer argue that an unmediated experience has taken place. Experience inevitably involves our work of perceiving and hence cannot be called direct. Hermann Cohen took this argument to its logical extreme. If no empirical encounter can take place without our employing a cognitive means of processing the sensory data, everything we know begins with the mind's creative act of structuring itself.

The second objection moves from the issue of the inevitable priority of reason to the related issue of selectivity. Surrounding us is a buzzing, booming environment that mostly we do not experience. We must be making some ongoing judgment as to whether what impinges upon us deserves our attention, credence, and response, or not. We also need to be able to identify the kind of experience we are having in order to be able to attend to it appropriately, say, to distinguish one of beauty from one of God. If experience always involves evaluation, then there can be no direct access to others that bypasses the intermediary activity of reason, religion's claims to the contrary notwithstanding.

I believe this debate largely has to do with who sets the rules for the use of certain words. Philosophic rationalists believe terms like "experience" and "knowledge" lose their dignity and authority when used nonrationally. Perhaps people do have "some sort of experiences" that may be cognitively unmediated, but no rational person should care much about them. Only those that have a significant cognitive component deserve a rational person's concern. The disagreement also hearkens back to the issue of how to define human being. As it were, the first principle of the rationalist philosophic credo limits what the rational animal will find truly significant to that which has rational structuring and content.

These arguments, which require logic and language to precede experience, are difficult to discuss in the kind of discourse I am carrying on in this book without appearing to grant them. I have been attempting to set forth in simple, discursive prose the content and structure of my belief; that is, I have been putting it in the form of ideas. If I now seek to present the ideas that lead me to reject the notion that rationality necessarily accompanies experience, I will simply be giving evidence that significant communication requires rational structuring. Even the syntax and vocabulary of our didactic style concedes this point. I have been highly conscious of this problem in writing about this issue, but without abandoning this pattern of communication I cannot escape from the charge. I can, however, call attention to the issue and indicate that though I am playing the rationalistic language-game here, I do not think it the only one worth our attention or even the best one for trying fully to understand the meaning of existence. I employ it because I believe it has a certain limited usefulness and even because I get great personal pleasure from doing so, but I do not let it structure my life.

Prerational, Personal Religious Experience

I begin my response with a *reductio ad absurdum*. If we set forth a strong version of the argument for reason's priority to or accompaniment of all experience, it as good as denies the possibility of having a truly new fundamental insight, such as of a sole, unique God for whom there had been no real prior language or concepts. This sense of the breaking in of the utterly new has often led religious thinkers to speak of revelation as in-spiration, receiving an understanding from without. For somewhat similar reasons, theologians do not customarily identify revelation with ordinary experience—the kind in which one might well argue mind is always implicated—but have tried to indicate something of its special quality. Thus, Buber tries to clarify the differences between I–thou and I–it address, keeping revelation different but, in the modern style, not so exceptional as, say, mystic communion would be.

The analogy with interpersonal relationships gives us some indication of why theologians can describe revelation as unmediated. Consider how we proceed when we must decide how to respond when someone for whom we care greatly asks us to do something that requires us to put very much at stake. Of course we shall want to bring our mind and experience to bear on the decision as fully as possible. That often does not bring us to a decision and makes our situation deeply disturbing. Often, we shall finally come to a decision because of who we know the other person to be, something we determine largely in terms of their relationship with us. How do we come to such a significant judgment, one that lies beyond the reach of our reason? We do so through what we have "known/sensed/felt/

intuited" the other to be and, at our best, by transcending our conditionings to confront them and ourselves directly. When pressed to say how we knew what we had to do, we may not be able to give an explanation of the kind that carries weight in our culture, but we will say we nonetheless "knew." Reason may have preceded and later refined the insight, but it did not rule the self at the critical moment of insight and decision.

Authentic relationship obligates and does so in a curious dialectic of particular importance for postmoderns seeking to illumine their experience of being commanded by God. Its oddity begins with its shared authority. Were one of the partners dominant, as in Orthodoxy, we would have something like the master-slave relationship, a figure we shy away from in recent centuries, translating *eved Adonai* as "God's servant" rather than the more literal "God's slave." Of course, our hesitancy has good biblical foundation, God being depicted there as attending to human will and not overriding human freedom. We moderns have amplified that view of human dignity to include the critical power to share in the decisions that affect one. The model of relationship reflects this enfranchisement of the person by indicating that rightful authority arises *between* the parties involved. What they mean to one another, just who they discover themselves and this other to be in this relationship, the special depth and quality of what has and now continues to transpire between them, all exercise normative power on them. For to be true to another they must carry the meaning they have gained from their relationship into deeds; inaction—or unseemly behavior—damages, perhaps destroys, what they have meant to one another.

Curiously, too, they do not surrender their autonomy in all this, though its connotations have somewhat changed. Now the self (*autos*) discovers its duty in the relation with the other—not, as in Kant, through universal reason. Here the "law" (*nomos*) arises from what freely passes between two fully dignified selves, neither subordinate to the other, each making its claim on the other simply by the act of relating. Formally, this equal participation in the relationship transcends other status differences between them. In a family, for example, one may love in this personalistic fashion persons to whom one customarily defers or who, for whatever honest reason, look up to one. Genuine relationship can occur despite such difference in status and without compromising the worth that inheres in each of them singly. Just as a relationship with someone one highly esteems will have a special normative effect, wholeheartedly loving God, the one God of the universe, will most powerfully command us, albeit by our personal response rather than by God's verbalized mandates.

What, then, does God "reveal" if not a detailed teaching that legend says has been kept in Heaven since before creation? God now makes known just what we make known in a relationship: self or, more familiarly, presence. God may be "right here," but we remain unaware of it. Revelation begins in our awareness but could not transpire if God did not also "come forth to meet us" and enter into personal intimacy with us. In response, we determine what we now must do, exercising our autonomy not as isolates but keeping faith with the God to whom we have been and to whom we yearn to remain close.

Can We Be Certain Now or Tomorrow?

If we grant the possibility of such unmediated knowing, how can we know the relationship is real and not an illusion? Recent religious history has been replete with frauds and our own lives have often been beset by self-delusion. If we do not carefully distinguish between spurious and authentic relationships, we become irresponsible about no less a matter than our relationship with God. A related unease arises from asserting religious continuity but then insisting that relationship's normative power arises only in the present. If this moment alone directs me and no past experience of relationship can be rationally identified, on what basis do we equate the God we encounter now with the God we—and our people—claim previously to have met?

In these issues rationalism asserts its undeniable virtues and casts light on the special problems created by nonrational exposition. I agree that where rational argument is appropriate, one's judgments can be made with considerable confidence—but that statement no longer carries the power it once did when rationalists seemed the children of light. Today granting authority to rationalism means accepting the assumptions of one or another system of thinking. With rationalists divided over what constitutes a proper rationalism, with that decision necessarily pre- and therefore nonrational, a nonrational approach to a given topic cannot be dismissed out of hand as it once was. The hermeneutic power of a nonrational approach to a given set of concerns may make it the preferable mode of setting forth that particular content. Thus, I have been arguing for its employment in religious thought because its power to uncover and illumine is less reductionist and more fully disclosive than the alternatives. It will not yield the kind of certainty that rationalisms produce in areas of their adequacy, but I, like many other caring Jews, do not find this cause to panic and fly to an orthodoxy or a rationalistic philosophy. Rather, the kinds of uncertainty it produces seem characteristic of the most humane forms of contemporary thought. Thus I agree with those who associate maturity not with a consistent set of certainties about the world or history but with an informed openness that allows for growth and change while demonstrating sufficent integrity to avoid the irresponsibility of relativism.

Rather than interpreting religion by abstracting reality into cognitive (mathematical) simplicities, I find it best explicated by proceeding in terms of the most complex reality we readily know, persons. The analogy to relationship clarifies why we believe a real God relates to us and why we can claim this association has continuity. To begin with, how do we know that someone we love is real and that we are not deluded about them? The simplest answer, that they look and act like a person, will not long do, for we mean something more than having a body or exhibiting certain behaviors. We often point to this something more by referring to a "real" or "genuine" person, a qualification we readily employ in daily affairs in judging whether we have been treated as persons or as things. When someone has related to us in full mutuality, we know that both our own personhood and that of the other are "real." In the afterglow of an event of genuine relationship, we have little doubt about it, though the passage of time can make us less certain, perhaps to the point of anxiety. Only another encounter can reassure us. In the exceptional case, a single meeting affects those involved to such depth that its certainty remains for all time. More commonly, even our moments of great significance give way to doubts. If we are to love, we must live with this fearsome alternation of knowing/not-knowing. Personhood does not allow more certainty than this, and even the records of the saints show this to be the common pattern of relationship with God.

We also easily speak of relationships extending through time despite the harsh reality that the immediacy of encounter begets only a temporary certainty. It sometimes manifests such quality that we hope it will recur, allowing acquaintance to ripen into friendship, perhaps even love, or, almost miraculously, the love that elicits the pledge of self for the life we call marriage. We cannot be certain this will ever happen, but we also know it sometimes does because we have had certain true relationships in our lives. So enduring relationships begin in the hope that the confirming meeting will recur and restore our assurance. If that does not happen, the relationship ends though no one can give a rule as to how much waiting makes sense. Should our expectation be rewarded, we have little difficulty identifying the present other with our old intimate, though we both change ceaselessly, as does our relationship. Being thus renewed in relationship we become empowered to endure its sad cycle of knowing, loss, hope, and occasional fulfillment.

Our relationship with God follows this pattern closely. We know God's reality not by reasoning about God but by that kind of human reach that opens us to God's presence. It too finds its staying power as it returns to overcome the skepticism that besets us in the face of the trials life thrusts upon us. Why should responsible people risk their lives on so "subjective" a judgment? Because, to begin with, this side of an orthodoxy we make no serious choice that is untouched by significant hazard. The record of the many rationalisms that in recent decades have betrayed their adherents' utter confidence confirms our wariness of intellectual rigidity. Our choice cannot realistically be limited to risk-free alternatives; the best we can do is to insure that the risks we undertake—here, accepting experience of God as self-validating—have safeguards that reasonably compensate for our mistakes and misapprehensions. For Jews, this means that the burden of this discussion shades over into the consequences of relational revelation for our lives, a theme I will begin to discuss in this chapter and continue in the next.

Two things, however, must immediately be said here. First, the ineffability of the experience that gives rise to our duties does not exempt them from subsequent rational scrutiny and evaluation. We have too often seen the privileged status of certain knowledge unleash reprehensible behavior—hence the imperatives deriving from our religious experience require intense, nonreductive, rational, public examination. Scrutiny is not absolute insurance against folly and mendacity, but it can, in fact, often save us from them.

The second matter has to do with the increased possibility of deception occasioned by God's never becoming an object to us. We cannot escape that hazard without endorsing idolatry, but the temptation waxes strong because of the eeriness of relationship with the incorporeal. With human beings, their physical presence implies their selfhood and our closeness. But we have no tangible indicator of the evanescent One so critical to our lives. Psychically and existentially, our poignant longing for the physical makes much sense, but it also confuses the two levels of address that the relational metaphor clarifies for us. Bodies never in themselves give us genuine knowledge of persons, nor can all the empirical evidence we can muster ever bring us into relationship. We can and do connect bodies with selves, often to good effect, but until the "it" becomes "thou" and the relationship that transcends the physical exists, we cannot know whether the intimacy that once passed between us still lives. Before the next encounter, all genuine living proceeds by faith—and that too has been the experience of the pious with God.

Can Personal Relationship Provide for Social Ethics?

I turn now to three ethical objections to revelation as relationship: one, that this personalism fosters relativism or anarchy but not social conscience; two, that its immediacy negates structure, continuity, and moral law; three, that it does not adequately control against the demonic in us.

Post-Enlightenment ethics, by beginning with individual autonomy, must specify how the self's freedom ought to be contained. Kantians hardly saw the issue, assuming that rationality itself included universal ethics. Today, as various contemporary rationalisms deny this premise, with libertarian radical individualism a particularly stimulating alternative, relativism and anarchy have become major problems for all rationalistic ethical theories. Relational revelation, because it manifests a similar regard for the individual self, shares the common plight of modern ethics.

Two traits above all keep this concept of revelation from the limitlessness of relativism. Once selfhood acquires full meaning only in terms of relations to other selves, our potential willfulness has a critical limit: every other self and the entailments of our relationship. If all that appears too privatistic, one must remember that selfhood in this theory can never be simply self-determining; it always remains linked to the God who undergirds all encounter.

This already begins to indicate why relational revelation necessarily mandates social concern; indeed, its dyadic understanding of selfhood is more inherently social than most modern ethical theories that begin with a monadic, Cartesian self and then must struggle to validate otherness and groups. Moreover, the I–thou address and normativity should not be thought of as limited to two partners, though it most commonly arises that way. Groups also experience genuine relationship whenever people involved in a similar activity or special event find themselves engaged with one another in a corporate yet personal sharing of meaning. Should it recur with some regularity, we shall be bound to the group in utter depth.

This experience should not be confused with group contagion or mass hysteria. In both, individuals lose themselves in the crowd by letting themselves be swept away by the mass mood (some people build their lives on this surrender of self to a larger whole). By contrast, reflection suggests that the exaltation that frequently is a by-product of an authentic group encounter does not become central to the experience and lead to a loss of self in the whole. Rather, our individuality remains intact as it expands by means of this involvement with many other selves. When God stands not as the shadowy background of the coming together but as the conscious center to and from which all the lines of relationship derive, the experience of community becomes even more intense. Religious groups that exemplify and communicate this experience exercise a compelling influence on us, validating our loyalty to them and their disciplines.

The reality of group relationship, small or great, serves as a further check on individual arbitrariness. It not only personifies the universal moral horizon, it gives us others with whom we share standards of humaneness and who might therefore be able to instruct us in our ethical perplexities. Community tradition, social by its very inclusiveness, endurance, and practice, now can come to us with great authority—but not with such absoluteness as to override our autonomy. The group can be wrong; it may have perverted or become insensitive to its central vision, the one that bound us to it. Then we must dissent or dissociate ourselves from it not because we anarchically trust only our own conscience but because, after serious deliberation, we find our living experience of what has bound us to this community moving us in another direction.

The possibility that at any moment we might overthrow the rules that once guided our life appears to substantiate the suspicion that this theory devalues the continuity that ought to mark a moral life. Accumulating an aggregate of decisions faithful to given moments does not deserve the ethical commendation of a lifetime's consistent growth in personal integrity. The issue can be extended to the realm of applied ethics. What will our ethics realistically amount to if it can only yield oases of justice but not policies and institutions that channel group activity through the great social wilderness of impersonal time?

The vice of flightiness and the sin of preserving one's purity by disdaining moral accommodation ought to be denounced by any Jewish theology seriously committed to the sanctification of history. Relational revelation meets this challenge by recourse to its theory of our bi-level address to the world. Genuine encounter involves no solipsistic lingering in the meeting but carries with it a commission to transform our lives and our world in terms of the ennobling quality we have experienced. Our autonomy then adopts, coopts, or creates structures to enable us to live the truths we have known directly or through our communities. These verities commandingly provide the framework of our individual and social existence as long as they remain true to their mandate, perhaps even renewing it in us as we carry out their prescribed activities. The stability they give to our lives never accords them ethical hegemony. We all have suffered too much from meaningless rites, soulless groups, barren convention, and self-serving institutions to deny the self ultimate primacy in its need/critique of social involvement. Nothing more is being asserted here than the continuing emphasis on voluntarism that lies at the heart of every democratic ethical theory. In this instance, however, the autonomy being celebrated arises in relationship with others (specifically, the Jewish people) and with God, and not in pristine individuality.

The philosophical version of the foregoing criticism denigrates personalistic revelation for its inability to generate moral law, that is, rationally compelling imperatives that could rightfully restrain impulse and direct will. But I do not see that any theory can satisfy this aspiration now that Kantianism has become only another possible mode of moral reasoning rather than the necessary pattern of living rationally. Reason surely remains our moral guide to responsibility, but only within the terms of the prerational ethical assumptions that are its basis.

Perhaps I can extend my case for personalism by showing how its second-level application can provide one with an I–it ethical principle. Its equivalent of the Kantian categorical imperative may be put this way: To the extent that you can, treat everyone as if they had been or now might be a thou you have known in encounter and create forms of interacting with them that reflect and foster that kind of personhood. I suggest that this principle has shown its moral power in our time as people have sought to include various social outsiders in their world and to create personal community wherever possible. One can usefully learn from applying these quasi-philosophic generalizations to many situations, but they are no substitute for the living dialogue with persons that gives this I–it theory the power to command.

The ethical critique reaches a climax in the charge that this theory does not adequately control the demonic in us. Any deprecation of this problem itself constitutes evil and every thinker must speak to it out of the humbling knowledge that our once-vaunted defenses against the demonic have shown themselves to be tragically weak in our time. Nonetheless, though the ultimate primacy of the self provides a ready opening for the devil, I must in all honesty maintain it. No theory is person-proof; the *yetzer* is that wily. All that we can do is seek to provide adequate checks on it. I do not know better ones than those I have been adumbrating: the immediate sociality of the self; the intimate linkage of self and God; pursuit of the unique quality of personhood in relationship; the second-level scrutiny of reason; the esteem of community opinion and humane tradition; the creation and renewal of personalistic structures and institutions; the provisional use of generalization in assessment; and a hermeneutic of suspicion with regard to exceptional claims for the self.

Can Relational Revelation Mandate Steady Jewish Action?

The Jewish objections to this doctrine of revelation introduce no new theoretical problems but only give particular form to some of those previously discussed. To introduce my discussion, I wish to reject the charge that Jews should be suspicious of a theory of revelation that applies to all humankind exactly as it applies to Jews. Classic Judaism, in its teaching about the Noahide covenant, asserted that all human beings had some knowledge of God and God's commandments. Any Jewish theology that does not adequately account for the religiosity of the Noahides must therefore be judged deficient. The Bible and Talmud do depict the Sinaitic revelation as a once-and-for-all-time occurrence. I agree with the vast majority of contemporary Jewry in finding the utter exceptionality of Jewish revelation introducing too great a mental gap between what we believe about human experience generally and what we nonetheless proclaim as uniquely true of our people. I therefore consider situating revelation to the people of Israel within the larger context of human revelation to be an important Jewish theological step forward.

Jewish critics of personalistic revelation charge it with invalidating a critical characteristic of Judaism, *halakhah*. As a logical observation, the indictment has merit: one cannot derive a legal structure from a theory that ultimately reserves authority for the self—even the self in relationship. But I reject the normative principle that authentic Jewish continuity requires the halakhic process. Our people did not lack Covenant-faithfulness in the millennium before the rabbinic period, when its primary religious structure appears to have been priestly and cultic. This precedent allows for the possibility that the rabbinic structuring of Jewish life that proved so effective until the Emancipation may now need to be drastically altered. Positively put, do the radically changed Jewish social status and cultural ethos that resulted from modernization prompt us to devise a more appropriate way of framing Jewish existence?

Two interrelated considerations, one practical and one theoretical, lead me to say "Yes." To begin with reality, almost all Jews who have modernized now consider Jewish law to be instructive rather than obligatory. Only the Orthodox and the few non-Orthodox ideologically committed to the necessity of *halakhah* discipline their lives by it. The remaining members of the caring community simply take for granted their right to determine what provisions of the *halakhah* they will and will not observe.

These Jews have negative and positive theoretical grounds for their insistence on autonomy. They do not believe God gave the Written and Oral Law and they remain unpersuaded that the Jewish desirability of the halakhic process should lead them to constrain their freedom by its rulings. Were there a non-Orthodox theory of revelation that indicated how God authorizes the corporate determination of individual Jewish duty, many might bend conscience to a newly flexible *halakhah*. But no one has yet provided one and the task seems presently undoable. The stumbling block remains the authority we have vested in selfhood. We have no compelling theories of corporate authority that still allow for something like the normativity we commonly grant to self-determination; mostly, we prefer to reason from self to society.

Moreover, to introduce "flexibility" into the halakhic process constitutes an unwarranted break with the classic halakhic process and this can be justified only by unconsciously asserting the right of a later generation to self-legislation, which is autonomy in another form. The rejoinder to this charge consists of citing the many precedents for the introduction of substantial changes into the *halakhah* as a result of social variation. But it is disingenuous to suggest that we are only doing the same thing today. The sages never cite progress in ethical thought or historical spiritual growth as a reason for halakhic change, and we come to every question with a self-conscious openness to the possibility of innovation they would have deemed heretical. Hence, a theology of "flexible" *halakhah* would have to validate our authority to make changes in ways that the overwhelming majority of those who today discipline their lives by its precepts would consider a break with the past.

As a result of this theological impasse, protagonists of the necessity of structuring non-Orthodox Judaism on a "flexible" *halakhah* have sought to save their case by asserting either of two positions: first, as David Novak asserts, that it is a dogma of Jewish faith; or, second, as Elliot Dorff and Neil Gillman humanistically argue, that the Jewish ethos requires us to live by *halakhah*.

The caring non-Orthodox Jewish community has indicated its rejection of both arguments by a non-halakhism it defends as a matter of conscience. As long as Jews continue to believe that a God-given dignity inheres in each single self, a *halakhah* that can require the significant surrender of "conscience" will be unacceptable. The issue can perhaps be put most clearly in terms of the immediate implication of the term *halakhah*: discipline—a notion made more explicit by its equivalent term, *din*, law or rule. The *halakhah* is not just something that the *rav* "says" but a ruling that, once he has specified it, the people are *required* to do, classically, by God's own authority. Any concept of *halakhah* that foregoes this notion of requirement should not call itself "*halakhah*"; that is, if one is using the term figuratively, one should expect the resulting "*halakhah*" to have only figurative authority, with the true legislative power reserved for the self. With so many Jews only willing to accept *halakhah* as *guidance*, I am convinced that we have come to an end of the period when Jewish living could still be disciplined by rabbinic *halakhah*. By contrast, I believe that the relational theory of revelation generates the possibility of creating its own pattern for giving form to Jewish life—its own "halakhic" structure—and I shall discuss it in the next chapter.

Does this theory of revelation so normalize God's commanding presence as to rob it of appropriate awesomeness and diminish the revelation at Sinai? But we cannot reclaim Sinai's power without reaffirming the most extraordinary miracle of the Bible—God personally communicating the Ten Utterances (and later writing the commandments as well as giving the Oral Torah). For moderns and postmoderns alike, the Sinai experience must be brought into the common range of human experience. The relational theory of revelation enables us to do so unreductively. It "explains" by presence how God and people communicate and it recognizes that this can happen to nations on special occasions. It also appreciates those uncommon moments when encounter occurs with such fullness that our lives can never be the same—and Sinai was just that for our people. No longer a miracle, it remains wondrous enough to draw the Jewish spirit to existence in Covenant.

I do not see it as a defect in this theory that identifying revelation with genuine relationship renders communication with God an ongoing, everyday occurrence. This is simply the reality behind common piety. Even we ordinary Jews know that now and again we stand in God's immediate presence and find ourselves specially obligated because of it. High on my list of things I wish for in Jewish life today is the existence of more Jews who regularly share such ordinary intimacy with God. The simplicity of these encounters will refresh the appreciation of the genius of the prophets, psalmists, and other biblical authors whose spirituality could not borrow, as ours does, from the prior experience of millennia. They broke new religious ground with such success that their words still inspire and instruct people the world over. Our little touch of revelation does not entitle us to hope that anything we discern will have the equivalent depth and staying power. Nonetheless, it will do what Jews have always known revelation to do: direct us to our duty as participants in the Covenant.

One critical problem remains. If we seek to be true to our postmodern intuition that our Jewishness is primary and not tangential to our existence, this theory of revelation must be restated to take into account the absoluteness of Jewishness. We can do so through the concept of the Jewish self, to which I now turn.

20   The Jewish Self

ODERN AND POSTMODERN non-Orthodox Jewish theologies diverge decisively in their views of the self's Jewishness. All the great modern systematizers considered it axiomatic that contemporary Jewish thought must be constructed on the basis of universal selfhood. To accommodate this concept, they willingly redefined Jewish responsibility in terms of the hierarchy of value it entailed: self first, Jewishness second. I rather see Jewish truth—the Covenant—as the primal, elemental ground of the Jew's existence. Without denying the spiritual validity of universal selfhood, I assert the need to rethink its meaning in Jewish terms. Jewish selfhood arises within the people of Israel and its Covenant with God. Put in this unqualified form, the definition not only includes Orthodox as well as non-Orthodox Jews but could be used by thinkers of either group, lending it an inclusiveness that helps persuade me of the conceptual value of this approach.

I detect something of this personalism when some contemporary *poskim* (halakhic decisors) claim the right to issue directives to the community simply on the basis of *daas Torah*. In these cases they assert their authority in terms of their general "knowledge/sense" of Torah, though they cannot validate their stand on this specific issue by citing direct halakhic precedents. I interpret this as pointing to the legislative authority of their personal intuition of our Jewish duty, one growing out of their learning and piety but finally valid as the insight of a Torah personality. I have in mind something similar, a non-Orthodox self that is autonomous yet so fundamentally shaped by the Covenant that whatever issues from its depths will have authentic Jewish character. The secular conception of autonomy must be transformed in terms of its Covenantal context. We will best understand what this means by tracing the cumulative threefold progression of self (secular) to self-God (universal religion) and thence to self/Israel/God (Judaism). Since this recapitulates much of the direction of this book, I will briefly review the foundation of the first two ideas and give the bulk of my attention to their culmination in the theory of the Jewish identity that mandates postmodern Jewish duty.

The Truth and the Limits of Secular Selfhood

The notion of the self-determining individual occasionally occurs in classic Jewish texts, but modern Western democracy so embel-

lished the notion that it gained utterly new spiritual power. The
resulting ideals of person and society it projected so enlarged the
Jewish soul that they made the pains of Emancipation well worth
bearing. We contemporary Jews may have jettisoned the optimism
that once sacralized modernization, but the very experience that has
made us more realistic has reinforced our steadfast devotion to
self-determination. Witnessing the moral failures of orthodoxies,
institutions, and collectives has reconfirmed our trust in the self as
the best critic of iniquity and our indispensable defense against social
tyranny.

Emancipated Jewry imported the notion of the self into Judaism
primarily under the rubric of ethics, which commended itself for
uniquely integrating freedom, duty, Jewish change, and social responsibility. The irresistible interpretive appeal of an ethical framework
may be estimated from the unanimity with which our thinkers made
it central to their theories of Judaism. Mordecai Kaplan's naturalism
provides even stronger testimony to the sovereign power of ethics
than does Hermann Cohen's neo-Kantianism, which identified ethics
with reason. Kaplan, who made folk culture the effective creator of
human value and thus always open to revision, insisted on one
exception to this rule: moral law. In Martin Buber's shift of thought
to personalism, the interhuman experience becomes the paradigm
not merely for duty but the whole of the religious life. Abraham
Heschel, despite making God's revelation, not human experience,
the fulcrum of his theology, intimately identifies the prophetic
experience of God's reality with the imperative to reach out to every
human being. On no other theme—not God, nor the people of Israel,
nor revelation, nor messianism, nor law, nor theological method—
do these thinkers so completely agree.

This key concern of modernism remains vital today as postmodern non-Orthodox Jews continue to feel issues of interhuman obligation addressing them with an unparalleled imperative quality.
Though they envision their Jewish duty as extending far beyond
universal ethics, no other realm of Jewish obligation regularly outranks it.

Though the thinkers to whom I referred echoed the Enlightenment notion of the self, they significantly changed its meaning and
that of its corollary terms by organically fixing them in a religious
context. In various ways, they all declared that the autonomous self
makes sense only in terms of each person's ineluctable bond with
God, the source of our dignity and the criterion of its correct use.
Our tradition spoke of this as the (Noahide) covenant, a term

whose legal origin conveyed a sense of seriously contracted specific obligations. Opposing a heteronomic understanding of it, I reinterpret the term through the metaphor of personal relationship, which communicates duty without depriving either participant of selfhood and autonomy—an experience as characteristic of direct relationship with God as with persons through whom we know God indirectly.

Martin Buber, who taught us this self-God paradigm, also believed that single selves could join in common encounter, turning, for example, ethnic groups into nations whose formative experiences still exercised normative power over their descendants. He therefore believed that Zionism made certain inescapable national-spiritual demands of contemporary Jews. Yet he insisted that the independent self remained the judge of the legitimacy of group injunctions and he never clarified how one could integrate group authority with such rigorous individualism. This interpretation of his thought does not enable us to take the step from self-God to self-Israel-God that would explain the postmodern intuition of the absoluteness attaching to Jewish identity.

Can the Noahide Self Take Jewish Particularity Seriously?

Because of Buber's continued liberal confidence in the single self (and despite the fact that he shifted its reference point from reason to relationship) I consider him more a transitional modern than a postmodern Jewish thinker. Rosenzweig sought to move Buber from this individualism and thus make possible a more authentic Jewish existence, but because Rosenzweig agreed that a postrationalist theory of Jewish duty needed to be grounded in the self, he faced the same difficulty. He finally integrated thought and intuition by dogmatically asserting that Jews must, in principle, accept the authority of the law, allowing practice to produce its personal confirmation. So to speak, he is the existentialist equivalent of what later emerged as the postmodern flight to Orthodoxy.

Rosenzweig's effort to add the law to the self-God relationship has a contemporary counterpart. Some thinkers suggest that if we derived our rulings on specific contemporary issues by classic halakhic methods utilized with non-Orthodox flexibility, we then would produce fully authentic *halakhah*. They variously argue that many factors might make such rulings authoritative to many despite the loss of the halakhic process's theological foundations: our continuing esteem of Jewish law; our respect for time-hallowed Jewish forms; our regard for Jewish scholars; our desire for non-Orthodox Jewish communal structure; and our willingness to accept an authentic Jewish discipline. Yet, to date, only a small minority of the non-Orthodox regularly subordinates its own good judgment to such rulings.

Autonomy lies at the heart of the decision about this suggestion. Why should thinking Jews consider giving up their self-determination to follow the rulings of decisors who have Jewish learning but otherwise no greater access to God's present will than the rest of us possess? The answer cannot be simply the cogency of their rulings, for these inevitably raise the question of the criteria they employ in reaching their decisions. Sometimes they are lenient, sometimes stringent, sometimes they insist on specific textual warrants, sometimes they substantially rely on interpretation. How do non-Orthodox decisors determine when a historical or ethical development requires us to change the law or resist changing it? For that matter, how can "history" require anything since it has no objective reality but depends entirely on the historian's theory of how we ought to structure events? (As applied to theology, this problem of the unknown criteria by which it is determined what traditional beliefs remain valid or must be discarded has been the chief criticism of the historical theologies of thinkers as diverse as Kaufmann Kohler and Louis Jacobs.) Judges have always manifested such methodological vagaries and have been enfranchised to do so by the authority vested in them. When God stood behind the operation of the *halakhah*, the self had no basis upon which to question given rulings. But without a non-Orthodox theology of halakhic process, what validates the old processes or simple learning in the face of conscientious Jewish doubt?

We cannot expect formal similarity to the past to empower even a responsive Jewish legal system without a convincing theory of authority to persuade us we ought to sacrifice our autonomy to it— and if we do not, it is merely wise counsel, not law. A modernized halakhic process could have considerable Jewish value, but we shall know what constitutes authentic "flexibility" only when we have theologically established its meta-*halakhah*. And only when we have been personally persuaded of the validity of its theory of Jewish decision making are we likely to make its rulings our law.

I think it unlikely that a non-Orthodox relegitimation of Jewish law would have either theoretical success or practical effect. I therefore turn first to the theological task and only then inquire what kind of Jewish discipline it engenders. I suggest we, whose Jewishness is primary to our existence, should reverse Buber's strategy. Instead of positing an axiomatic universal selfhood in whose terms we then seek to validate Jewishness, we seek to interpret our elemental Jewishness by the culturally compelling metaphor of selfhood, that is, by explicating the nature of a Jewish self.

Five Premises for Jewish Duty

Like all humankind (the *benei noah*), Jewish selves (the *benei yisrael*) have a grounding personal relationship with God; but where the *benei noah* relate to God as part of a universal covenant, the *benei yisrael* have a particular, ethnic Covenant with God. Being a Jew may then be described in this metaphor as having an individuality that is elementally structured by participation in the Jewish people's historical relationship with God. In the ideal Jewish self one can detect no depth, no matter how intensely one searches, where the old liberal rift between general self and particular Jew still occurs. Jewish selfhood arises as ethnic existentiality while remaining an individuality dignified by autonomy; in this case autonomy is properly exercised in terms of its ultimate situation in the Jewish people's corporate, historic relationship with God.

In contrast to contemporary privatistic notions of selfhood, the Jewish self, responding to God in Covenant, acknowledges its essential historicity and sociality. One did not begin the Covenant and one remains its conduit only as part of the ongoing people of Israel. Here, tradition and ethnicity round out the universal solidarity of humankind which this particularity grounds in its myth of the Noahide covenant. With heritage and folk essential to Jewishness, with the Jewish service of God directed to historic continuity lasting until messianic days, the Covenanted self knows that Jewish existence must be structured. Yet as long as we honor each Jew's selfhood with a contextually delimited measure of autonomy, this need for communal forms cannot lead us back to law as a required, corporately determined regimen. Instead, we must think in terms of a *self-discipline* that, because of the sociality of the Jewish self, becomes communally focused and shaped. The result is a dialectical autonomy, a life of freedom-exercised-in-Covenant. It differs so from older non-Orthodox theories of folk discipline—Zionism or Kaplanian ethnicity—or personal freedom—Cohenian ethical monotheism or

Buberian relationship—that I wish to analyze in some detail its five major themes.

First, the Jewish self lives personally and primarily in involvement with the one God of the universe. Whereas the biblical-rabbinic Jew was almost entirely theocentric, the contemporary Jewish self claims a more active role in the relationship with God. In the days of buoyant liberalism this self-assertion overreached to the point of diminishing God's active role, sometimes countenancing supplanting God with humanity writ large. Postmodernity begins with a more realistic view of our human capacities and a determination not to confuse the junior with the senior partner. Knowing Who calls and keeps us as allies endows each self with a value it could never give itself even by extraordinary achievement. To believe we bestow meaning on ourselves by our deeds inevitably destroys us, for no one can successfully keep filling up the relentless now of personhood with estimable accomplishment. When we live in Covenantal closeness with God—asked only to be God's helpmeet, not God's equal in goodness—we acquire unique dignity and power and can hope to remain whole even when burdened by the world's injustice and our own heavy sins.

This consciousness of ongoing intimacy with God precedes, undergirds, and interfuses all the Jewish self's other relationships. It ties us to God's other partners for more than pragmatic or utilitarian reasons and gives us an ineradicable stake in humanity's welfare and destiny. It binds us with particular intensity to other Jews with whom we share a special dedication to God.

Yet the Covenant that affirms us also subjects us to judgment in terms of the quality learned through our personal involvement with God. What we do as persons, lovers, friends, citizens, humans, Jews, must live up to it or be found wanting. Wherever the Jewish self sees faithfulness to God imperiled, Covenanthood requires it to be critical as well as supportive, perhaps even temporarily withdrawing from others in order to remain true to what once made them close. This applies with particular force to the people of the Covenant. Pledged to live most intensively with God, this people and its communities must always stand under special scrutiny even as they also deserve our special love.

Community, Tradition, and Messianic Hope

Second, a Jewish relationship with God inextricably binds selfhood and ethnicity, with its multiple ties of land, language, history, traditions, fate, and faith. By this folk rootedness Covenantal Jewish identity negates the illusion that one can be loyal to humanity as a whole but not to any single people, and it rescues the messianic hope from being so abstract as to be inhuman. Ethnic particularity commits the Jewish self to the spirituality of sanctifying history through gritty social and political struggles. Internally as well, each Jew becomes implicated in this people's never-ending struggle to hallow grim social circumstances or the temptations of affluence and show itself another faithful Covenant generation.

Nowhere can Jews hope to better fulfill the multilayered responsibilities enjoined on them by the Covenant than in the land of Israel organized as a politically sovereign, self-determining nation, the State of Israel. Every Jewish self must face the Covenantal challenge of the desirability of moving there to join the Jewish people in working out its uniquely full response to God's demand that we sanctify social existence. Jews who do not find themselves able to fulfill this behest must nonetheless live by a particularly intense tie to the land of Israel and measure their Diaspora fulfillment of the ethnic obligations of Jewish selfhood by the standard of the State of Israel's Covenant accomplishments.

Ethnicity also has a certain normative force. As the Jewish self ponders a decision, it must attend seriously to the attitudes and practices of other Jews in this matter. They share the same Covenant, serve the same God, and reflect the same folk experience and aspiration. Often, what Jews have been told to do and what they now value will commend itself as Covenantal wisdom. When the Jewish self has some ambivalence about its accepted path, loyalty to the folk will often cause the Jewish self to sacrifice personal predilection for folk unity. That most easily takes place when a community standard makes possible common ethnic activity—e.g., a folk, not a personal, Jewish calendar—or makes demands that hardly can be called onerous or defiling—e.g., *kiddush* over wine or grape juice and not the whiskey or spring water one might prefer. For the Jewish self, then, Covenant means Covenant-with-all-other-Jews, past and present.

For all the inalienable ethnicity of the Jewish self, it surrenders nothing of its individual personhood. In a given matter, the Covenant people may be inattentive to its present duty to God or, in a given situation, an individual Jew of certain talents and limitations may find it Covenantally more responsible to go an individual way. Now Covenanted selfhood requires conscientious self-examination in the light of community standards to determine whether this dissent of the Jewish self is willfulness or an idiosyncratic sensitivity to God. I shall return to this theme later in this exposition.

Third, against the common self's concentration on immediacy, the Covenant renders the Jewish self radically historical. Our Jewish relationship with God did not begin with this generation and its working out in Jewish lives has been going on for millennia. Social circumstances and Jewish self-perception have changed greatly in this time yet the Jews we encounter in our old books sound very much like us. Different social circumstances aside, the underlying relationship between God and the people of Israel has remained substantially the same. For one thing, the same religious moments decisively shape our Covenant sensibility—Exodus, Sinai, settlement, Temple, Exile, return, destruction of the Second Temple, Diaspora, the rise of the rabbis, medieval triumph and trial, which we extend by Emancipation, Holocaust, and Third Commonwealth. We too live by Jewish memory. For another thing, reading our classic texts inevitably points up the constancy of human nature with its swings between folly and saintliness. Jews then behaved very much as Jews do today. Hence, much of what they did as their Covenant duty will likely still lay a living claim on us. For the Jewish self, then, Covenant means Covenant-with-prior-Jewish-generations.

Many modern Jewish thinkers deprecated the idea of such a spiritual continuity. They thought our vastly increased general knowledge made us more religiously advanced than our forebears and optimistically taught that each generation knew God's will better than the prior one, a notion they called progressive revelation. Postmodern thinkers, such as myself, reverse the hierarchy. On most critical religious issues, no one writing today can hope to command the respect the authors of the Bible rightly continue to elicit. Moreover, since their life of Covenant was comparatively fresh, strong, and steadfast, where ours is often uncertain, weak, and faltering, we should substantially rely on their delineation of proper Covenantal existence. The biblical and rabbinic texts have every Jewish right to exert a higher criticism of the lives of each new generation of Jews, so classic Jewish learning must ground Jewish selfhood as firmly as does personal religious experience.

In one critical religious respect, however, we stand apart from prior generations: our conviction that we must exercise considerable self-determination. If some respect for Jewish individuality had not always characterized Jewish spirituality, we would be astonished at the luxuriant display of change and innovation we find in Jewish religious expression over the centuries. Our radically transformed social and intellectual situation elicits a corollary reinterpretation of Covenant obligation. In particular, our sense of linkage with God prompts us to identify spiritual maturity with the responsible exercise of agency. Hence, we find it necessary to take initiative in untraditional fashion in order to be true to what our Jewish self discovers in Covenant. Here, too, our sacred books make their authority felt by challenging us to ask whether our deviance has grown out of Covenantal faithfulness or trendy impulse.

Fourth, though the Jewish self lives the present out of the past, it necessarily orients itself to the future. All the generations of Jews who have ever been, including us, seek the culmination of the Covenant in the Days of the Messiah. The glories of the Jewish past and the rewards of the Jewish present cannot nearly vindicate Israel's millennial service of God as will that era of universal peace, justice, love, and knowledge of God. A Jewishness satisfied merely to meet the needs of the present but not radically to project Covenantal existence into the far future betrays the hopes of the centuries of dedication that made our spirituality possible. The Jewish self, by contrast, will substantially gauge the Covenantal worthiness of acts by their contribution to our continuing redemptive purpose. For the Jewish self, then, Covenant means Covenant-with-Jews-yet-to-be, especially the Messiah.

I can provide a personal analogy to the manner in which a vision of the far future limits the self in the immediate exercise of its freedom: the attainment of personal integrity. One can hope to accomplish that only over the years, for though the self constantly reconstitutes itself in the present, it also persists through time. Living detached from previous experience and with minimal concern for the future denies the chronological character of creatureliness and ignores our most creative individual challenge, to shape an entire life into humane coherence. The responsible self will cultivate the forms, habits, and institutions indispensable to long-range fulfillment. And when, in our frailty or indecisiveness, our autonomy falters before life's demands, we can hope these structures will carry our fragile self through the dark times with integrity unimpaired. All this is true of every human being but, I suggest, more intensively so for the Jewish self, whose integrity involves messianic steadfastness to God as part of the Covenant between God and the Jewish people.

Nonetheless, our Covenantal future-directedness may also compel us to break with an old, once valuable but now empty Jewish practice. For Jewish selfhood also requires us to assure the Jewish future by making our way to it through the presently appropriate Covenantal act. Even then, the awesome endurance of Jewish traditions will dialectically confront us with its question as to the staying power of the innovation we find so necessary.

The Compelling Selfhood of the Jewish Self

Fifth, yet despite the others with whom it is so intimately intertwined—God and the Jewish people, present, past, and future— it is as a single soul in its full individuality that the Jewish self exists in Covenant. I can illustrate my meaning best by using myself as an example. I must not hide from the fact that it is I, personally, who am making all these assertions. I believe God has objective reality—but I also do not know how anyone today can objectively make that assertion. I likewise believe that what I have been saying about Judaism is true regardless of my accepting it or not, that it would still be true and make rightful claims upon Jews even were I to come to deny all or any part of it. I proclaim the truth of the Covenant between God and the Jewish people, but I know I can only speak from my own premises and perspective even as other people must do from theirs. None of us can escape from radical finitude to a conceptual realm of unconditional truth. The self, free and self-determining, must then be given its independent due even though, as a Jewish self, its autonomy will be exercised in Covenantal context. At any given moment it is ultimately I who must determine what to make of God's demands and Israel's practice, tradition, and aspiration as I, personally, seek to live the life of Torah in Covenantal faithfulness. For the Jewish self, then, Covenant means Covenant-with-one's-self.

Before I turn to the issue of how Jewish selfhood could lead to a new sense of corporate Jewish duty, I want to say something about the gap between the ideal of the Jewish self and the realities of being an individual Jew. I have been describing more a spiritual goal than a present condition, my version of what Rosenzweig called our need to move from the periphery of Jewish living back to its center. By the standards of this ideal, fragmentariness and alienation characterize most Jewish lives today; our lives commonly reflect more the brokenness of humanhood in our civilization than any integrating

Jewish vision. This diagnosis leads to a therapeutic goal: bringing Jews to the greater wholeness of Jewish selfhood, a reconstruction of Jewish life that begins with helping individual Jews find greater personal integration, one that ineluctably involves them in community as with God. This constitutes the obverse of Kaplan's emphasis on changing our pattern of Jewish community organization so as to foster a healthy Jewish life.

How might this ideal, so individualistically based, bring a critical mass of Jews to communal patterns of Covenantal observance? It cannot be created by a contemporary version of heteronomous law as long as we continue to accept the personal and spiritual validity of self-determination. But if Jews could confront their Judaism as Jewish selves and not as autonomous persons-in-general, I contend that they would find Jewish law and lore the single best source of guidance as to how they ought to live. Rooted in Israel's corporate faithfulness to God, they would want their lives substantially structured by their people's understanding of how its past, present, and future should shape daily existence. But as autonomous Jewish selves, they would personally establish the validity of every halakhic and communal prescription by their own conscientious deliberation. We would then judge their Jewish authenticity less by the extent of their observance than by the genuineness of their efforts to ground their lives, especially their actions, in Israel's ongoing Covenant with God. The more fully they integrate their Jewish selves, the more fully will every act of theirs demonstrate their Jewishness.

With autonomy then an integral part of Jewishness, some subjectivity will inevitably enter our Jewish practice, leading to a greatly expanded range of Covenantally acceptable ways of living as an authentic Jew. Moreover, our simultaneous responsibilities—to self, to God, to the Jewish past, present, and future, and to humankind as a whole (through our continuing participation in the covenant of Noah) will frequently clash with one another, leading to different views as to which should have greater weight. For these reasons I avidly espouse Jewish pluralism in thought and action. In our contemporary cultural situation I am more anxious about the corporate than the personal aspect of Jewish selfhood and therefore eagerly await the day when enough Jewish selves choose to live in ways sufficiently similar that we can create common patterns among us. A communal life-style, richly personal yet Jewishly grounded, would be the Jewish self's equivalent of *halakhah*.

Does my call for a community openness so tolerant of individuality destroy our character as a distinct people? Has not autonomy escaped from its Covenantal containment and again manifested its anarchic and therefore ultimately un-Jewish character?

I cannot deny the risks involved in the path I am suggesting but any theory that makes democracy a spiritual principle of our Judaism will face something of the same risks—and I do not believe any large number of Jews today will accept a nondemocratic theory of Jewish duty. Moreover, the act of passing substantial power from the rabbis to the community has, for all its weakening of community discipline, also produced unique human benefit. The demand that everyone in our community tolerate other Jews' radically differing views has produced a harmony among us unprecedented in Jewish history; our contemporary distress at Jewish interreligious conflict testifies to our ideals and to our distance from the Jewish past, when surly antagonism often reigned among us. Though Covenantally contextual individualism will surely amplify Jewish diversity and threaten communal solidarity, there will never be any question about its directly authorizing and commending Jewish democracy.

An Odd but Instructive Case

I can make my meaning clearer by providing some concrete examples of how I apply this standard (though I acknowledge that others might utilize the same theory to reach other conclusions). I begin with a somewhat unusual matter: how an Orthodox Jew should face the issues created by the medical treatment of dwarfism. The *halakhah* imposes no special disabilities upon Jewish dwarfs, and while the condition is troublesome to those who have it and often a heavy burden for their relatives, it does not constitute a threat to life deserving of exceptional halakhic consideration. Some halakhic urgency for the treatment of dwarfism arises from the greater than usual difficulty dwarfs have in conceiving children.

The special halakhic difficulty once raised by dwarfism arose from the hormone with which it was treated. Before it had been synthesized, the hormone had to be collected from human corpses, bringing the laws of respect for the corpse into conflict with the desirability of curing a non-life-threatening condition. Various decisors discussed how the incisions should be made in the corpses so as to create the least disfigurement, wishing to be as respectful as possible while fulfilling the law's higher concern with a significant human need.

The non-Orthodox Jewish self would think about this issue in somewhat different fashion. A corpse, the physical remains of the self, surely deserves respectful treatment. Indeed, with lessening concern for the dead—fewer people saying *kaddish* and visiting graves—Jews need to be reminded that we do not know disembodied persons. However, when one thinks primarily in terms of selfhood, there will be little doubt that the needs of a living person override respect for a corpse. One can surely be a Jewish self as a dwarf, yet the selfsame psychosomatic view of the self that authorizes honoring corpses makes us appreciate the trials of dwarfism. Hence I would rule with little hesitation that the suffering of the dwarf, not respect for the corpse, would be our primary Covenantal concern here.

Fortunately, we find little difference in the practical outcome of applying Orthodox and Covenantal procedures. But, hypothetically, had rigorous *poskim* imposed such stringent conditions on cutting into the corpse as to have impeded the collection of the hormone, I would have demurred. I do not believe our tradition implies, our community wants, or God requires our giving the corpse such precedence over the living—and in this theoretical situation I could not accept the *halakhah*.

The classic cases of the *agunah* (deserted wife) and *mamzer* ("bastard") trouble us very much more than does dwarfism because they can create a radical distinction between what the *halakhah* can allow and what non-Orthodox Jews perceive as our Jewish duty. If required, observant Jews will repress whatever stirrings of autonomous rebellion they may feel in these cases so as to faithfully follow God's law. The Jewish self I have described will far more likely react indignantly at the inability of Jewish legal authorities to respond to what they too know to be clear-cut human and Jewish values. To maintain proper legal procedure an *agunah* can be debarred from remarrying and establishing a fully ramified Jewish home. Or, in consequence of a parental sin, someone ruled a *mamzer* cannot contract a marriage with a *kosher* Jew. These disabilities contravene some of our most primary Covenantal responsibilities. The Jewish pain attached to them intensifies when we think of the Holocaust. Is there much in our hierarchy of Jewish duty that takes priority today over contracting a Jewish marriage and creating a Jewish family?

The Covenantal trauma created by these laws cannot be assuaged by mitigation, by suggesting that compassionate decisors will limit the number affected or that accepting the few unresolved cases will allow us to maintain familial unity among Jews. In fact, Orthodox decisors continue to declare some people *agunot* and *mamzerim* and apply the consequent Jewish legal disabilities to them. As I understand the range of my obligations under the Covenant, I do not believe God wants some Jews to relate to other Jews by categorizing and treating them as *agunot* and *mamzerim*. Thus I will abet Jews seeking to fulfill their Covenantal responsibilities outside these laws. As a pluralist, I oppose any suggestion by the non-Orthodox that Orthodox Jews should be asked to compromise their understanding of God's law for the sake of communal unity. I do, however, find it troubling that while the *halakhah* has kept some laws such as "an eye for an eye" in force but practically inoperable, contemporary *poskim* have not yet demonstrated such creativity in this area.

The issue of women's rights in traditional Jewish marriage and divorce law disturbs Jews like me far more because, committed so fundamentally to the concept of personhood, I consider women's equality a critical matter for contemporary Judaism. Again the mitigations do not persuade. But I cannot usefully say more. Non-Orthodox Jewish women have reminded us that they must be allowed to speak for themselves and they increasingly do so to those who will listen.

Exercising Responsibility as a Jewish Self: Four Instances

I can now make some generalizations about Covenantal decision making. Should our various Covenantal obligations appear to conflict, our duty to God—most compellingly seen in the treatment of persons—takes priority over our responsibilities to the Jewish people or the dictates of Jewish tradition. I acknowledge only one regular exception to this rule, namely, those cases that clearly involve the survival of the Jewish people. Without Jews there can be no continuing Covenant relationship, and it is the Covenant, not universal ethics, that grounds the autonomous Jewish self.

What should an autonomous Jew do when confronted by a conflict between a divinely based responsibility to persons and another one that directly contributes to the survival of the Jewish people? I cannot generalize about how the Jewish self should proceed when it must compromise one of two values that have shaped it fundamentally, but I can compensate by indicating how I respond to four such situations.

Many years ago, as I was struggling with the old liberal identification of Judaism with universal ethics, I realized the ethical unsupportability of the Jewish duty to procreate. Bringing a child into the world to bear the name Jew potentially subjects that child to special danger. All the joys and advantages of being a Jew cannot ethically compensate for loading this ineradicable disability on another. Yet the Covenant absolutely depends on Jewish biologic-historic continuity until the Messianic Days. For all its ethical difficulty then, I believe I have a clear Covenantal responsibility to proclaim the duty to have Jewish children.

Since many Jews believe that anything that limits the marriageability of all Jews critically affects Jewish survival, why do I then resist establishing one community standard for Jewish marriages and divorces? I do so because I believe our people will survive without a uniform marriage and divorce law. I base this conclusion on the fact that, despite their abandonment of the *halakhah*, the overwhelming majority of Jews worldwide still manifest a will to Jewish continuity. Without a relatively uniform standard of practice in family matters, Jewish life will not continue as it did when it had reasonable consensus in this area; but our people, as such, will survive. Reserving the supererogatory survival category for exceptional situations, I therefore cannot invoke it to override my Covenantal sense of human obligation in this matter.

Then why will I not perform intermarriages when by some accounts more than half of the resulting families raise their children as Jews? Why do I not accept their will to be Jewish as a viable means of Jewish survival and thus remove the Jewish bar to my simple human responsibility, uniting in marriage two people well suited to one another though of different religions? I am moved by such arguments and acknowledge that my "Yes, but . . ." response may appear even more subjective than usual. My positive response to such people's Jewish concerns leads me to reach out to them with warmth and gladly accept their children as Jews when they manifest Covenant-loyalty through education and participation. But I cannot be so approving as to officiate at their weddings, for it falsely symbolizes and communicates to them and others my understanding of Covenantal obligation. The relation between God and the Jewish people is mirrored, articulated, and continued largely through family Judaism. Jews like me must then necessarily prefer a family structure fully espousing the Covenant to one that seeks to do so but with inherent ambiguity. Moreover, I understand myself as a rabbi authorized to function religiously within the Covenant community only on behalf of the Covenant.

My rabbinic colleagues who differ with me on this issue do so because they read the balance between human and Jewish obligation differently than I do. They believe, erroneously in my opinion, that performing intermarriages will help win and bind these families to the Jewish people. Because I may well be wrong and because I respect their reading of their Covenant-responsibility, my pluralism makes itself felt here and I associate myself with them in full collegiality.

But it does not extend to those rabbis who now not only officiate at intermarriages but do so as co-officiants with Christian or other clergy. In so doing, they symbolize and communicate that it makes no difference what religion one espouses. They thus dissolve the Covenant of the *benei yisrael* into that of the *benei noah*. That clearly constitutes a threat to the survival of the Jewish people and its Covenant, and exceeds my liberally capacious pluralism. My Jewish self may not be able to state just where the boundaries of its openness lie, but in this instance it has no difficulty in identifying their transgressors.

Because I know myself to be related to God as part of the people of Israel's historic Covenant with God, I can be true to myself only as I, in my specific individuality, am true to God, to other Jews, to the Jewish tradition, and to the Jewish messianic dream. And while that truth is found more in the doing than in the thinking, it is by reflection on what constitutes true Jewish doing that Jews in every age have kept themselves alive to their responsibility as partners in the Covenant.

Afterword

WHILE WRITING this book I often became conscious of the stream of personal history flowing through me onto these pages and thus into the future.

My father grew up in the home of his maternal grandfather, Hershel Ahron-Yena's, who was a Slobodka *musmakh, moreh horaah*, ordained and certified to give others ordination. My great-grandfather had served as Rav of Sokoly in Lomza *gebernyeh* and then had a small *yeshivah* of his own there. My father reported that Hershel hated Hasidim and would cross the street if he saw a Hasid approaching. Loving Hershel, my father steered me gently toward the rabbinate and claimed that, if he looked away when I spoke in a synagogue, he could hear Hershel.

My mother met my father in the United States, having immigrated here from Koroscmezo, Hungary, a town she believed was somewhere near Jassy. Her father had died sometime after World War I, and when I got around to asking about him as I got older, she recalled very little. I was named after him, *Yehiel*, "God will live," a prophetic name for an American boy who would grow up wanting to be a Jewish theologian and would spend much of his life explaining that God was not dead. The only thing my mother remembered about Yehiel's Jewish practice was that each *Shabos* he would put on a *zaydeneh kapoteh*, a silk kaftan and, I think she added, a *shtraymel*.

I am, then, the product of an intermarriage between Litvak rationalism and Hungarian Hasidism. Perhaps that explains my determination to be as rational as I can about what I know to be my nonrational Jewish faith. In any case, from time to time as I wrote I would muse about what Hershel and Yehiel would make of the Judaism that I, who bear their influence, have given exposition here. But I was far more concerned about my grandchildren's generation. They may be as Jewishly different from me as I am from Hershel and Yehiel but I hope that I will help them move confidently into their Jewish identity even as my parents and their parents did for me. *Zekher tzadik livrakhah*, "the memory of the righteous is for blessing."

Glossary

AGGADAH   The texts in rabbinic literature which are not *halakhah* (see below); often homilies, folklore, anecdotes, and maxims

AGUDAT YISRAEL   International Orthodox organization, founded in 1912 to continue the traditions of the East European *yeshivah* world and to oppose political Zionism

AGUNAH   A women legally debarred from entering a marriage because her husband cannot or will not grant her a divorce, or whose husband's death cannot be properly established

ALIYAH   Immigration to the land of Israel

BAAL (pl. BALLEI) TESHUVAH   A sinner who has repented; used today to describe nonobservant Jews who have become observant

BAR/BAT MITZVAH   A boy/girl who has reached 13 (some congregations observe the traditional maturity of girls at 12 years and 1 day) and now stands under the obligations of Jewish law; also used for the ceremonies celebrating this milestone

BENEI NOAH   "The children of Noah"; humankind

BENEI YISRAEL   "The children of Israel"; the Jewish people

BERAKHAH   A blessing

BET MIDRASH   "House of study"; where adults gather to study texts

BILDUNG (German)   "Formation"; well-rounded education

BRIT   Covenant; often, specifically, the rite of circumcision

DAAS TORAH   "Knowledge of Torah"; that which entitles a great sage to give authoritative guidance on matters not specifically dealt with in classic legal texts

DAVVEN (Yiddish)   To pray in the East European manner

EMANCIPATION   The social and political enfranchisement of the Jews that took place in Europe during the 18th and 19th centuries

EN SOF   "Without limit"; in mystical theosophy, that aspect of God which is utterly beyond human comprehension

FRUM (Yiddish)   Pious, observant

GHETTO   Legally segregated section of a city in which alone Jews could live

GOY   "Nation"; gentile, non-Jew

GUSH EMUNIM   "Bloc of the Faithful"; Israeli Orthodox political group dedicated to settling Jews in the Occupied Territories

HAVURAH (pl. HAVUROT)   Small, face-to-face associations of Jews; in recent decades, alternative Jewish communities

HALAKHAH   The legal texts in rabbinic literature; Jewish law generally

HASKALAH   The movement for secular Jewish Enlightenment, which began in the 1770s and is generally linked to Hebrew or Yiddish culture

ḤILLUL ḤASHEM "Profanation of God's name"; figuratively, a shameful act

INTIFADA The name given by the Palestinians of the Occupied Territories to their anti-Israel campaign of the late 1980s

KABBALAH Jewish mystical tradition and literature

KERIAT SHEMA The formal, liturgical recitation of the *Shema* (see below)

KIDDUSH The blessing over wine on Sabbaths and festivals

KOSHER "Ritually acceptable"; proper, legitimate

LAAZ A foreign, non-Jewish language

LAW OF RETURN Israeli law granting the right of automatic entry to all immigrant Jews

MAMZER (fem. MAMZERET) The Jewish legal equivalent of "illegitimacy"; effectively, someone debarred from marrying a *kosher* Jew

MEGILLOT "Scrolls"; used to refer to the five biblical books: the Song of Songs, Ruth, Lamentations, Ecclesiastes, and, particularly, Esther

MELLAH Specifically the Jewish quarter in Morocco, but often used for its equivalent in other North African areas

MENTSH (Yiddish) "A human being"; an admirable person

MIDRASH Biblical interpretation; also, specifically, books in this genre

MIKVEH Ritual bath

MINYAN (pl. MINYANIM) The quorum of ten adult, male Jews required for full religious worship

MISHNAH The first authoritative compilation of the Oral Law, completed ca. 200 C.E., which provides the basis for the later talmudic discussions

MITZVAH (pl. MITZVOT) "Commandment"; good deed

MOTZI The blessing over bread

ORAL LAW, or ORAL TORAH Traditionally, that aspect of God's revelation at Sinai not revealed in written form but formalized and gradually put in writing, beginning in the 2nd century C.E.

PIKUAḤ NEFESH "Saving a life"; the halakhic provisions for exceptions to the law when a life is at stake

POSEK (pl. POSEKIM) Decisor; a sage whose determinations are authoritative

RABBIS In its restricted sense, the sages cited in the Talmud

RAV "Master"; a rabbi whose decisions one accepts as law

RESPONSUM (pl. RESPONSA) A formal, written response by a sage to an inquiry

SEFIROT In kabbalistic theosophy, the ten emanations of God

SHABOS (Yiddish) The sabbath

SHEKHINAH God's Presence

SHEMA The central avowal of Jewish faith; in a restricted sense, "Hear, O Israel, *Adonai* is our God, *Adonai* alone/is One"; in liturgical usage combined with other passages from the Torah

SHIKSA A gentile woman

SHTETL   A small Jewish settlement of Eastern Europe

SHTRAYMEL (Yiddish)   The broad-brimmed black hat, often trimmed in fur, favored by Hasidim on festive occasions

SHUL (Yiddish)   Synagogue

SIMHAH   "Rejoicing"; a celebration

TALMUD   The classic texts of rabbinic literature, essentially discussions of the Mishnah but with many additions; that of the land of Israel, known as the Jerusalem Talmud, was compiled about 350 C.E. but the more authoritative (and larger) version was compiled in the Babylonian academies about 500 C.E.

TESHUVAH   "Turning"; the movement away from sin and back to God

TORAH   The first five books of the Bible; more broadly the Bible and thus all the religious instruction which flowed from it

TORAH MISINAI   "Torah from Sinai"; God's revelation, particularly the Oral Law

TZEDAKAH   Charity; righteousness

TZIMTZUM   "Contraction"; in Lurianic theosophy, God's prelude to creation

WRITTEN LAW, or, WRITTEN TORAH   The first five books of the Bible

YESHIVAH (pl. YESHIVOT)   Academy for talmudic study

YETZER HARA   The will-to-do-evil

YETZER HATOV   The will-to-do-good

YIDDISHKAYT (Yiddish)   Eastern European Jewish folkways and culture

ZOHAR   "Splendor"; the classic text of *kabbalah*, written in Spain about 1275 C.E.

Two Bibliographical Notes

I

HAVING WRITTEN on these themes as far back as 1957, I drew on some of my papers to help me with this systematic statement of my theology. A few survived with some revision though most of the others supplied only a line of reasoning or some verbal prompts. Readers interested in seeing the continuity and change in my ideas over these decades will find the previous incarnation of the relevant chapters below, thanks to the permissions given by the holders of the various copyrights:

Introduction: "The Changing Forms of Jewish Spirituality." *America*, April 28, 1979.

Chapter 4. "The Problem of the Form of a Jewish Theology." *Hebrew Union College Annual, 1969–70*. Cincinnati: Hebrew Union College Press, 1970 and "The Idea of God," *Central Conference of American Rabbis Yearbook, 1957*. New York: Central Conference of American Rabbis, 1957.

Chapter 5. "Liberal Judaism's Effort to Invalidate Relativism Without Mandating Orthodoxy." *Go and Study, Essays and Studies in Honor of Alfred Jospe*, Samuel Fishman and Rafael Jospe, editors. Washington: B'nai Brith Hillel Foundations, 1980.

Chapter 6. "Beyond Immanence: How Shall Liberal Jews Educate for Spirituality?" *Religious Education* 75, no. 4, July–August, 1980.

Chapter 7. "Affirming Transcendence: Beyond the Old Liberalism and the New Orthodoxies." *The Reconstructionist* 46, no. 6, October 1980.

Chapter 8. "A Jewish 'Rumor of Angels'." *Sh'ma*, 16/37. September 19, 1986.

Chapter 10. "Liberal Jewish Theology in a Time of Uncertainty." *Central Conference of American Rabbis Yearbook, 1977*. New York: Central Conference of American Rabbis, 1977.

Chapter 12. "The Autonomous Self and the Commanding Community." *Theological Studies* 45, no. 1, March 1984. Another part of this article was used for chapter 16.

Chapter 14. "The Chosen People Concept as It Affects Life in the Diaspora." *Journal of Ecumenical Studies* 12, no. 4, Fall 1975.

Chapter 15. "Covenant Theology—Another Look." *Worldview*, March 1973.

Chapter 16. "The Dialectic of Jewish Particularity." *Journal of Ecumenical Studies* 8, no. 3, Summer 1971.

Chapters 17 and 18 were originally written for this book and presented as papers at conferences. The former was published in somewhat different form as "The Enduring Truth of Religious Liberalism," in *The Fundamentalist Phenomenon*, Norman J. Cohen, editor (Grand Rapids: Eerdmans, 1990). The latter, also with variation, will appear as "Autonomy and Community" in *The Proceedings of the Academy for Jewish Philosophy*, vol. 1, a new series to be published by SUNY Press, Albany.

Chapter 20. "The Autonomous Jewish Self." *Modern Judaism* 4, no. 1, February 1984.

II

IN RESPONDING to the ideas of other thinkers I have had these principal works in mind:

Ahad Haam. *Ahad Haam: Essays, Letters, Memoirs.* Oxford: East and West Library, 1946.
———. *Kol Kitvei Aḥad Haam.* Tel Aviv: Devir, 1949.
———. *Selected Essays of Ahad Ha-'Am.* Philadelphia: Jewish Publication Society, 1936.
Baeck, Leo. *The Essence of Judaism.* New York: Schocken Books, 1961.
———. "Mystery and Commandment." In *Judaism and Christianity.* Philadelphia: Jewish Publication Society, 1958.
Buber, Martin. *At the Turning.* New York: Farrar, Straus & Young, 1952.
———. *Between Man and Man.* New York: Macmillan, 1948.
———. *Eclipse of God.* New York: Harper & Brothers, 1952.
———. *Good and Evil.* New York: Charles Scribner's Sons, 1953.
———. *I and Thou.* Edinburgh: T. & T. Clark, 1937.
———. *Israel and the World.* New York: Schocken Books, 1948.
———. *Moses.* Oxford: East and West Library, 1947.
———. *The Prophetic Faith.* New York: Macmillan, 1949.
Cohen, Arthur A. "Eschatology." In *Contemporary Jewish Religious Thought*, edited by Arthur A. Cohen and Paul Mendes-Flohr. New York: Charles Scribner's Sons, 1987.
Cohen, Hermann, *Reason and Hope.* New York: W. W. Norton, 1971.
———. *Religion of Reason.* New York: Frederick Ungar Publishing Co., 1972.
Eisen, Arnold. *Galut.* Bloomington: Indiana University Press, 1986.
Fackenheim, Emil L. *God's Presence in History.* New York: New York University Press, 1970.

———. *The Jewish Return into History.* New York: Schocken Books, 1978.

———. *Quest for Past and Future.* Bloomington: Indiana University Press, 1968.

———. *To Mend the World.* New York: Schocken Books, 1982.

Fisch, Harold. *The Zionist Revolution.* New York: St. Martin's Press, 1978.

Green, Arthur E. "Judaism as a Spiritual Language: A Jewish Mysticism for Our Age." *Manna* 19, Spring 1988.

———. "Reconstructionism." *Reconstructionist.* 56, no. 1, Autumn 1990.

———. "The Role of Jewish Mysticism in a Contemporary Theology of Judaism." *Shefa Quarterly* 1, no. 4.

———. "Spirituality." In *Contemporary Jewish Religious Thought,* edited by Arthur A. Cohen and Paul Mendes-Flohr. New York: Charles Scribner's Sons, 1987.

Greenberg, Irving. *The Third Great Cycle in Jewish History.* New York: National Jewish Resource Center, 1981.

———. *Voluntary Covenant.* New York: National Jewish Resource Center, 1982.

Halkin, Hillel. *Letters to an American Jewish Friend.* Philadelphia: Jewish Publication Society, 1977.

Hartman, David. *A Living Covenant.* New York: The Free Press, 1985.

———. "Reflections on Jewish Faith in a Secular World," *Immanuel* 8, Spring 1978.

Heschel, Abraham Joshua. *God in Search of Man.* Philadelphia: Jewish Publication Society, 1956.

———. *The Insecurity of Freedom.* New York: Farrar, Straus & Giroux, 1966.

———. *Israel, an Echo of Eternity.* New York: Farrar, Straus & Giroux, 1969.

———. *Man Is Not Alone.* Philadelphia: Jewish Publication Society, 1951.

———. *The Prophets.* Philadelphia: Jewish Publication Society, 1962.

Jacobs, Louis. *A Jewish Theology.* New York: Behrman House, 1973.

Kaplan, Mordecai, M. *The Future of the American Jew.* New York: Macmillan, 1948.

———. *Judaism as a Civilization.* New York: Reconstructionist Press, 1957.

———. *The Meaning of God in Modern Jewish Religion.* New York: The Jewish Reconstructionist Foundation, 1937.

———. *Questions Jews Ask: Reconstructionist Answers.* New York: Reconstructionist Press, 1956.

Kaufman, William E. *Contemporary Jewish Philosophies.* New York: Reconstructionist Press and Behrman House, 1976.

Klatzkin, Jacob. *Teḥumim.* Jerusalem: Devir, 1928.

Kohler, Kaufmann. *Jewish Theology*. Cincinnati: Riverdale Press, 1943.
Kushner, Lawrence. *Honey from the Rock*. San Francisco: Harper & Row, 1977.
———. *The River of Light*. Chappaqua: Rossel Books, 1981.
Lachover, F., and I. Tishby. *Mishnat Hazohar*, vol. 1. Jerusalem: Mosad Bialik, 1957.
Petuchowski, Jakob J. *Heirs of the Pharisees*. New York: Basic Books, 1970.
———. *Zion Reconsidered*. New York: Twayne, 1966.
Plaskow, Judith. *Standing Again at Sinai*. San Francisco: Harper & Row, 1990.
Reines, Alvin. *Polydoxy*. Buffalo: Prometheus Press, 1987.
Rosenzweig, Franz. *On Jewish Learning*. New York: Schocken Books, 1955.
———. *The Star of Redemption*. New York: Holt, Rinehart & Winston, 1971.
Rubenstein, Richard L. *After Auschwitz*. Indianapolis: Bobbs-Merrill, 1966.
———. *Morality and Eros*. New York: McGraw-Hill, 1970.
Samuelson, Norbert. Two unpublished manuscripts, tentatively entitled *The Doctrine of Creation out of the Sources of Judaism* and *The First Seven Days*.
Schulweis, Harold M. *Evil and the Morality of God*. Cincinnati: Hebrew Union College Press, 1984.
Slonimsky, Henry. *Essays*. Cincinnati: Hebrew Union College Press, 1967.
Steinberg, Milton. *Anatomy of Faith*. New York: Harcourt Brace, 1960.
Steinsaltz, Adin. *The Thirteen Petalled Rose*. New York: Basic Books, 1980.
Umansky, Ellen. "Females, Feminists, and Feminism: A Review of Recent Literature on Jewish Feminism and the Creation of a Feminist Judaism." *Feminist Studies* 14, no. 2, Summer 1988.
Woocher, Jonathan. *Sacred Survival*. Bloomington: Indiana University Press, 1986.
Wyschogrod, Michael. *The Body of Faith*. New York: Seabury Press, 1983.
———. "Faith and the Holocaust." *Judaism* 20, no. 3, Summer 1971.
———. "Judaism and Conscience." In *Standing before God*, edited by Asher Finkel and Lawrence Frizzel. New York: Ktav, 1981.
———. "The Impact of Dialogue with Christianity on My Self-Understanding as a Jew." In *Die Hebräische Bibel und ihre zweifache Nachgeschichte*, edited by Erhard Blum, Christian Macholz, and Ekkenard W. Stegemann. Neukirchen-Vluyn: Neukirchener Verlag, 1990.

Index

Abbaye, x

Abraham, 227, 230–31, 250; Covenant with, 2, 188 (*see also* Covenant)

activism, 26, 48–50, 122, 151, 166–67, 196, 202–4, 223

"address" (Buber), 269–72, 277–78

Adler, Alfred, 160

aesthetics, and observance, 86–87, 254–55

afterlife. *See* immortality

aggadah, xi, 2–3, 57, 61, 218–19

agnosticism, ethical, 176; Jewish, 15, 32–33, 44, 74; about science, 137

Agudat Yisrael, 47

agunah, 70, 249, 296–97

Ahad Haam [pseud. Asher Ginzberg], 67, 69, 173–75, 208–9

AIPAC, 262

Akiba, 247

aliyah (immigration to Israel), 43–44, 47–48, 206, 260–61, 263, 290

Altizer, Thomas J. J., 33

Anti-Defamation League, 262

antinomianism, 180, 212–13

antisemitism, 144–45, 183, 186, 199–200, 203, 217, 233

apologetics, x, 199, 227

Aquinas, Thomas, 119, 170

assimilation, 10, 73, 182, 228, 255. *See also* intermarriage

atheism, Jewish, 33, 44, 135

Atman, 102

Auschwitz, 79, 119

authenticity: as criterion in theology, x, 1, 59, 156, 208, 226, 294; existentialist, 176; Holocaust as criterion of Jewish, 78

authority, in culture, 17, 22, 25–26, 237–53, 266, 281; in Judaism, 10, 17–18, 98, 101, 123, 223–25

autonomy, 17–19, 31, 170–81, 256, 264, 273–74; self, and group, 221–23

Baeck, Leo, 35, 64–65, 84, 142, 145, 207–8

berakhah, 111–12, 140–41, 260

Bereira, 262

Berger, Peter, 108–9

Berkovits, Eliezer, 242

Besht, x

Bible, 73, 75–76, 92, 140, 223, 251, 291. *See also* Torah

Bible (citations): Genesis 1–11, 227; Genesis 1–3, 137, 168, 198; Genesis 1, 140; Genesis 4:7, 164; Genesis 9, 185; Genesis 10–11, 229; Genesis 31:42, 100; Exodus 20:2–17, 243, 283; Exodus 23:9, 186; Leviticus 19:19, 247; Deuteronomy 5:6–21, 243, 283; Deuteronomy 6:4, 218; Deuteronomy 11:13–21, 34; Jeremiah 1:13–14, 269; Amos 8:1–3, 269; Jonah, 185; Psalm 13:6, xiv; Psalm 139:21–22, 240; Psalm 144:15, xiv; Job, 147; Song of Songs, 250; Ecclesiastes, 147; Esther, 219

biblical criticism, 15, 117, 237–39, 250–51

blasphemy, 34, 36, 79, 92, 131, 219, 229

blessings. *See berakhah*

Bradley, F. H., 75

Buber, Martin, 15–17, 35, 68–71, 88–89, 103–5, 128–31, 142–44, 146, 147, 151, 161–63, 178–81, 208, 212–14, 267–74, 285–86

Buddhism, 56, 126; Zen, 102

Cartesian. *See* Descartes, René

Cassirer, Ernst, 171–72

Central Conference of American Rabbis, ix, 237

Chmielnicki pogroms, 34

chosenness of Jews, 2, 144–45, 195–206, 207–20. *See also* ethnicity; particularism

311